With
Your
Words
    in
    My
    Hands

McGill-Queen's Studies in Ethnic History

Series One: Donald Harman Akenson, Editor

1 Irish Migrants in the Canadas
A New Approach
Bruce S. Elliott
(Second edition, 2004)

2 Critical Years in Immigration
*Canada and Australia
Compared*
Freda Hawkins
(Second edition, 1991)

3 Italians in Toronto
*Development of a National
Identity, 1875–1935*
John E. Zucchi

4 Linguistics and Poetics
of Latvian Folk Songs
*Essays in Honour of the
Sesquicentennial of the Birth
of Kr. Barons*
Vaira Vikis-Freibergs

5 Johan Schroder's Travels
in Canada, 1863
Orm Overland

6 Class, Ethnicity, and
Social Inequality
Christopher McAll

7 The Victorian Interpretation
of Racial Conflict
*The Maori, the British,
and the New Zealand Wars*
James Belich

8 White Canada Forever
*Popular Attitudes and Public
Policy toward Orientals
in British Columbia*
W. Peter Ward
(Third edition, 2002)

9 The People of Glengarry
*Highlanders in Transition,
1745–1820*
Marianne McLean

10 Vancouver's Chinatown
*Racial Discourse in Canada,
1875–1980*
Kay J. Anderson

11 Best Left as Indians
*Native-White Relations in the
Yukon Territory, 1840–1973*
Ken Coates

12 Such Hardworking People
*Italian Immigrants
in Postwar Toronto*
Franca Iacovetta

13 The Little Slaves of the Harp
*Italian Child Street Musicians
in Nineteenth-Century Paris,
London, and New York*
John E. Zucchi

14 The Light of Nature
and the Law of God
*Antislavery in Ontario,
1833–1877*
Allen P. Stouffer

15 Drum Songs
Glimpses of Dene History
Kerry Abel

16 Canada's Jews
(Reprint of 1939 original)
Louis Rosenberg
Edited by Morton Weinfeld

17 A New Lease on Life
Landlords, Tenants, and
Immigrants in Ireland
and Canada
Catharine Anne Wilson

18 In Search of Paradise
The Odyssey of an Italian Family
Susan Gabori

19 Ethnicity in the Mainstream
Three Studies of English
Canadian Culture in Ontario
Pauline Greenhill

20 Patriots and Proletarians
The Politicization of Hungarian
Immigrants in Canada, 1923–1939
Carmela Patrias

21 The Four Quarters of the Night
The Life-Journey of
an Emigrant Sikh
Tara Singh Bains and Hugh
Johnston

22 Cultural Power, Resistance,
and Pluralism
Colonial Guyana, 1838–1900
Brian L. Moore

23 Search Out the Land
The Jews and the Growth of
Equality in British Colonial
America, 1740–1867
Sheldon J. Godfrey and
Judith C. Godfrey

24 The Development of Elites
in Acadian New Brunswick,
1861–1881
Sheila M. Andrew

25 Journey to Vaja
Reconstructing the World of
a Hungarian-Jewish Family
Elaine Kalman Naves

Series Two: John Zucchi, Editor

1 Inside Ethnic Families
Three Generations of
Portuguese-Canadians
Edite Noivo

2 A House of Words
Jewish Writing, Identity,
and Memory
Norman Ravvin

3 Oatmeal and the Catechism
Scottish Gaelic Settlers in Quebec
Margaret Bennett

4 With Scarcely a Ripple
Anglo-Canadian Migration into
the United States and Western
Canada, 1880–1920
Randy William Widdis

5 Creating Societies
Immigrant Lives in Canada
Dirk Hoerder

6 Social Discredi
Anti-Semitism, Social Credit,
and the Jewish Response
Janine Stingel

7 Coalescence of Styles
The Ethnic Heritage of St John
River Valley Regional Furniture,
1763–1851
Jane L. Cook

8 Brìgh an Orain /
A Story in Every Song
The Songs and Tales
of Lauchie MacLellan
Translated and edited
by John Shaw

9 Demography, State and Society
   Irish Migration to Britain,
   1921–1971
   Enda Delaney

10 The West Indians of Costa Rica
   Race, Class, and the Integration
   of an Ethnic Minority
   Ronald N. Harpelle

11 Canada and the Ukrainian
   Question, 1939–1945
   Bohdan S. Kordan

12 Tortillas and Tomatoes
   Transmigrant Mexican
   Harvesters in Canada
   Tanya Basok

13 Old and New World
   Highland Bagpiping
   John G. Gibson

14 Nationalism from the Margins
   The Negotiation of Nationalism
   and Ethnic Identities among
   Italian Immigrants in Alberta
   and British Columbia
   Patricia Wood

15 Colonization and Community
   The Vancouver Island Coalfield
   and the Making of the British
   Columbia Working Class
   John Douglas Belshaw

16 Enemy Aliens, Prisoners of War
   Internment in Canada
   during the Great War
   Bohdan S. Kordan

17 Like Our Mountains
   A History of Armenians
   in Canada
   Isabel Kaprielian-Churchill

18 Exiles and Islanders
   The Irish Settlers of
   Prince Edward Island
   Brendan O'Grady

19 Ethnic Relations in Canada
   Institutional Dynamics
   Raymond Breton
   Edited by Jeffrey G. Reitz

20 A Kingdom of the Mind
   The Scots' Impact on the
   Development of Canada
   Edited by Peter Rider and
   Heather McNabb

21 Vikings to U-Boats
   The German Experience in
   Newfoundland and Labrador
   Gerhard P. Bassler

22 Being Arab
   Ethnic and Religious Identity
   Building among Second
   Generation Youth in Montreal
   Paul Eid

23 From Peasants to Labourers
   Ukrainian and Belarusan
   Immigration from the
   Russian Empire to Canada
   Vadim Kukushkin

24 Emigrant Worlds and
   Transatlantic Communities
   Migration to Upper Canada in
   the First Half of the Nineteenth
   Century
   Elizabeth Jane Errington

25 Jerusalem on the Amur
   Birobidzhan and the Canadian
   Jewish Communist Movement,
   1924–1951
   Henry Felix Srebrnik

26 Irish Nationalism in Canada
Edited by David A. Wilson

27 Managing the Canadian
Mosaic in Wartime
*Shaping Citizenship Policy,
1939–1945*
Ivana Caccia

28 Jewish Roots, Canadian Soil
*Yiddish Culture in Montreal,
1905–1945*
Rebecca Margolis

29 Imposing Their Will
*An Organizational History
of Jewish Toronto, 1933–1948*
Jack Lipinsky

30 Ireland, Sweden, and the Great
European Migration, 1815–1914
Donald H. Akenson

31 The Punjabis in British Columbia
*Location, Labour, First Nations,
and Multiculturalism*
Kamala Elizabeth Nayar

32 Growing Up Canadian
Muslims, Hindus, Buddhists
Edited by Peter Beyer
and Rubina Ramji

33 Between Raid and Rebellion
*The Irish in Buffalo and Toronto,
1867–1916*
William Jenkins

34 Unpacking the Kists
The Scots in New Zealand
Brad Patterson, Tom Brooking,
and Jim McAloon

35 Building Nations from Diversity
*Canadian and American
Experience Compared*
Garth Stevenson

36 Hurrah Revolutionaries
*The Polish Canadian Communist
Movement, 1918–1948*
Patryk Polec

37 Alice in Shandehland
*Scandal and Scorn in the
Edelson/Horwitz Murder Case*
Monda Halpern

38 Creating Kashubia
*History, Memory, and Identity in
Canada's First Polish Community*
Joshua C. Blank

39 No Free Man
*Canada, the Great War, and
the Enemy Alien Experience*
Bohdan S. Kordan

40 Between Dispersion
and Belonging
*Global Approaches to
Diaspora in Practice*
Edited by Amitava Chowdhury
and Donald Harman Akenson

41 Running on Empty
*Canada and the Indochinese
Refugees, 1975–1980*
Michael J. Molloy, Peter
Duschinsky, Kurt F. Jensen,
and Robert J. Shalka

42 Twenty-First-Century
Immigration to North America
Newcomers in Turbulent Times
Edited by Victoria M. Esses and
Donald E. Abelson

43 Gaelic Cape Breton Step-Dancing
*A Historical and Ethnographic
Perspective*
John G. Gibson

44 Witness to Loss
Race, Culpability, and Memory
in the Dispossession
of Japanese Canadians
Edited by Jordan Stanger-Ross
and Pamela Sugiman

45 Mad Flight?
The Quebec Emigration to the
Coffee Plantations of Brazil
John Zucchi

46 A Land of Dreams
Ethnicity, Nationalism, and
the Irish in Newfoundland,
Nova Scotia, and Maine,
1880–1923
Patrick Mannion

47 Strategic Friends
Canada-Ukraine Relations from
Independence to the Euromaidan
Bohdan S. Kordan

48 From Righteousness to Far Right
An Anthropological Rethinking
of Critical Security Studies
Emma Mc Cluskey

49 North American Gaels
Speech, Story, and Song
in the Diaspora
Edited by Natasha Sumner
and Aidan Doyle

50 The Invisible Community
Being South Asian in Quebec
Edited by Mahsa Bakhshaei,
Marie Mc Andrew, Ratna Ghosh,
and Priti Singh

51 With Your Words in My Hands
The Letters of Antonietta Petris
and Loris Palma
Edited and translated
by Sonia Cancian

With Your Words

in My Hands

The Letters of Antonietta Petris and Loris Palma

EDITED AND TRANSLATED BY

Sonia Cancian

FOREWORD BY Antonietta Petris
AFTERWORD BY Donna R. Gabaccia

MCGILL-QUEEN'S UNIVERSITY PRESS
Montreal & Kingston • London • Chicago

© McGill-Queen's University Press 2021

ISBN 978-0-2280-0552-0 (cloth)
ISBN 978-0-2280-0553-7 (paper)
ISBN 978-0-2280-0714-2 (ePDF)
ISBN 978-0-2280-0715-9 (ePUB)

Legal deposit first quarter 2021
Bibliothèque nationale du Québec

Printed in Canada on acid-free paper that is 100% ancient forest free (100% post-consumer recycled), processed chlorine free

This book has been published with the help of a grant from the Canadian Federation for the Humanities and Social Sciences, through the Awards to Scholarly Publications Program, using funds provided by the Social Sciences and Humanities Research Council of Canada.

We acknowledge the support of the Canada Council for the Arts.
Nous remercions le Conseil des arts du Canada de son soutien.

Library and Archives Canada Cataloguing in Publication

Title: With your words in my hands : the letters of Antonietta Petris and Loris Palma / edited and translated by Sonia Cancian ; foreword by Antonietta Petris ; afterword by Donna R. Gabaccia.
Names: Container of (expression): Petris, Antonietta. Correspondence. Selections. English. | Container of (expression): Palma, Loris, –2007. Correspondence. Selections. English. | Cancian, Sonia, 1965– translator, editor.
Series: McGill-Queen's studies in ethnic history. Series two ; 51.
Description: Series statement: McGill-Queen's studies in ethnic history. Series two ; 51 | Includes bibliographical references and index. | Letters translated from the Italian.
Identifiers: Canadiana (print) 20200405527 | Canadiana (ebook) 20200405578 | ISBN 9780228005537 (paper) | ISBN 9780228005520 (cloth) | ISBN 9780228007142 (ePDF) | ISBN 9780228007159 (ePUB)
Subjects: LCSH: Petris, Antonietta—Correspondence. | LCSH: Palma, Loris, –2007—Correspondence. | LCSH: Italians—Correspondence. | LCSH: Immigrants—Canada—Correspondence. | LCSH: Immigrants—Italy—Correspondence. | LCGFT: Personal correspondence.
Classification: LCC FC106.I8 W58 2021 | DDC 971.004/51—dc23

Set in 11/14 Warnock Pro with TT Bells
Book design and typesetting by Lara Minja, Lime Design

For my parents, Maria and Luciano,
and my children, Arianna and Lorenzo

Contents

Foreword xiii
Antonietta Petris

Acknowledgments xix

Figures xxv, 147

Introduction: Love in the Midst of Migration 3
Sonia Cancian

Part One

"Neither Here nor There"
The Letters from September 1948 to December 1948

1 "That day an abyss opened under my feet"
Mobility in the Immediate Postwar Era 65

2 "I will know how to wait knowing this is the last time"
Writing and Waiting across National Boundaries 84

3 "This is America for the crazy!"
Linguistic Currents in Postwar Montreal 101

4 "Christmas trees are everywhere"
Reconciling a New Christmas Celebration 123

Part Two

"Worlds Apart, and Near to Heart"
The Letters from January 1949 to July 1949

5 "A new year, a new life"
Optimism and Melancholy Gazing into the Future 161

6 "Imagine your Nietta, sadder than ever"
Traumas of Separation and Displacement 178

7 "It almost feels like you are already here"
The Metonymy of Writing and Feelings of Proximity 195

8 "Did you think I was sleeping here?"
Women's Agency in Migration 214

9 "You are lovely, season of springtime"
The Poetics of Nature and Writings of Distant Love 232

10 "Come on, my darling, it's your turn now"
Leaving for Love 255

Afterword 271
Donna R. Gabaccia

Bibliography 283

Index 299

Foreword

Antonietta Petris

MY COLLABORATION began four years ago, after the death of my husband, my companion for over sixty years. What remains of us are our letters, letters that I have cherished for many years. We wrote to each other every day. When Sonia Cancian asked me if I wanted to publish these letters, I hesitated at first. I wasn't sure I was ready to revisit my past so soon after my husband's passing. Gradually, I came to change my mind and agreed.

My love story began immediately after the end of the Second World War. I was nineteen years old, living in Ampezzo Carnico, a small town in Northern Italy where I was surrounded by the affection of my grandparents, my aunts and uncles, and my doting mother. My father had immigrated to Canada in 1928. It was 1946, and I was happy. The war was over, and the sufferings and anxieties that came with it had ended. Finally, we could live in peace. Like everyone my age, I wanted to enjoy myself. With friends we organized day trips to the mountains; the dance halls were always packed. A general feeling of euphoria filled the air! I had many friends, including a young man named Nicola, whom I had known since we were children.

One day, I saw Nicola walking alongside a young man who I later learned was from Venice. His name was Loris. His employer, the Società Adriatica di Elettricità (also known as the SADE), had sent him to the area of Ampezzo Carnico to convalesce over the summer from a bout of malaria, a consequence of the war. From that day onward, any opportunity to see me was good enough. It was obvious that he liked me. On my part, I had no interest in tying myself down to anyone, least of all to someone who lived so far away. He lived in Venice and I lived in Ampezzo. I was certain that once he would leave my little town he would forget me. Fate, however, had other plans.

One evening, as he accompanied me home – I remember this as if it were today – he held me in his arms and whispered, "I love you," and we kissed passionately. The sky was filled with stars, and the moon illuminated everything around us. We could see the mountains far ahead and hear the sound of crickets chirping. It all seemed like a dream. One week later, Loris returned to Venice. Soon after, I received his first letter, then the second, the third … In those years, no other means to communicate existed for us. It was August 1946. The days followed one after the other, and the desire to see each other grew more intense. "I will come down at Christmas," Loris wrote, "and we will be engaged to be married. My *mamma* and *papà* will join us." When that day finally came, I was so excited my heart beat very loudly. At his arrival, I ran toward him, and we gazed intently into each other's eyes. We could not believe that all of this was actually happening to us. On Christmas Day, the day of our engagement, we were reunited, happy to be together. After Christmas dinner, Loris gave me a beautiful diamond ring – the same ring I wear on my finger today.

Those were marvellous days. The town was covered with snow. We had fun tobogganing and throwing snowballs at each other like two kids. (We were kids! We were just twenty years old.) And then, we separated again. This time, we promised we would see each other in Venice. In a letter I received a few days after his return home, Loris wrote, "You will meet my family. I will be your guide to the treasures of this city, a city which is like no other in the world." And so, it was. There are no words to describe the first time I saw Venice from a distance … it was a dream, and I was in awe. To see Venice for me was a breathtaking experience, especially since I had lived all my life in a small town in the Alps (a town that remained very dear to me, nonetheless). We took walks on Piazza San Marco and along La Riva degli Schiavoni, and we visited museums. One evening – one magical night – Loris said to me, "Wear your most beautiful gown tonight. I am taking you to the *teatro*, we are going to La Fenice." We were going to see *Madama Butterfly*, our favourite opera. The theatre was stunning. Shortly after the curtains opened, the sublime music of Puccini began to move us to another place and time. The opera *Madama Butterfly* is about a young Japanese girl who waits many years for her sweetheart's return; the waits are long, and the separations are constant. In some ways, this love story was no different from ours.

This is where another chapter of my life began. Earlier, I mentioned my father who had immigrated to Canada in 1928. For many years, we had not received news from him. This was especially the case during the war years. One day, my mother received a letter from my father announcing his return to Italy. We were happy, but at the same time, we worried. Yes, because I had never met my father. He had left Italy when I was six months old, and I only saw him again when I was twenty years old. That may seem like an incredible story, but it's true. My mother waited for him for twenty years. Their only means of staying in touch was letters. I remember when he arrived at the train station of Venice. There we were, Loris, my mother, and I, waiting on the platform for his train to arrive. From a distance, I saw a tall man, wearing a grey hat and a dark coat, approach us. Loris turned to me and said, "That is your *papà*." In those first few seconds, I wanted to run away, far, far away, but instead, I stood there unable to whisper a word. How could I call this man "*papà*," a man I had no memory of having seen before?

With time, I came to know him, even though it wasn't easy. There was always something between us. He would often speak of America, of his life over there. Never did I think that one day I would leave Italy to follow him. He stayed six months with us. Then, he was gone again. This time, he reassured my mother that he would never leave her alone again. In fact, shortly after his departure, he wrote asking us to join him in Canada. I had no intention of leaving my home in Italy, and I especially had no desire to leave Loris. My mother was not going to leave without me. What would we do? What solution was in store for us? A period rife with tensions, uncertainties, and worries followed as we endeavoured to resolve the problem. Even in this case, fate followed its course.

In the meantime, Loris and I continued to write to each other. He too had trouble dealing with this new uncertainty. One day, I received a letter from him in which I read these exact words: "If you wish, I will come too, I will join you there, and we will be happy." And so, he had decided to leave his world – his Venice, his family, and his work. This is where the saddest part of my life began.

Finally, after much consideration, my mother decided to join my father with me, of course. I don't remember all the details because many years have passed since. However, I cannot forget the day we left my hometown of Ampezzo Carnico, especially the moment we left my home, and we said goodbye to our dear ones. As we embraced one last time, I thought I would probably never see them again. Even today, as I write these words, my heart aches. Loris travelled with us to Rome, where we would board our transatlantic flight. He stayed with us until the final moments prior to our departure. There we were at Ciampino International Airport, tearfully saying goodbye and ardently promising that we would see each other again soon, very soon, we hoped.

After three days of travelling by airplane, we arrived in Montreal. My father greeted us at the airport with his friends. I looked around me, watching people. I heard them speaking but I could not understand a word. All of this made my head spin. I was exhausted. The next morning, I woke up in my little room and that was when I realized how far I actually was from my home. I closed my eyes and cried.

Several days ago, inside a drawer I found one of the first letters that I wrote to Loris while in Canada. I think it accurately describes my state of mind of those early moments: "Every part of me reaches out toward you, and all I do is dream with my eyes wide open of my Italy, the place that saw me as a very happy child and young woman. We cannot forget everything that was our world until yesterday, where we played, the places where we cried, the classrooms in which we were taught, and the places we learned to love, in one word, the spaces in which we lived." From that day onward, everything became the same as in our previous epistolary exchanges: the writings, the carefully constructed words, the fear of losing each other, and the burning desire to realize our dream. Even today, I clearly see myself writing diligently to Loris, on many evenings late into the night. To Loris I described everything about myself: my activities and reflections in a given day. It felt as though I was sitting next to him, and I could hear his every breath. Yet, alas! How far away we were from each other in reality!

Over time, I slowly adapted to my new life in Montreal. There always seemed to be something new to discover. What interested me most was learning the language of the country so that I could communicate with others and understand what they were telling me. Months passed, and the arrival of Loris loomed far despite my father's efforts to advance the process of the sponsorship application. The procedures were very slow in those years. Immigrants were subjected to a medical examination and to other regulations that I don't remember precisely. Finally, after nearly one year of anticipation, Loris arrived in Canada. Close to six months later, on 17 December 1949, we were married. What made this all possible was our determination, our love, and the letters that kept us in touch despite the enormous distance between us. From that day onward, we lived a life together.

June 2011
Translated by Sonia Cancian

Acknowledgments

LIKE A CAREFULLY FOLDED HANDKERCHIEF tucked inside the pocket of a worn jacket, the letters of Antonietta Petris and Loris Palma have travelled with me for several years. During much of my research and teaching in Canada and overseas, I turned to the letters of Antonietta Petris and Loris Palma for analysis, evidence, and inspiration. Throughout this period, I was privileged to be hosted by a number of institutions providing me with financial support and a place to work and engage with colleagues. In Montreal, I am grateful to William Straw and the colleagues and staff at the McGill Institute for the Study of Canada, Graham Carr and colleagues and staff at the Department of History, Concordia University, Geneviève Rail and the Research Associates group at the Simone de Beauvoir Institute at Concordia University, Deirdre Meintel and the colleagues and staff at the Groupe de recherche de diversité urbaine (CEETUM) at l'Université de Montréal, and more recently, Pascal Brissette and Stéphan Gervais, and colleagues and staff at the Centre de recherches interdisciplinaires en études montréalaises, and Nancy Marelli and the Archives Out Loud group at the Italian-Canadian Archives of Quebec.

The Immigration History Research Center Archives at the University of Minnesota was an important intellectual home for me, and I am grateful to Donna R. Gabaccia, Daniel Necas, and the archivists, students, volunteers, and staff who cheerfully welcomed me as a postdoctoral fellow. The Digitizing Immigrant Letters Project, led by Donna Gabaccia, Daniel Necas, and myself, was created when few letter collections were available on websites.

Ahead of its time, the global and multilingual Digitizing Immigrant Letters Project features series of letters written both by immigrants and to immigrants expressing emotion and intimacy among loved ones separated by migration. Four letters from the Petris-Palma collection are featured in the digital project.

For providing an enriching environment in the various phases of the book, I am also grateful to Anne-Marie Motard at the Direction des Relations Internationales, Études Montpelliéraines du Monde Anglophone, and Isabelle Felici at Langues, Littératures, Arts et Cultures des Suds, and the colleagues and staff at l'Université Paul-Valery Montpellier 3 in Montpellier, France; Franca Roncarolo, Roberta Ricucci, and colleagues at the Dipartimento di Culture, Politica e Società at l'Università degli studi di Torino in Turin, Italy; and Jyoti Grewal, Belkeis Altareb, Sabrina Joseph and colleagues at the University College and the College of Humanities and Social Sciences at Zayed University, Dubai, United Arab Emirates. For the intellectual sustenance and support at the Research Center, History of Emotions at the Max Planck Institute for Human Development in Berlin, I am grateful to Ute Frevert, staff members, particularly Karola Rockmann, Anja Berkes, and the late Christina Becher, and the numerous colleagues with whom I enjoyed friendly and constructive exchanges on the manuscript. As a member of the institute, I also benefited from taking part in the Challenges of Migration, Integration and Exclusion Group of the Max Planck Society, and I thank Marie-Claire Foblets and colleagues for the enriching conversations we shared on the challenges of migration and mobility.

As I write these words of gratitude, the weeks and months before the Coronavirus pandemic appear distant, reflecting a time when visits and travel were a normal part of our daily lives. This kind of physical travel has now, only temporarily I hope, been overshadowed nearly entirely by digital communications. When I look back on the numerous conferences, workshops, and seminars in which I participated in person (including a TEDx Talk presentation in Lausanne, Switzerland), I feel fortunate. While digital communications are effective in creating a form of co-presence in the face of geographic divides, physical presence affords important opportunities for a fuller, more in-depth human experience of contact, still a basic human need. These academic

Acknowledgments

xxi

meetings have provided me with critical exchanges to reflect, engage, revise, and consider new methodological and analytical questions regarding the letters of Antonietta Petris and Loris Palma.

Good friends make for good work, and I would be remiss if I didn't thank the friends and colleagues whose kindness and clear thinking commingled with a great deal of enthusiasm have encouraged me during the writing of the book. A special thank you is extended to Cawo Abdi, Shamma Aldabal, Silvia Cassamagnaghi, Kerry Choun, Marija Dalbello, Francesco D'Arelli, Lorenzo del Pio, Emily Deschaine, Patrizia Diana, Luca Donner, Norbert Finzsch, Wladimir Fischer, Marion Froger, David A. Gerber, Nancy L. Green, Haven Hawley, John Kantara, Laurence Kirmayer, Ursula Lehmkuhl, Peter Leese, Johanna Leinonen, Ingrid Liekens, Royden Loewen, Soňa Mikulová, Daniel Necas, Mark Nicholls, Francesca Pala, Goffredo Palmerini, Massimo Pamio, Michel Peterson, Jeffrey Pilcher, Alessandra Pipan, Bruno Ramirez, Susy Ricciardelli, Françoise Perrenoud Rossier, Margaret Scarborough, Francesca Sorcinelli, Maura Sorcinelli, Annemarie Steidl, Aisling Sweeney, Liz Stanley, Sylvie Taschereau, Makoto Harris Takao, Tamara Turner, Simone Wegge, and Roberto Zorfini. A considerable number of people contributed in various ways to the book project, and in my recollection, I may have left some people out. In no way does this oversight diminish my gratitude for their contribution.

A special word of appreciation to Marcelo Borges, Donna Gabaccia, Mary Anne Poutanen, Linda Reeder, Vishanthie Sewpaul, and Elizabeth Zanoni who have provided astute comments and suggestions on earlier readings of the manuscript. As always, they have shown great generosity, wisdom, and fortitude in their friendship and in their intellectual engagement, and I am deeply grateful to them.

For their professionalism and commitment, I am grateful to McGill-Queen's University Press. I especially thank Jonathan Crago whose dedication and support to this project have been unparalleled. I also thank Kathleen Fraser and everyone at the press who made this book possible. A special thank you also to Paula Sarson for her meticulous and graceful copy-editing, and to Catherine Marjoribanks for her attentive work on the index. For their careful readings and insightful suggestions, I extend much gratitude to the two anonymous reviewers. The book is significantly improved as a result of their generous observations. For

xxii   Acknowledgments

their assistance in collecting additional information and photographs, I thank the daughters of Antonietta and Loris, Nelia Palma and Wanda Palma. I take this opportunity to gratefully acknowledge the support of François Crépeau, the Hans & Tamar Oppenheimer Chair in Public International Law at McGill University, whose support made the in-depth indexing possible for the book.

Finally, I thank my beautiful family. An affectionate thank you to my brothers and their families, and especially my sister Nadia and brother-in-law Nunzio for their encouragement. I hope that for my youngest nephews, Luciano and Dante, these letters will one day serve as an inspiration. I am immeasurably grateful to my parents, Luciano Cancian and Maria Lemmo Cancian, whose unconditional love and support sustain me always, and to my children, Lorenzo and Arianna, whose unwavering love and encouragement are constant sources of strength and inspiration.

In an epoch when the world pulsates with uncertainty, there is no better time than now for love. And, with love, I extend an enormous debt of gratitude to Antonietta Petris. This book would not have been written without the extraordinary participation of Antonietta, whose determination and optimism have been a source of inspiration. When I speak with Antonietta today, she often reminds me that the days we worked on the letters together were *"una parentesi della mia vita con Sonia"* (A parenthesis of my life with Sonia). These days were an important chapter of my life, as well, dear Antonietta.

Letter excerpts have appeared in the following publications: Sonia Cancian, *"My Love, How Different Life Is Here ...'*: A Young Italian Woman's Impressions of Postwar Montreal," in *Engaging with Diversity: Multidisciplinary Reflections on Plurality in Quebec*, edited by Stéphan Gervais, Raffaele Iacovino, and Mary Anne Poutanen (Bern: Peter Lang, 2018); Sonia Cancian, "The Language of Gender in Lovers' Correspondence, 1946–1949," Special Issue: "Gender History across Epistemologies," *Gender & History Journal* 24, no. 3 (November 2012): 755–65; Sonia Cancian, "'My Dearest Love ...': Love, Longing and Desire in International Migration," in *Migrations: Interdisciplinary Perspectives*, edited by Michi Messer, Renee Schröder, and Ruth Wodak (Vienna and New York: Springer-Verlag, 2012, 175–86); Sonia Cancian, "Love in the Time of Migration: Lovers Correspond Between Italy and

Canada, 1948–1957," Érudit: Diversité Urbaine 10, no. 2 (printemps/ Spring 2011): 91–109; Sonia Cancian, *Families, Lovers, and Their Letters: Italian Postwar Migration to Canada* (Winnipeg: University of Manitoba Press, 2010); and the Digitizing Immigrant Letters Project, Immigration History Research Center Archives, University of Minnesota Libraries, accessible at the University of Minnesota, https://ihrca.dash.umn.edu/dil/.

Antonietta and Loris, Montreal, summer 1950. Unless otherwise noted, photographs are in the private collection of Antonietta Petris.

Antonietta and Loris on their first hiking trip together with friends. Rifugio Tita Piaz, Ampezzo, August 1946.

Antonietta hiking in the area of Forni di Sopra, in 1947–48, when her father returned to Ampezzo after a twenty-year absence. A dedication is written on the back of the photograph: *"Il mio più bel sorriso a Loris che sempre amo Nietta"* ["My most beautiful smile for Loris whom I love forever, Nietta"].

Loris, at a photo studio in Venice, 1946.

Loris walking to work, Venice, August 1946.

Venice, late 1940s.

Home and neighbourhood of Loris's family, Venice, December 2013. PHOTO: SONIA CANCIAN.

Loris and his friends on the train headed to a soccer match to support the Venezia team, 1947–48.

Antonietta and Loris after a performance of Puccini's *Madama Butterfly* at La Fenice, Venice, February 1947.

Antonietta and Loris at the Lido, Venice, June 1947. Antonietta had travelled to Venice and stayed with a friend. During this period, the couple saw each other nearly every day.

A reunited family: Antonietta and her mother and father after twenty years of separation, Ampezzo, early 1948.

Via Braccioletta (Via Brazzoletta), Ampezzo, September 1990.

With
Your
Words
in
My
Hands

I listen to his breath, warm upon the night air, and somehow I am comforted. He does not mean that it does not hurt. He does not mean that we are not frightened. Only that: we are here. This is what it means to swim in the tide, to walk the earth and feel it touch your feet. This is what it means to be alive.

Madeline Miller, *Circe*

Introduction

Love in the Midst of Migration

Sonia Cancian

Today I begin to miss you and wait for you, to wait for the blessed day when you hold me again in your strong loving arms. It hurts very much, Nelson, but I am glad it hurts so much because this hard pain is love and I know you love me too. You so near and so far away, so far and so near, my beloved one.

Simone de Beauvoir, *A Transatlantic Love Affair*

My dear Antonietta,
I am taking advantage of a little free time to send you these two lines and to tell you how much I think of you constantly and truthfully with affection. I hope you and your mamma received my letter. I hope the letter convinced you a little more of my love. I spend my days thinking of everything that our future will bring and I can hardly wait to tell you about it. Believe in the love that I feel for you so that you too can begin to love me; I would not be doing this if my love were not genuine. Forgive me for writing to you with a pencil. It was all I had to write to you. Absolutely convinced that I will be seeing you on Saturday, I send you my most affectionate greetings and a sincere kiss.
Your Loris

THUS BEGAN THE CORRESPONDENCE between Antonietta Petris and Loris Palma on Thursday, 22 August 1946. As Loris penned these first lines to his love, he could not imagine that in a few years' time, Antonietta would leave permanently for Canada. Two years of continuous writing and occasional visits between Ampezzo and Venice would first pass before a new kind of correspondence would flourish, a steady stream of transatlantic correspondence whose paper and envelopes were embedded with renewed hope, joy, affection, resilience, and longing. As Antonietta makes clear in her foreword, nothing could have prepared her and Loris for the fierce yearning that ensued in their long-distance separation. For Antonietta, the memory of this separation had become so pronounced that it led her to declare over sixty years later that the separation "wasn't easy ... we pushed forward with determination, with the desire to move ahead and reach our objective, and we did it! But, it cost us dearly."[1]

This book presents an extraordinarily rich collection of love letters written during a migration process. The letters belong to Antonietta Petris and Loris Palma, a couple who wrote avidly to each other during their transatlantic separation from September 1948 to July 1949. The letters of Antonietta Petris and Loris Palma are as much about love as they are about migration. Written just a few years after the end of the Second World War, the collection shows how women and men navigated their transnational lives on a day-to-day basis between Canada and Italy. The correspondence highlights the workings of a transnational family life as well as the meanings and aspirations attached to work in Italy and Canada during the postwar years. How kin and non-kin relations were managed across borders, and how gender relations and dynamics were meditated and negotiated in the letters in a transnational framework can be gleaned from the epistolary narratives.

Emotions also figure prominently in the letters, and the ways in which they were identified, negotiated, and reflected upon represent another cornerstone of the letters. Significantly, the letters testify to the transnational nature of migrant lives of women and men before the connected presence of today's world. They show that migration was not a one-way process that involved the shedding of ties to the homeland, but rather that it was a process that deeply and intimately linked the sending and receiving families and communities through the intimate lives of people across space and time.

Migration made transnationalism a normal dimension of life for many, perhaps even most, working-class families in Italy in the nineteenth and twentieth centuries. Family discipline, economic security, reproduction, inheritance, romance, and dreams transcended national boundaries and bridged continents.

Donna R. Gabaccia, *Italy's Many Diasporas*

In this introduction, I discuss many of the themes threaded in the letters, ranging from the diverse dynamics involved in a migration process, including kin and non-kin relations; gender norms, roles and expectations; and the emotional energies associated with love, longing, nostalgia, hope, and other emotions that imbue the letters; to the practices of maintaining a correspondence; the different faces of separation; and the labour of staying in touch. In this four-part introduction, I begin with how the letters were first identified, and my work involved in recovering the epistolary voices in collaboration with Antonietta Petris. In this section, I elaborate upon the interrelationship of love and migration that emerges from the letters. Second, I draw a biographical sketch of Antonietta Petris and Loris Palma, and the couple's initial period of courtship prior to their transatlantic separation, which also involved long periods of separation and intense letter-writing. Third, I briefly situate the letters in relation to the scholarship in the fields of history of Italian migration to Canada, the history of emotions, gender history, and studies on migrant correspondence. Next, I discuss the intersectionality between the oral memory associated with the letters – based on oral history interviews and conversations with Antonietta – and the textual memory embedded in the letters. In the final section of the introduction, I reflect on the challenges I faced in the process of translating the letters from Italian to English.

The full collection of letters follows the introduction. Each of the ten chapters is introduced with a brief commentary on themes woven into the individual chapters. The themes vary considerably, moving from the meaning of migrating to America, to the reflective practice of writing letters and language dynamics particular to postwar Montreal. The themes of Christmas celebrations in Canada, the experience of melancholy, the passage of time, and the trauma of separation and displacement are briefly illustrated. The meanings of presence and co-presence and the materiality of the letters are also explored. They are followed by observations on gender and women's agency in a migration process, and nature and its correlation to literacy. The heartbreak in leaving behind a family and the social death that the migration of a loved one initiated among family members and significant others is discussed in the final chapter. The afterword by Donna R. Gabaccia ponders the powerful popular association of emotionalism with the Italian nation, and the relationship between the national and emotional in the letters of this young couple.

Letters in a Shopping Bag

I first came across a small portion of the letters of Antonietta Petris and Loris Palma in 2003 during the fieldwork research for my doctoral study on Italian migrant correspondence in Canada. I had contacted Loris Palma, who was then the director of a Venetian cultural association based in Montreal. Loris agreed to participate in the study and offered to loan me a few of the letters he had received from his family following his immigration to Canada in 1949. Buried in the package of letters was a handful of the letters he and his then fiancée, Antonietta, had exchanged while he was waiting to immigrate and join her in Montreal in 1948–49. Loris and I kept in touch over the years following that first meeting.

In the fall of 2007, just days prior to the defence of my doctoral dissertation, I learned that Loris had died in August of that year. His family reiterated to me how much Loris had valued his participation in my research, to the point that even in his final days he had spoken about it to his family. Shortly after, I met with Antonietta and her daughters to share memories of Loris and the letters he had loaned me for the study. I discovered then that the couple's letter collection was much larger than I had been led to believe. Other scholarly obligations interceded with a postdoctoral fellowship waiting to be taken up at the University of Minnesota, but the promise to meet Antonietta again held fast. The opportunity materialized in the fall of 2010, when Antonietta and I met in her home in Saint-Léonard, a municipality to the east of Montreal renowned for its prominent Italian community. Antonietta met me in earnest and showed me the letters that she and Loris had exchanged while they were engaged. On the day of my visit, there they were, hundreds of letters heaped into a shopping bag!

Leafing gingerly through the pile of letters, I was immediately struck by the sheer volume and the fairly intact state in which they had been preserved. Many of the letters were still in their original envelopes with only the stamps cut away. The shopping bag contained most of the letters that Antonietta and Loris had penned to each other over two periods of their lives. The first period comprises the letters written shortly after the couple had met in Ampezzo Carnico, when they had first begun to write to each other between Ampezzo Carnico and Venice, from August 1946 to September 1948. The second period began after Antonietta and her mother immigrated to Montreal on 21 September 1948 while Loris remained in Italy, promising to join her at the earliest opportunity. I remember being struck by the breadth and depth of the epistolary narrative as it unfolded before my eyes. Even today, after having read them countless times, I remain in awe of the letters and the authors' epistolary worlds.

Privacy and intimacy were important to Antonietta and Loris. A number of the letters included greetings from the writers' respective parents, but only on occasion were salutations added at the end of a letter by the parents themselves. When asked about the place in which she found herself writing to Loris most often, Antonietta recalls reading and writing the letters usually in the kitchen when it was quiet, or in her bedroom. While we can assume that most immigrant letters were shared among family members and friends, as David Gerber notes, in this case, given the nature of the letters, it appears that the sharing of letters beyond the letter writers was more the exception than the rule.[2]

The power of the letters between Antonietta and Loris is still evident today. Discovering this chorus of epistolary voices in the early twenty-first century when letters appear to many individuals as synonymous with a nostalgic past, coupled with the presence of one of the correspondents is a rare encounter, and not surprisingly, it transformed my initial enthusiasm into a veritable exhilarating experience as a scholar throughout the project. Antonietta was as thrilled as I was in re/discovering the letters, and this further galvanized the experience. In January 2011, as I began to read and sort the letters, and the possibility of turning them into a book emerged, Antonietta became an important voice to the project. In the beginning, I visited Antonietta every two or three weeks. As visits diminished with the passage of time, the connection remained between us. When we met, our conversations took us to the letters, her family, Loris's family, and the stories in and around the letters. No sooner had I begun to visit Antonietta than a friendship bloomed, and conversations between us reflected a spirit of collaboration.

We began reading the letters together – starting from the first one penned by Loris on 22 August 1946, with the words, "I am taking advantage of a little free time to send you these two lines and to tell you how much I think of you constantly and truthfully with affection."[3] Whether reading through the letters on my own, or with Antonietta, we quickly became absorbed by them. A thousand and one questions emerged as I inquired with Antonietta about her life, their lives apart, their lives together, and the lives of the letters. In December 2013, on my way back from a conference in Padua, I had the opportunity to travel to Ampezzo Carnico and Venice. In Venice's Corte Coppo, I imagined a young Loris seated at a desk by his bedroom window reflecting on his next lines for Antonietta. In Antonietta's Ampezzo, I met with one of Antonietta's childhood friends as well as her much-loved cousin, Nadia. Both offered insights on the love story of Antonietta and Loris. During the day, I walked along the town's Via Nazionale envisioning the young couple radiating with joy as they strolled with their friends on many a cool summer evening just after the war. The house on Via Braccioletta (Via Brazzoletta) where Antonietta had lived with her family before immigrating to Canada was still there, well cared for.

Introduction

But can we not argue with equal justice that geography enables love to blossom? A dialectics of distant love and nearby love prompts the question: How much nearness and how much distance can love survive?

Ulrich Beck and Elisabeth Beck-Gernsheim,
Distant Love

Long-distance love and migration have weighed upon lovers since "time immemorial."[4] Myths, legends, and stories of untold Ulyssess and Penelopes inform our imagination about couples separated by the forces of mobility. The paradoxes of separation and reunion were frequently evoked in the feelings of longing, frustration, tension, joy, and melancholia; these, and other emotions, have shaped the experience of separation. The significance of these emotions is profound. As Marcelo Borges, Linda Reeder, and I note in the collection of essays *Emotional Landscapes: Love, Gender, and Migration*, loves that have been lost, found, embittered, and celebrated are woven through the stories told by those who cross borders and oceans and those who greet them on the other side.[5] The letters of Antonietta and Loris illustrate transnational love experienced moment to moment. This love was understood by Loris as "the most arduous enterprise because love blinds you, you are transported by the passion of being loved, love is the fruit of self-analysis so that you will not commit any wrongs. Love is the virtue of human strength, the virtue that withstands pain and gives life to sorrow" (10 October 1948). To Antonietta, this love of a lifetime is aptly captured over sixty years later in this volume's foreword, in which she highlights her desire to write to Loris and tell him, "everything about me: my activities and reflections in a given day. It felt as though I was sitting next to him, and I could hear his every breath. Yet, alas! How far away we were from each other in reality!"

The story that the letters of Antonietta and Loris tell is a noteworthy precedent for the countless epistolary love stories that have remained tucked away in family archives for years – in dust-covered shoeboxes or carton suitcases – or simply lost altogether. The letters are also testimony to the love stories situated in the present and in the future where distance and separation continue to be markers of relationships the world over. For countless families, individuals, and lovers, love was a force that frequently infused the experience of migration with determination and strength. Couples were no different from individuals and families navigating the uncertainties and anxieties, seeking the reassurances, appreciating the joys, and mitigating the discontentment and sorrow that accompanied being separated from loved ones as a result of migration. Love was also a curse. It inflicted wounds that were opened again and again at the minutest of detail, reminding couples of their longing for, dreaming, and missing of each other. This love resurfaces in the letters of Antonietta Petris and Loris Palma. Again and again, this love is re/plenished, re/idealized, re/imagined, and continuously re/negotiated during the lovers' separation between the cities of Venice and Montreal in the years 1948–49. Complete and two-sided, the letters in *With Your Words in My Hands: The Letters of Antonietta Petris and Loris Palma* offer a rich and rare epistolary voice of an ordinary couple and their transnational love unravelled on paper.

The title of the book merits brief clarification. The words "with your words in my hands" are drawn from a letter written by Antonietta on 25 October 1948. In this letter, Antonietta explicates to Loris how his words were the breath of life for her as she read the letter over and over again until she fell asleep thinking of him with the letter in her hands. This gave Antonietta the feeling that for a fleeting moment, the distance between her and Loris had collapsed. The elements of the handwritten letter, its calligraphy, style, punctuation, contents, and the movement of her hands physically grasping the letter, underscore the interconnectedness of the letter's materiality and message together with the emotions running through it, and the experience embodied by the correspondents. This materiality of absence and longing is a theme that has captured the imagination of artists, notably in Johannes Vermeer's *Girl Reading a Letter at an Open Window* (c. 1657–59), Jean Raoux's (1677–1734) *La Liseuse*, and Jacques-Louis David's *The Death of Marat* (1793).

In the narrative, the couple's identities are "retrospective," a concept I borrow from philosopher Rosi Braidotti, who explains its significance in relation to the maps that we draw, "but only of where we have already been and consequently no longer are."[6] In this sense, migration drove the emotions of a loved one, and love drove their migration. This retrospective representation is crystallized in the epistolary collection exchanged between Antonietta and Loris, a young, literate couple with working-class and artisan origins. How did the couple navigate the tensions of separation and distance following Antonietta's migration? How did the writers create a sense of presence in absence? The letters of Antonietta and Loris not only feature reflection, resilience, and reification that defined their love at a distance but also they underscore the emergence of transnational strategies – material, emotional, and relational – that the correspondents employed to reassure continuity in their ties. Through the ink on the page, agency emerges with each correspondent asserting with tenacity the successful outcome of their migration.

Lovers Caught in the Throes of Distance

Antonietta Petris (commonly referred to as Nietta or Tetina in Loris's letters) was born on 18 September 1927 in the town of Ampezzo, also known as Ampezzo Carnico, located in the Province of Udine in Italy's northeastern Friuli-Venezia Giulia region. Natives of Ampezzo, Antonietta's parents, Vittorio Petris and Lucia Martinis, married in early 1927. An only child, Antonietta grew up in an extended household, surrounded by the affections of her mother, her maternal grandparents and an uncle. As Antonietta poignantly notes in the book's foreword, with the exception of letters and parcels, her father had been absent for most of her life, having departed for France in 1928 and later Canada.

Vittorio Petris had spent much of his young adult life travelling with his father throughout Germany and the former Czechoslovakia in search of work. Just six months after Antonietta was born, he immigrated to France, and from there crossed the Atlantic Ocean to reach the French islands of Saint-Pierre and Miquelon, less than twenty kilometres away from Canada's easternmost province, Newfoundland and Labrador. Once his work contract had ended, Vittorio travelled to Montreal where he eventually settled in 1929, at the start of the Great Depression. Over time, he and a business partner started a masonry and stonework company in Montreal. During his twenty-year absence, his wife Lucia Martinis managed the family home in Ampezzo Carnico like so many "white widows" that Linda Reeder discusses in her book *Widows in White*. The arable land and farm animals that the family owned allowed them to live without major economic hardship in Vittorio's absence right until the end of the Second World War.[7] While in Montreal, Vittorio did not forget his family in Italy, although letters were exchanged far less frequently. A story shared in the Petris-Palma household recalls when Lucia bought a radio with the money that her husband had sent her. It was the only radio in town, and townsfolk and neighbours gathered in their house on Via Braccioletta to listen to the evening news.[8] In the meantime, Antonietta attended the local school and completed grade school under the law, *Legge Gentile* enacted in 1923. Though Antonietta regrets not furthering her studies, especially given her interest in Italian literature, at the time she was introduced to the needle trade. At the home of her seamstress-teacher, Antonietta learned to sew clothes, and she gained an appreciation of opera. Each time she visited her teacher Rosina, she would return home with several opera libretti in her hands. She read them avidly. The music and lyrics of the operas of Verdi, Mascagni, Puccini, and others served as inspiration throughout Antonietta's life, especially after meeting Loris for the first time in Ampezzo in the summer of 1946.

The youngest of five children, Loris Palma was born in the heart of Venice on 10 October 1927. His mother, Cornelia Dureghello, and father, Luigi Palma, were both natives of Venice. His father worked on ships as a steward, and his mother took care of the family while under the guidance of her mother. Before and after the Second World War, the family lived on Corte Coppo in Venice's popular San Marco district. During the war, the family moved to Marghera, one of Venice's boroughs just eleven kilometres away.[9] After completing his first year at the religious institute Collegio Salesiano, in San Donà di Piave, Loris was forced to drop his classical studies. Instead, he completed two diplomas in mechanical and electrical technology at the Istituto Berna, in Mestre. During the war, he became employed at the SADE, the Società Adriatica di Elettricità in Porto Marghera, where his brother had been working before being drafted. A passion for theatre and opera music came easily to Loris. He was a kindred spirit to his grandfather,

Introduction 13

who had worked as a craftsman skilled in carpentry and toolmaking at the Teatro La Fenice and had access to the prestigious theatre. Throughout the years, Loris's grandfather provided both his daughter and, later, Loris access to the Fenice. Loris's fascination with the Fenice, Venice's Goldoni, and other theatres persisted into adulthood.

Once in Montreal, Loris continued to nurture his interest in opera music and the arts. In 1993, he co-founded along with Dino Fruchi and Carlo Caramelli, the Société de diffusion du patrimoine artistique et culturel des Italo-Canadiens to promote Italian-Canadian art and culture. The group began with Guido Nincheri's artwork, and when they realized the scope of his work – found in churches in Montreal and throughout Canada and New England – they focused their attention on the artist and his work by holding conferences and speeches, and lobbying for recognition from the City of Montreal, the Canadian government and the artist's Italian native city of Prato.[10] Shortly upon arriving in Montreal in July 1949, when refrigerators were still a rarity, Loris started working by delivering ice blocks to homes in the Montreal area. From there, he began working for a Montreal electrical firm situated in the northern regions of Labrador, Churchill Falls, and Chesterfield Inlet. In 1954, Loris was hired by the City of Montreal's Public Works division, where he continued to work until 1963.

In that year, Loris and Antonietta and their two daughters gathered their things and moved to Italy with the intention of returning to live near Loris's family and becoming part of the socio-economic fabric of a now buoyant Italy. They proceeded to live in Mestre, which would provide them easy access to Loris's family, who by then had resettled in the town of Mogliano Veneto. In the summer of 1964, just fourteen months after moving from Montreal, the family's trajectory changed course again. As his work obligations were taking Loris to Milan more frequently and the need to move his family to Milan became more urgent, Antonietta and Loris made the decision to permanently return to Montreal, where Antonietta's parents awaited them. Over the years, Antonietta and Loris travelled home to Italy to visit their families and friends. Montreal, however, remained their home.

"Not even for a moment did I stop thinking of you": *A Glance at the Letters*

The letters of Antonietta and Loris are imbued with remarkable expression and reflection. The letter writers longed, loved, despaired, and hoped as they faced the challenges of uncertainty and love in a world that only a few years earlier was immersed in the violence and destruction of the Second World War. The archive of letters is significant for several reasons. First, two sides of the correspondence shape the collection, a rarity in the field of migrant letters. Second, the letters evince a remarkable range of expression and engagement between the writers and their worlds. Third, the letters exemplify the flourishing of a "modern love," increasingly understood as fundamental in many marriages in the postwar period. Last but not least, the letters show the construction and meaning-making process of relationships at a distance, part of a way of life for millions of individuals and their families in the postwar period for whom "family discipline, economic security, reproduction, inheritance, romance, and dreams transcended national boundaries and bridged continents."[11] Over much of the twentieth century, migration was conceptualized predominantly as a one-way movement, despite migrant mobilities. The recent transnational turn in migration studies has underscored the increased connectivities between sending and receiving societies due to cheaper air travel and affordable communication technologies.

The letters of Antonietta and Loris provide strong evidence that lives in pre-polymedia times were intimately transnational. They weave the story of a young couple's emotions and experiences from the moment of Antonietta's arrival in Montreal to Loris's final letter composed as he was about to begin his journey for Canada. Eighty-two letters comprise this book, that is, approximately 170 double-sided sheets that evoke despair and resilience, sadness and joy, longing and delight, and jealousy and tension. Both sides of the correspondence exchanged between Antonietta and Loris have been preserved relatively well; only a few letters are missing. The writing in pen and pencil is for the most part legible with some exceptions. All of the letters have been scanned digitally and a handful are part of the Digitizing Immigrant Letters Project at the University of Minnesota's Immigration History Research Center's Archives.[12]

Introduction

As is generally the case with love letters, the letters do not elaborate only on love – its associated emotions and the hyperbolic expression – but also on the writers' multifarious worlds, both real and imaginary. Melodramatic overtones are reflected in the couple's letters, both as models of impossible and attainable loves and in the individual style adopted by the correspondents. Descriptions abound over the couple's concerns about their families' well-being, their evolving responsibilities at work, their aspirations and ideologies, and their identities as they came of age just a few years following the end of the Second World War. How did the couple cope when the distance proved to be too much? What kind of emotional discourse did they develop as they expressed themselves on paper? While the telegraph and telephone existed at the time, they were seldom used; the costs were prohibitive. Letters, on the other hand, were the most accessible and affordable form of staying in touch. Countless letters could be written and delivered across the ocean at affordable costs. But writing letters also entailed risks: misreadings of the letters' content, unusual delays, frustrations, and unexplained silences that were inevitably read as loss of interest between the correspondents.

When we think of the role of time in these letters, sociologist Liz Stanley's term "flies in amber quality,"[15] is appropriate, as these letters "do things with and to time."[14] As Stanley explains, "When a letter is read, its reader of course knows that time has passed and the 'moment' of its writing has gone; but at the same time, the present tense of the letter recurs – or rather occurs – not only in its first reading but subsequent ones too."[15] In this sense, letters are very similar to photographs: they not only hold memory they also represent the moment of their production.

Italy and Canada: The War and Immediately After

The letters were written in 1948 and 1949, a unique historical juncture in both Italy and Canada. It was the end of the Second World War, a war which for over five long years, Italians fought on two opposing sides, the Allied and the Axis forces. With the war fully under way, particularly between 1943 and 1945, the situation in the peninsula quickly deteriorated with increasing food shortages and rations, a flourishing black market amid deafening enemy raids, carpet bombings, armed military forces everywhere, and rampant confusion, chaos, and violence. With the men drafted into the war and others fighting in the mountains as resistance fighters, many women became heads of their households.[16] Similar to other women whose husbands had emigrated overseas for work, Antonietta's mother ran single-handedly the household in Ampezzo. This engendered contacting state bureaucracies, making decisions for the well-being of her household and family, and managing the household budget.

The end of the war came on 2 May 1945. Women were granted the right to vote in early 1945, and the country's general elections in 1948 voted in favour of a new democratic republic. Evidence of the war was everywhere: the rubble from destroyed buildings and bridges, a broken transportation system, and countless injured, bereaving, and traumatized Italians trying to make sense of their losses and widespread depravation. Despite these difficulties immediately after the war, peace brought some semblance of normalcy.[17] Like Antonietta and Loris, young men and women flocked to the theatres, concerts, dance halls, and sporting events, and in some cases, despite the clergy's disapproval, as they endeavoured to put the war behind them. People were once again gathering in cafés and strolling through the streets, giving a sense that, "something had started, even if its wheels were still squeaky ... the old automobile of a city began to move."[18]

Levels of education for Italians were beginning to rise following the war. In 1951, just a few years after Antonietta and Loris had started writing to each other, roughly 59 per cent of the Italian population had received elementary school education like Antonietta, and a small minority (only about 3 per cent) had been conferred a diploma of higher education similar to Loris's. Across the nation, illiteracy stood at a staggering 13 per cent, compared to the current less than 1 per cent.[19] Millions of Italians moved from their rural homes to new urban settings, from the southern regions of the peninsula to Italy's northern triangle – Genoa, Milan, Turin – and over seven million migrated to countries in Northern Europe, or to Canada, the United States, South America, and Australia. Exponential growth (fuelled also by migrant remittances) materialized into an unprecedented "economic miracle" with rapid, dramatic changes transforming this period of great

Introduction   17

optimism.[20] The love stories featured in the *fotoromanzi* magazines gained currency from the late 1940s onward, as going to the movies became more widespread, and the television made its way into Italian homes after 1954.[21]

Writing Emotions on Paper: A Historical Moment

The letters of Antonietta Petris and Loris Palma are part of an emotional historical juncture. After the Second World War and its catastrophic repercussions in Europe, romantic love, as Claire Langhamer and others argue, became viewed as a way of binding self-actualizing individuals to the social contract of marriage amid concerns about family disintegration.[22] For many couples like Antonietta and Loris, married love promised more than companionship, it offered a dynamic emotional connection in which shared projects and life changes could be achieved together.[23] Their affective lives and preoccupations are reflected in the letters. Tensions and gratifications around family and work also punctuate the letters amid a flurry of emotions, all part of the couple's resolve to keep a pulsating connection between them. Antonietta and Loris maintained a relationship of distant love, as characterized by sociologists Ulrich Beck and Elisabeth Beck-Gernsheim.

At its core, the notion of distant love is marked primarily by geographical distance in which "the lovers live many miles apart, in different countries even on different continents."[24] While the term is theorized for a contemporary, globalized context, it can be applied to historical contexts. With physical proximity not possible, the couple believed there were other ways for them to feel connected across distance; one of these was manifested through language.[25] As Antonietta reminded Loris on 14 November 1948, the flow of letters "must be constant, lively and continuous because if one day that disappears, it will be over." The couple's awareness of language also signalled their sensitivity toward the other, and their effort to avoid misreadings in the letters. Shades of self-censorship emerged in the process of writing, as each writer first faced within themselves the tensions and frustrations, uncertainties and satisfactions that regularly emerged in their lives. Antonietta and Loris were familiar with writing letters. As Antonietta Petris discusses in her foreword, writing letters had already become a way of life for them in August 1946, upon Loris's completion of his assignment in Ampezzo and subsequent departure for Venice. They wrote fervidly, constantly, as "the desire to see each other grew more intense."[26]

I now turn to a short summary of the story that marks these letters written at the outset of their relationship, an important precedent to the letter collection in this volume. Set in Venice and Ampezzo between August 1946 and September 1948, the synopsis provides a narrative behind the letters, a glimpse into the couple's first period of courtship and engagement before their transatlantic separation.

An Epistolary Precedent: The Letters between August 1946 and September 1948

With the war over in May 1945, the people of the commune of Ampezzo clung to a new life in which fear and suspicion belonged to the past.[27] The final withdrawal of the Nazi troops and the Cossack troops, who had been promised the territory by the Third Reich, was marked by the descent of the partisans returning from the mountains, flags waving atop the church towers, and the open countryside exuding tranquility once again."[28] At war's end, a feeling of euphoria hung in the air. It was accompanied by an ardent desire for peace and a fresh start:

> After all the fears that had stolen even the dimmest of sunrays, and all the anxieties that had poisoned the breath of every home and every family, a happiness exploded verging on madness. A time of absolute pervasive happiness abounded. There was dancing everywhere, on the squares, under the pergolas, on makeshift wooden stages ... and the heartfelt words of forbiddance voiced by the priests and bishops were viewed as meaningless.[29]

In this first year after the end of the war, Loris Palma was stationed in the neighbouring village of La Maina (Sauris), working on the completion of the Diga del Lumiei (completed in 1947), the most ambitious hydroelectric dam project in Europe at the time. At the end of a typical workday, Loris and his co-workers bicycled to Ampezzo to meet with their friends. To Antonietta and her friends, the presence of the young men of the SADE[30] symbolized not only a renewed vitality for the town but also hope for the future.

From the day Antonietta and Loris first set eyes on each other in the summer of 1946, the couple grew increasingly fond of each other. Together with their friends, they went hiking on the trails of the Monte Tinisa surrounding the valley. They danced at the local dance hall and took evening walks on Ampezzo's main street Via Nazionale. Indeed, these were happy days for the young couple: "Do you recall how happy I was on the eve of our famous excursion? We laughed so hard and joked around so much together! I will never forget these days!" wrote Antonietta in a letter to Loris on 13 September 1946. As the summer months of 1946 drew to an end, Loris's assignment in Ampezzo was completed. On 22 August 1946, he returned home to Venice, where he resumed work at the central offices of the SADE. Through their separation and occasional visits, the couple's attachment flourished. Longing, nostalgia, and hope marked their relationship now: "Imagine, my dear Antonietta, how I must feel, so far away from you, as I longingly look back to our hours together. As I left Ampezzo – with both of us distraught over my departure – you were constantly with me, on my mind and in my heart, for the entire journey," wrote Loris just hours after leaving Antonietta in Ampezzo on 30 August 1946.

No sooner had Loris departed Ampezzo than the young couple began to plan their formal engagement. "I am certain these months will pass quickly, and in December we can begin to set the foundation for our life together with the official engagement," wrote Loris optimistically on 30 August 1946. Certainly, the knowledge that they would soon be engaged helped to alleviate the hardships of being apart. Both agreed that writing would be crucial in sustaining their love, as Loris remarked in a letter to Antonietta, "The hardships we are facing must be relieved by our writings, and especially, by your writings of love ... they give me moral and physical strength" (1 September 1946). Antonietta was moved by the intensity of Loris's words. Yet she worried. Would the magical city of Venice and its "beautiful women" sweep him away from her affections? "Write to me often, very often, tell me what you are doing, where you are going, and I will do the same," she pleaded. While their hearts, bodies, and souls yearned for an imminent reunion, family and work obligations kept the couple apart for several months at a time.

The couple turned to writing to reflect upon their future while seeking solace: "It's eleven at night ... Only when I write to you do I feel you close to me ... I now live solely for our future" (3 September 1946). Nostalgia surfaced frequently in their letters. One evening, sparked by the pleasure of listening to opera music with her friends, Antonietta reminisced how "the music transported me to the place where I told you I belong to you, do you remember how beautiful it was? ... Suddenly a storm broke out and we took refuge in a little rustic house together with A ... and M ... and we sang together, we were so happy! ... I will wait for you constantly and faithfully just like the little Japanese girl waited for Captain Pinkerton" (20 September 1946). For his part, Loris rekindled fond memories of his stay in Ampezzo: "on the second evening that we met ... I asked you if you were engaged, or had ever been ... there, in that moment, my eyes were glued onto yours, and I resisted not to close them for fear that I might lose you" (25 September 1946).

In October 1946, Antonietta received a letter from her father, who by then was firmly settled in Montreal. The news could not be more devastating to the couple. Antonietta advised Loris, "He is planning to stay for a little while when he comes down. Oh! I can't go on, my heart tightens and I am breathless just thinking that I will need to leave you, ... no one, Loris, will separate me from you. I will write to my *papà* and inform him about us" (16 October 1946). Upon receiving this news, Loris was equally disheartened: "I was not expecting such a powerful blow, I never imagined such a precarious situation ... everything is in the hands of your *papà* and *mamma* ... I believe that going ahead with this will destroy two lives ... Imagine my state of mind ... Please write to your *papà*, as a good *papà* he will know how to relate to your situation, and in that way, things can return to the way they once were" (19 October 1946). At this early stage of their relationship, a transatlantic separation was nothing other than a bad omen. Antonietta was already too familiar with the meaning and consequences of a transatlantic separation. She had lived it from a very young age, watching her mother living apart from her father, a topic I return to in more detail later.

Introduction

The letters that followed this moment describe the desire for a highly coveted reunion in December when the couple would celebrate their engagement with their families. The anticipation was overwhelming and poetic: "Another twenty days await, Loris, ... you will see Ampezzo at its best, covered in snow, where everything is white, the mountains, the countryside, the rooftops, just imagine it ... each snowflake is an image of a butterfly in the sky" (8 December 1946). With both families' approval, including her absent father's, Antonietta and Loris were formally engaged on 25 December 1946.

In the next twelve months, the couple corresponded and visited each other as frequently as possible. Discussions about Canada came up now and then, to the point that Loris, too, was enthusiastic about the possibility of moving to Canada. "We spoke so much about it on numerous evenings that I believe in the future more and more," wrote Loris (11 March 1947). As with other prospective migrants, *L'America* symbolized a mythical place where a new life together would finally begin, a vast land where the couple could build a future with the support of Antonietta's parents, a place where, in the words of Loris, "I will work, we will work together, I will do everything possible to reach our dream of being happy and together. If I were the President of Canada, I would change the laws immediately," he wrote, so that he could join them at the earliest (30 April 1947).

Vittorio Petris returned home in December 1947, after twenty years of being away. For migrants like Vittorio, leaving for France and subsequently for Canada in the interwar period signified the pursuit of greater economic security. While the 1920s represent a period of restrictive migration worldwide, Italy's migrations remained as high then as in the 1880s and 1890s, with about 200,000 to 400,000 Italians immigrating per year until 1928.[31] Still, twenty years is a long time, and absence leaves its mark. While the impact of that long absence upon family members varied, for Antonietta, it was indelible. Loris, who was present at the family's moment of reunion at Venice's Santa Lucia train station, later recalled that fateful day: "The meeting was difficult, emotionally difficult, because the daughter did not know her father. There she was, closer to me than to him. Finally, we broke the trance and things necessarily became easier. To tell the truth, I was the one to recognize him on the train ... a gentleman wearing a hat, a long

American-style coat, you could distinguish him, yes and no, but from his features, I knew it was him."[32]

The visit of Antonietta's father opened the possibility of migrating to Canada for Antonietta and her mother, Lucia: "*Mamma* has decided, she is even interested in inquiring about the paperwork involved for us, God, it feels impossible to me, and yet, it will happen" (21 January 1948). Antonietta had agreed as well, certain that Loris would follow (as he had promised), noting in the same letter, "Do you think it will bring us luck? Yes, isn't that right?" Vittorio Petris returned by ship to Montreal on 12 April 1948, leaving his wife and daughter once again, but this time, with the near-certainty of an imminent reunion.

In the letters that followed, Antonietta discussed both her excitement and her ambivalence of travelling to a "new world." She described some of the complex immigration procedures, which comprised of blood tests, X-rays, and an interview at the Canadian Consulate in Rome, along with changes in dates of departure, and whether they should travel by airplane or by ship. The thought of leaving Loris, however, eclipsed all other concerns when she wrote on 13 July 1948: "My darling, but how, how can I leave you?" Finally, with the date of departure confirmed for Antonietta and her mother, Loris travelled to Ampezzo on 11 September to spend their final days together before accompanying them to Rome. On 21 September at Rome's Ciampino International Airport, mother and daughter boarded their flight, which would take them to Montreal over three days.[33]

"There will be a day in which everything will smile upon us": The Letters from September 1948 to July 1949

With the arrival of Antonietta and her mother in Montreal, the immediate family was reunited. The family's first objective had been met. The second objective now awaited: Loris's anticipated arrival in Canada. The letters presented in this volume begin with Loris's first missive written forty-eight hours after Antonietta's flight to Montreal; they conclude with Loris's last letter dated 7 July 1949. This first letter, dated 23 September 1948, earnestly describes his immediate emotional aftermath following her departure. The dramatic despair with which he details his downward spiral marks one of the most compelling moments featured in the correspondence. Aptly describing a lover's depth of sorrow, Loris penned, "It was as though I had died" (23 September 1948), as he returned home to his family in Venice, traumatized by the void that suddenly darkened his existence. In the same letter, he revealed it had been a day in which "an abyss had opened under my feet."

The separation from Loris proved no less troubling for Antonietta. In her first letter to Loris, she described an inconsolable tightening of the heart compounded by an acute breathlessness. In the same letter, however, she also showed immeasurable resilience and fortitude, as she wrote to him about how much more she treasured his love, "as strong and as deep as the ocean" (26 September 1948). In this letter and many subsequent ones, there was a promise of unification that was reinforced with words like, "you will see that in one way or another, you will come here." To demonstrate the seriousness of her commitment, Antonietta discussed in detail how she was taking action in regard to his joining her, advising him that she had met the agent who would assist her and her father to complete the Canadian sponsorship application for him. On 30 September 1948, Antonietta received Loris's first letter in Montreal, and her excitement was overwhelming, as she wrote, "I started to read it. Of course the first time I didn't read it, I devoured it." Flowing through the letters is a jumble of emotions that surface time and again.

ARRIVALS

In the weeks that followed her arrival, Antonietta explored Montreal in the company of her parents and their friends, sharing first impressions with Loris while careful to reassure him that "never, not even for a moment did I stop thinking of you" (26 September 1948). The Atlantic Ocean now stood between them and the separation was steeped in uncertainty. Still, the flow of communication was constant. The letters covered a plethora of topics, including family ties, work and military obligations for Loris, and new friendships, new work and cultural experiences, including learning English for Antonietta. Her observations included curiosities about the way people drank coffee, the music on the radio, and any social events she attended in Montreal's vibrant Italian community. Antonietta also travelled outside of ontreal and described her impressions, piquing Loris's curiosity about Canada, while she continued to update him on her trips to the travel agent and the immigration office. Antonietta's experience of culture shock is evidenced in these descriptions. The letters also provide insightful accounts of the intimate experience of settlement and the pull of the homeland that coloured this experience.

Antonietta wrote about the excitement and challenges she experienced in the garment-making industry (in the factory and at home), including her desire to contribute to the couple's future: "Since Tuesday I have been working in a large factory. I wanted to try it even though my *mamma* and my *papà* did not agree with me, I hoped to succeed ... so that I would feel that I am contributing to our future together." Antonietta's agency and relative freedom were also underscored, making evident that she was capable of working even though her parents didn't want her to. As well, nostalgia and self-awareness undergird the letters in remarkable ways, with lines like: "Those words that skidded across the ocean waves delivered your thoughts as they travelled toward me one metre at a time. They have dispatched your sorrow, your agony, your discouragement ... I have read and understood your sorrow and your love" (2 October 1948), followed by declarations of love, "here I am to you, for you, as always, heart, soul, and all of me" (8 October 1948).

TRANSNATIONAL TIES

Soon after the initial shock of their separation, writing became once again a regular occurrence in their lives. Writing was not only a vehicle of communication but also a space for respite and confidences, as one of the lovers reminisced: "A month has passed since we said goodbye, ... since then, one month has passed since this tribulation began, one month since we were together in Rome, walking side by side, happily, cheerfully, and all too conscious of what awaited us in a few short days" (17 October 1948). Concerns over an imminent war and Loris's military duty, coupled with descriptions of her new home, her impressions of life in Montreal were also remarked upon in the letters.

Throughout the correspondence, words of encouragement were constant between them: "You must be strong to persevere this rugged path, light will follow this darkness" (Loris to Antonietta, 20 October 1948), as were affective reassurances: "I adore you, my darling, I love you so very much, remember me and love me forever, tell me over and over again for me to be sure that you have not changed, and that you have not changed your mind" (25 October 1948). Despite the plethora of encouragements and declarations, tensions also surfaced in the couple's letters. The postal silence from two weeks or more of no mail triggered anxiety, uncertainty, and desolation: "There is no place for me to find peace. You can imagine why, can't you? Not even today did I receive news from you. I am devastated and disheartened in a way I cannot describe. Why, tell me, why do you do this?" (6 November 1948).

At the same time, information about new immigration regulations was shared, injecting renewed hope for an imminent reunion: "they have now introduced a new law, the fiancée can sponsor her fiancé provided the marriage takes place within 30 days of his arrival in Canada" (14 November 1948). In the weeks before and after Christmas, new experiences were detailed in Antonietta's letters, ranging from a visit to one of Montreal's largest department stores to the lighting of Christmas trees, giving Loris a sense of how Christmas was celebrated in Montreal. In the meantime, for Loris, upsetting news in the family encouraged him to write to Antonietta, "proceed as soon as possible with the application" (16 December 1948), with the promise that "our next Christmases will witness us together forever" (25 December 1948).

MAKING MONTREAL HOME

The year 1949 ushered in a series of news and entanglements. Across the spectrum of emotions, nostalgia predominated in a letter of 1 January 1949: "Oh memories of years past, why do you torment me?" While there still was no date in sight, the couple sensed a reunion approaching, and their impatience intensified, as the same letter shows: "A thousand letters are proof of our constant struggle to start our new life, a thousand letters have documented the advent of our long-awaited day, and all year our letters have asked, when will that day come?" With these questions, thoughts frequently turned to past memories as on 3 January 1949: "Even 1948 has ended, a new year is about to begin, a year filled with grace and joy for us, we hope; the beginning of last year was far more beautiful for us, it was a time that witnessed us together and jubilant in Ampezzo's small dance hall, do you remember, my darling?"

Regret in feeling that perhaps they had not loved each other enough while in Italy compounded their longing, leading them to feeling envy of "couples walking with their arms wound around each other" (3 January 1949). The need for solitude also emerged, and with it, feelings of fading. *Fading* in amorous relationships is described by philosopher Roland Barthes as a painful ordeal in which lovers appear to withdraw altogether from contact "without such enigmatic indifference even being directed against the amorous subject or pronounced to the advantage of anyone else, world or rival."[34] Still, Antonietta and Loris persevered. Antonietta continued to work in the clothing industry, attend language classes, and participate in social and cultural events with her parents as the immigration application for Loris advanced. By his account, Loris continued to work at the central offices of the SADE, attend evening classes, and follow his favourite soccer team, while tending to his parents and siblings. Throughout, the cries of nostalgia and melancholy grew louder over the ensuing months: "your absence, the more time passes, the more I feel it" (9 January 1949).

Antonietta had never experienced a Canadian winter before her arrival to Montreal, and described it in detail to Loris. She was reasonably confident that the freezing conditions would not dissuade Loris from joining her: "it takes me over half an hour to reach the factory by tram, the streets are impossible to walk on, they are covered in ice and snow" (1 February 1949). In the letters, Antonietta also detailed fragments of conversations with friends at work. By relaying these conversations to each other, Loris and Antonietta created a feeling of *co-presence* – a term employed by anthropologist Loretta Baldassar to describe how people maintain a sense of presence across distance through a variety of means, including the virtual, the physical, the imagination, and by proxy.[35] In doing so, the writers underscored the unaltered presence in their lives. For instance, in one letter Antonietta invited Loris to imagine himself in Montreal, writing on 16 January 1949: "we must see each other soon ... if we must suffer, it's much better to suffer together, whether here or at the end of the earth."

At the same time, she did not shy away from advising him of the hardships he would likely face in the first months of his arrival: "my

Loris, don't worry, and don't give up, the first months will be hard for you, as they have been for everyone, but then you will get used to it" (20 January 1949). With spring nearly approaching, Antonietta's family moved to a large apartment, "a lovely apartment composed of 5 rooms, electric heating, and all the necessary amenities" (15 February 1949). By then, Loris's immigration application had been submitted to the appropriate government offices, and a response was expected in several weeks' time. Descriptions of intense curiosity and imaginary worlds followed as on 15 March 1949 with words like, "Can you imagine what those days will be like?" During the Easter holidays in "sweet April," Loris had visited Antonietta's family in Ampezzo. Here, he had been surrounded by nature's familiar sights and sounds reminiscent of a time when the couple was together, as Loris wrote on 19 April 1949: "to return here is akin to fuelling a fire that has already been kindled." And he described the nature around him while reflecting on her absence: "this awakening grew more intense with your absence."

Spring and summer brought their share of highs and lows. On 4 May 1949 the ALI (Avio Linee Italiane, SA) airplane that carried the Torino (Grande Torino) soccer team crashed into the hill of the Basilica of Superga, just outside the city of Turin. There were no survivors. The team comprising many members of the Italian national football team was returning home after a match in Lisbon.[36] The desolation that Loris described in his letter represents both a personal and national grief. Shortly after, Antonietta announced that she had in her hands his boarding ticket. It was time to begin the travel preparations, firm up departure dates, arrange a meeting with the family of Antonietta's father in France, purchase gifts or items for Antonietta's family, visit Antonietta's family in Ampezzo, and say goodbye to co-workers, friends, and family members.

Loris was the first and only member of his immediate family to immigrate abroad, and his departure was especially devastating to his mother. The promise of Antonietta's love was the deciding force, and he was determined not to renounce it. In his last letter to Antonietta before travelling, the excitement of leaving his home is palpable, as he wrote on 7 July 1949: "Everyone is thinking of you, my darling, they are thinking of how happy you and your parents are as the wedding day approaches, and you will be married, to whom? I don't know? (laugh) I don't know?

(laugh) Try not to laugh too hard now, great news and surprises are about to reach you." Loris left for Paris on 11 July 1949 and from Le Havre sailed on the ss *Saturnia* for Quebec. He arrived on 25 July 1949 at the Port of Quebec, where Antonietta and her parents awaited him. There, they finally embraced and began their new life together.

Italian Postwar Migration to Canada: A History

The migration of Antonietta and Loris was motivated by love and the opportunity for a bright future. Their love story unfolded at the outset of a mass migration movement that for the most part reflected what historian James Hammerton calls a "migration of austerity," a typical occurrence in the postwar years.[37] Given the centrality of love as the primary motivating factor for Loris's migration, the love letters also engage with the concept of "discretionary migration," a trend in migration that Hammerton argues was more typically occurring in the later decades when there was greater affluence involving a "global drama of moving love stories."[38] In these letters, the depths with which the fulfillment of a romantic love was regarded is the primary motivation for migration and reunification. With love as the major factor motivating Loris to migrate to Canada, the path, as the letters show, was arduous, yet not impossible. For inspiration, the couple turned to Italian opera's melodramatic love stories as referents to their story. Both correspondents also seemed very aware of the need for resilience in the face of uncertainty. Both were cognizant that should their desire or commitment for the other diminish over the course of their separation, their story could collapse. Antonietta would have likely remained in Montreal and Loris would not have made the life-changing decision to leave his family and his beloved Venice.

In the century between 1876 and 1976, twenty-six million Italians immigrated beyond the peninsula's borders mostly to Europe, the Americas, and Australia. The postwar period alone witnessed seven million Italian women and men immigrating to similar destinations on a temporary and permanent basis. The letters of Antonietta Petris and Loris Palma are a remarkable collection written in the early years of the largest migration movement from Italy to Canada. This movement, defined by one historian as "one of the world's great

Introduction 29

voluntary migrations of the postwar,"[39] entailed the migration of approximately 430,000 to 470,000 men and women leaving Italy for Canadian destinations between 1946 and 1971,[40] with 23.2 per cent settling in Quebec, a large majority in Montreal.[41] Antonietta and her mother were among the earliest group of Italians arriving in Montreal after the Second World War. By the late 1950s, the number of Italian families immigrating to Montreal had soared to the point that by 1971, Italians represented a whopping 6 per cent of the total Montreal population.[42] Family affective ties were at the centre of this movement in significant ways.

From 1900 to 1930, over 115,000 Italian men migrated to Canada; women represented only 11 per cent of arrivals from Italy in the three decades with approximately 15,000 women migrating to Canada.[43] Many had come with the intention of working temporarily on the railways, and in the timber and mining camps. With the arrival of Italian women, and in the case of married men, their wives and children, a more permanent structure began to emerge in Italian communities – known at the time as "colonies" in Canada's major urban centres, Montreal and Toronto.[44] Very quickly vibrant Little Italies clustered in specific neighbourhoods exhibiting, as historian Donna Gabaccia notes, many of the social and cultural characteristics of the villages from which Italians came. In sum, these enclaves offered, "a lively street life, with vendors of food and businesses with Italian-language signs; crowds of children playing as women watched from open windows; men gathered around their clubs, cafés and bars; casual sociability within and between homes; workplaces dispersed among the residences; a Catholic church; and occasional street processions in honour of homeland saints."[45]

Montreal's Little Italy – also known as "La Petite Italie" – is the neighbourhood where the most important Italian parish was erected in Montreal. The Catholic church Madonna della Difesa, also known as Notre-Dame-de-la-Défense, was completed in 1919. Designed by artist Guido Nincheri and architect Louis-Roch Montbriand, it was built by the Italian immigrant community of the Molise region to commemorate the apparition of the Madonna della Difesa in Casacalenda, Campobasso. The church, the oldest and most important of Canada's Italian community, celebrated many of the first Italian marriages in Montreal, including the marriage of Antonietta and Loris in 1949.[46] The church served the community in critical ways, providing much-needed support in Italian, Catholic Mass in Italian, two schools, and an active community centre, the Casa d'Italia (completed in 1936).[47] This was the world that Antonietta's father frequented during the twenty years he was away from his family. This was also the world he imagined his wife and daughter living in upon joining him in Montreal.

As the Great Depression and the Second World War gave way, the late 1940s, and especially the 1950s and 1960s, witnessed unprecedented numbers of Italians arriving in Canada.[48] Ties with families across the oceans were reactivated and reconnected. In Antonietta's case, the end of the war witnessed the return of her father from Canada. His arrival in December 1947 signalled a family reunification with his wife and daughter, not in Italy, as perhaps Antonietta had hoped, but in Canada. Similar to other migrant households, a family-based migration was restored, and "family and kinship networks were at the root for the extensive migration chains that linked villages and towns in Italy to cities in Canada."[49] A new family-based sponsorship policy ensued in 1947 with the purposes of fostering national growth, and developing the nation's resources amid a larger domestic market.[50]

Immigration was encouraged, however, not without caution. In his oft-quoted speech, Prime Minister W.L. Mackenzie King stressed that the country's absorptive capacity would determine how many immigrants would be allowed into Canada from year to year so that "a fundamental alteration in the character of our population" would not occur.[51] Economic and population growth characterized Canada shortly after the Second World War. A buoyant economy was emerging, and new infrastructure (roads and electrical power facilities), buildings, schools, highways, and hospitals were being built to meet the needs of a growing population. Montreal emerged as Canada's "open city," a prevalently French-speaking city immersed in a highly industrialized economy combined with the demographic, economic, and social importance of an English-speaking minority.[52]

As demand for labour grew amid pressures from the international community, Canada liberalized its immigration laws. One outcome introduced in May 1947 entailed the widening definition of relatives: legal residents in Canada – able to receive and care for relatives –

could now sponsor family members well beyond the nuclear family. This directive made possible the sponsoring of Loris, who was by then formally engaged to Antonietta.[53] Italians benefitted from this policy to the extent that over 90 per cent of all Italians immigrating to Canada as part of the family sponsorship program made up the second largest group after British nationals as the source of Canadian immigration.[54]

The letters of Antonietta and Loris provide a bottom-up approach in revealing ways in which individuals – like others that I discuss in earlier studies – faced, fathomed, and negotiated their migration or the migration of a loved one in an early phase.[55] The emotional and physical challenges that migration created become apparent in the couple's moment-to-moment intimate lives. How memory and nostalgia undergirded their separation, and how migration contributed to a plethora of possibilities and uncertainties in their projections into the present and the imagined future are among the wealth of insights gleaned from the letters. A careful review compels readers to consider closely, and feel – through words, gestures, and reflections – what migration for love may have represented.

Emotions in the Letters and the Literature

The question of "what did it *feel* like?" directs us to the history of emotions, a rapidly expanding field that provides a fascinating perspective into the letters of Antonietta and Loris. While emotions and their meanings have piqued the curiosity of scholars, including philosophers, theologians, and scientists, over the past two millennia, in recent decades, historians of emotions have investigated more closely how emotions change and how their meanings differ across time and space. Historian Lucien Febvre is credited for invigorating an interest in emotions among historians.[56] More recently, through the introduction of concepts – from Carol and Peter Stearns' emotionology to William Reddy's emotives and emotional regimes and Barbara Rosenwein's emotional communities – new parameters have been introduced to identify change and causality in different kinds of emotions (fear, anger, jealousy, love, honour) across historical contexts and geographies. The impetus to understand the human experience from an emotional perspective has been so significant that the scholarship in the field has exploded, and an "emotional turn" emerged.[57] New inquiries and debates about what emotions are and whether they are understood in binary terms, as human biological universals or cultural constructions of varying degrees, or more of an "integrated biocultural world," have been among the broad questions generated in the field.[58] Understanding emotions, how they were experienced and represented, what aroused them, in what form, and with what effects across historical and cultural temporalities and spaces shape recent historical studies of emotions.[59]

Letters of intimacy exchanged between migrant lovers invite readers to enter a whirlwind of emotional constellations as they were experienced, reflected upon, constructed, and understood by the corresponding couples. The world of correspondence, writes Luisa Passerini, was a world different from actual life. And the love that the authors agonized and delighted over in their letters was a love that was drawn upon and expanded in the world of correspondence.[60] This particular universe was in many ways, a world of its own, separate from the realities of the lovers' day-to-day lives. It was a world that was "at once internally consistent, vital and self-supporting."[61] In contexts of long-distance migration, as in the case of Antonietta and Loris, letters were a vital communication device that spanned the intimate and public worlds of individuals and their communities both geographically and culturally as well as emotionally and intimately.[62]

In the letters, sentiments were pondered and elaborated; they were also normalized and heightened.[63] Translated into words that the heart, body, and soul of the writers *felt*, attention to the emotions in the letters offers a view onto the tensions and changes that distance and separation imposed onto a couple. An emotional lens offers a perspective into the life of the correspondents' minds. Ego-documents like letters point to the interplay of emotions and distance, as well as gender.[64] Equally relevant, they invite us to examine the emotional labour that writing intimately involved across transnational spaces.[65] Here, emotions are also mediated – to borrow from Baldassar – by various degrees of co-presence.[66] For instance, emotions are negotiated and illustrated virtually through the words of confidences, intimacy, and longing; by proxy, through the discussions about objects (photographs and letters), events, and loved ones; and through the lovers' imaginary leap, engendered through their embodied emotional experiences, and the spiritual (prayer and appeal to God) and the literary-musical (lyrics of arias identified and appropriated to the lovers' story) references in the letters.

In the letters, the body served as a window into the spirit of the lovers.[67] By articulating reflections of her or his body's undulations, the writers created a transparency of feeling directed to the correspondent as further proof of their despondent or glowing state. Writing was an inextricable emotional, melodramatic experience that shaped and was shaped by the state of mind and body of the lovers, extending beyond the hyperbolic expressions that typically characterize love letters.[68] Loris's description of the impact of Antonietta's departure is an appropriate example here: "That day an abyss opened under my feet, and I had to pay careful attention not to plunge inside, yes, my spirit and my heart were not normal, my body had never before felt a similar fatigue, my legs failed to hold me steady, rather they were there to vacillate my body back and forth" (23 September 1948). In addition to underscoring a synchronicity between the emotional mind and body, this excerpt is one of several identified in the letters that offer an inter-subjective emotional experience between the writers and readers.

To borrow an expression from historian Javier Moscoso, these letters offer, for instance, "a cartography of misery,"[69] whereby the emotional experience is one of suffering and pain, culturally meaningful sensations that are configured according to the principles of performative representation in which both victim and spectator co-exist.[70] In the letters, the spectator, "can, against all logic, experience the sensations of another, enter into the body of another, and somehow be one being with him or her."[71] The victim, by contrast, also modulates his or her experiences in accordance with outside evaluations and expectations, making his experience of feeling both natural and learned.[72] The pain in these words alludes to a despair that is analogous to a melancholy (viewed as a combination of longing and nostalgia[73] among other associations described by Freud and Kristeva) that imbued the letters while underscoring the sociability of painful events and their meaning in the creation of communities.[74] The expressions and metaphors are indicative of the couple's epistolary complicity. They wrote both aware and hopeful that the expressions on paper would resonate with the other and communicate an immediate understanding, underscoring once again the ties that bound them.

Gender and the Letters of Antonietta and Loris

Love, migration, and gender are intertwined themes in the letters of Antonietta and Loris. As historians and other scholars have shown, gender plays a critical role in the shaping of migrant experiences of the self in the world, and the attitudes and norms that shape them. While recognizing migrants as emotional and sexual beings is paramount, the consideration of "the intersectionality of love, sex, and emotion in framing mobility behavior" is as critical as experiences that are "culturally, socially, and economically sited and interdependent, both 'at home' and 'away.'"[75] An examination of the emotional landscapes of migration through a gender lens, therefore, more accurately captures the multiplicity of spatial and temporal connections that characterize migrants' lives.[76]

Gender and emotions intersect in complex ways in the intimate language identified in the letters. Sherry Simon notes, "The recourse to letters itself follows a feminist agenda in exploring the domain of the intimate."[77] By carefully observing the language and its meanings, I endeavour to discern how gender attitudes and norms were reinforced and negotiated in the letter writers' imagining of their lives in the past, present, and future. Intimate letters illustrate ways in which young couples accepted, negotiated, and challenged expected gender ideologies in their relationships both within sending and receiving societies, including transnational contexts like Canada and Italy, through the language they used in their letters. Since the mid-1970s, feminist scholars have analyzed gender in language systems employed verbally and in writing, and they have argued that language fundamentally reflects and creates a culture's unconscious.[78]

Traditional divisions of labour were underscored in the couple's gendered projections of their lives together in Montreal. Normative roles learned before migration were reiterated and resisted after migration, as anthropologist Sarah Mahler and others argue in studies on communication and transnational relationships, underscoring the point that gender relations prior to migration affected migration,

Introduction 35

settlement patterns, and ongoing relations between men and women.[79] For instance, once Loris's father was laid off work, the responsibility was placed on Loris to continue working and provide for his parents and his two sisters at home. Loris viewed his new familial duties connected to his future life with Antonietta as proof of his breadwinning capabilities as a husband. In the letters to Antonietta, he iterated that the fulfillment of his duties with his immediate family was an assurance of his commitment and love for Antonietta as a future provider-husband: "I became more understanding, more reasonable, more responsible. All of these are privileges that add to my experience, so that one day you will sing about your friend who is very aware of family consequences ... he will love you even more" (23 January 1949).

In their correspondence, gender ideologies were also resisted. For instance, in a letter penned on 29 November 1948, Antonietta proceeded to describe to Loris her hunting experience in the company of her father and his business partner in the Laurentian Mountains, a few hours' drive north of Montreal: "What luck they had! .... I did not do anything, I had a small rifle with no cartridges (don't laugh); ... and I called out an expression that still makes him laugh." While admitting that hunting was not an activity she enjoyed for herself, her description underscores two other points: first, that Loris's presence was increasingly normalized among her friends and family, and secondly, that once in Montreal he would be invited to join the other male members of the family. In the latter case, Antonietta felt it necessary to remind him that his place was by her side rather than with her father: "They're already talking about turning you into a hunter ... of crabapples!? As *Signora* C ..., the wife of my *papà*'s partner keeps telling me, 'When your Lorenzo will be here, I urge you not to let him go with these two rascals, keep him home, make sure he stays with you, and he doesn't go hunting on Sundays.'"

Loris's letters to Antonietta are imbricated with a patriarchal language to show, unconsciously or not, characteristics of self-restraint and protection more frequently assigned to men. In comparison to Antonietta's language, Loris's tone is also more instructional and disconsolate, though no less dramatic. By contrast, Antonietta's language is more aligned with typically feminine characteristics, that is, nurturing, sensitive to the needs of others, spontaneous, and dynamic. While both authors sought support and offered reassurance to one another, Antonietta demonstrated an acute awareness of herself and her surroundings, revealing time and again resourcefulness in the pursuit of her dream. In the process, she revealed a "resistant centre" in making sense of the new challenges they faced with the Atlantic Ocean separating them: "I started to read it. Of course the first time, I didn't read it, I devoured it, I understood just a few sentences ... and I cried, I cried so hard that tears rolled down and my chest heaved in desperate sobs. That cry, however, brought me serenity, it melted the knot that had been constantly tightening at my throat, ... I will learn to accept this new torment and wait with patience" (30 September 1948).

A gender lens throws light on an additional element identified in the letters: excerpts and references to arias of Italian operas like Giacomo Puccini's *Madama Butterfly* and Gaetano Donizetti's *L'elisir d'amore*.[80] The excerpts that the couple selected for inclusion in their letters reflect the characters and situations with which they identified, similar perhaps to the way a couple today might turn to a particular love song that mirrors their feelings and their relationship in that moment or while reminiscing. The melodrama here is imbued with questions of politics and religion, as well as with gender and sexuality.[81]

With the increasing popularity of opera in Italian society in the nineteenth century, Susan McClary notes, operatic representations contributed to the development and dissemination of moral codes, values, and normative behaviour.[82] On occasion, for instance, Loris used operatic references to reaffirm the affections of a devoted fiancé, as in the letter of 13 December 1948 in which he referred to the aria, "una furtiva lagrima" in Donizetti's *L'elisir d'amore*: "Isn't this the greatest poem of all, because to love and to die calls for a tribute to joy and sorrow, both ripening and cultivating love." Similarly, in a letter written a few weeks following their separation, Antonietta highlighted the strength and perseverance she endeavoured to adopt, in citing *Madama Butterfly*'s female protagonist, Cio-Cio San, "I recall the Butterfly's words, 'and I wait a long time, and does not weigh on me the long waiting'" (8 October 1948). The letters evince the intimate gendered worlds of the authors and illustrate ways in which Antonietta and Loris believed they would comply with or negotiate in response to the gender norms and roles of Italian society of the late 1940s. They did this as they imagined a future together in Canada.

Family was critical in creating continuity and connecting people to the past and future.[83] Familial affection, longing, and memory were central to maintaining these connections, and during this postal age, they were frequently channelled through letters. As I show in an earlier study, the level of kinship support that was sustained transnationally through migrant correspondence was remarkable and highly diffused.[84] In the letters of Antonietta and Loris, dynamics of familial support are evidenced in several family situations elaborated in the letters. One of these relates to Antonietta's concern over her grandmother's well-being. Here, she asks Loris to visit her family over the Christmas holidays and report back to her: "Today, D ... wrote to us telling us that *la nonna* [my grandmother] is feeling very down ... If you can, please do your best to visit them at Christmastime so that you too can tell me how she is doing, and how she seems to you, I am very worried about her" (14 November 1948).

In urging Loris to act on her behalf, Antonietta underscored her family's approval of their relationship as well as the bonds forged between the respective families.[85] As bonds were reified across borders, they contributed to the shaping of a transnational emotional community, a community defined by historian Barbara Rosenwein as the same as social communities, including families and neighbourhoods in which systems of feeling are uncovered.[86] Communities, particularly intimate communities in the day-to-day of migrants and their transnational loved ones have been explored through the notion of "transnationalism from below," with public issues of labour, capital, and citizenship being prioritized in earlier studies of the transnational and diasporas.[87] As Donna Gabaccia and Loretta Baldassar suggest, "a focus on intimacies across borders, whether transnational or diasporic, unfastens the boundaries of the private sphere by locating it in a space larger than that of a single nation."[88] In this case, the private sphere was primarily set in two households, in Canada and Italy, and the socio-historical and cultural communities that surrounded them.

Migrant Correspondence: A Historical Inquiry

The emotional communities of migrant correspondent couples writing in the mid-twentieth century like Antonietta and Loris[89] are imbued with a strong sense of "spiritual communion," a state of being described by David Gerber in the correspondence of Mary Ann Archbald that mystically broke down the barriers of time and space for a limited period as she wrote to her friend Margaret.[90] A spiritual communion between the lovers in this collection is manifest in the ubiquitous questions and answers, the voices of self-reflexivity and awareness, the detailed descriptions of the authors' emotional highs and lows, the emotional energies diffused in their words, and in the materiality of the letters. Through these literary devices, a spiritual communion was made real as each of the correspondents transcended the temporal and spatial separation between them. The spiritual intimacy shared between them is at times so palpable that it virtually jumps out of the letters' pages and into the readers' subjective worlds.

The letters of Antonietta and Loris constitute both love letters and migrant letters. Love letters are, in the words of one literary scholar, "the expression, par excellence, of sentiment" transporting us to the eternal and the repetitious, to the fleeting and the unexpected, but also to everyday life with its codes and banalities.[91] An "early type of transnational social space,"[92] the migrant letter surmounted physical and temporal geographic barriers to create and maintain emotional and affective ties between people who were separated. While the main purpose of love letters, broadly speaking, was closely tied to the maintenance of an affective connection between the writers, migrant letters had multiple functions: they justified leaving home, they established migration chains, and they helped others understand what the migration experience could potentially mean for them, should they decide to give it a try. In letters, immediate and extended family members and others sometimes requested money, in others, and sometimes in the same letters, emotional and intimate bonds were reified.

In other cases, silence, omissions, and even just money alone, replaced letters, jeopardizing the suspension of close ties.[93] While the literacy skills of many working-class migrants and their loved ones varied from rudimentary to more advanced, separation by migration

Introduction 39

served as powerful motivation for individuals to improve their writing skills. Antonietta and Loris both came from families who were literate. Beyond their formal education, Antonietta and Loris continued to nurture their passion for reading and writing. This is evident not only in their literary syntax and style but also in their choice of words and expressions, and in the subjects discussed, that extended beyond family and everyday preoccupations to include music, cinema, theatre, opera, the writing of the self, and nature and the seasons (underscored in chapter 9). As they penned their thoughts, they brought together constellations of emotional, imaginary, cultural, economic, spiritual, and political worlds.[94]

While letters are unquestionably fragmentary and mediated like other biographical documents, they are composed in specific socio-historical and familial contexts. Similarly, they are composed through a subjective and personal lens within a larger cultural universe of memories, norms, and traditions. With the exception of notes addressed to family members at the letters' closings, the letters in this volume were directed to the lovers themselves. These letters were written with elements of poetic conviction, and their remarkable literariness and emotional élan provide access to the reflective and imaginary worlds of the young couple writing between Montreal and Venice.

In the experiences of absence and presence evoked in the letters, the writers' transnational worlds, understood as "the process by which immigrants forge and sustain simultaneous multi-stranded social relations that link together their societies of origin and settlement,"[95] transpire, along with their words, gestures and norms, identities, ideologies, and more. Reading their letters may inspire an engagement with the authors' worlds and more contemporary transnational lives. The narratives in the letters transport readers to universes that are both familiar and distinct from the contemporary world. The personal is political. In this case, by demarginalizing the world of ordinary lovers like Antonietta and Loris – a shift away from the ubiquitous publication of love letters of professional writers – I bring a unique genre of everyday letters to the centre of migration experiences. This epistolary auto/biography written with candour and simplicity, especially in Antonietta's case, is anything but simple.[96] Their narratives contribute to humanizing the experience of migration through the migrants' own words. They usher a much-needed understanding of the challenges that overwhelming numbers of migrants and their significant others faced in the past and currently face in the present. The worlds and voices that are brought to light in this collection provide a glimpse into the interior and exterior dilemmas of migrants and their loved ones of the past and the present. It is my hope that the letters will evoke a heightened empathy and awareness of the infinite emotional, social, and physical hardships of ordinary women and men who in the past and in more recent years have migrated abroad, leaving their homelands and their significant others behind.

The transnational letters of Antonietta and Loris presented in their entirety in this volume facilitate a reading of separation and its undoings while privileging the voices of the migrants and their significant others. For this reason I have chosen to present the letters in a collection format, rather than through an analytical lens that I adopted in my earlier studies on migrant letters. The collection format, which featured letters in their relative entirety with editors' deletions, was commonly adopted in studies of migrant letters from at least the first decades of the twentieth century. This includes the widely cited five-volume study *The Polish Peasant in Europe and America* (1918– 1920) by the American and Polish team of sociologists William Thomas and Florian Znaniecki. With the work of immigration historians George Stephenson, Marcus Lee Hansen, and Theodore Blegen that followed in the 1920s, the migrant letter increasingly gained currency as an important source for representing a more inclusive, democratic history of nations.[97] Historians of the New Social History in the 1960s began to appreciate, as well, the analytical potential of many of the textual deletions that had been formerly considered trivial, such as health, family gossip, friendship, personal inquiries, and salutations and greetings.[98] With few exceptions, and for practical limitations, many of the published collections presented only one side of the correspondence, that is, the letters of the men and women who immigrated. In many of these collections, the letters of those who remained in the homeland, if available, had been left out of the migration epistolary narrative.[99]

Increasingly from the 1970s onward, historical studies analyzed themes around work, family, and settlement in urban and rural communities. From the late 1990s, these themes were complemented by analytical approaches that examined dreams, nostalgia, absence, politics, and separation. The emergence of digital humanities in the early 2000s drew an interest in publishing migrant letters in digital platforms. With the expanding field of history of emotions, a further shift resulted in an invigorated scholarship on migrant correspondence.[100] This collection of migrant love letters contributes to the scholarship of migrant correspondence in significant ways. Drawn together, the historical studies developed in the last few decades are aligned with two fundamental methodologies that have shaped the scholarship in the twentieth century, that is, the analytical approach and the less common letter collection approach.

The letters in *With Your Words in My Hands* will be of interest to researchers, teachers and students, and the general public. The book will draw interest on questions of personal narratives, transnational intimacy, migration, and settlement, among other areas in history, anthropology, sociology, language and literature, human geography, political science and law, gender studies, family history, and the history of emotions. The book invites readers to explore the epistolary lives of migrants and to further appreciate issues related to migration, correspondence, intimacy, identity, belonging, melancholy, resilience, gender, agency, and presence. Among other aspects, the letters offer reflections on epistemology, the practice of letter-writing and its co-relations with affective ties, and mobility. Finally, a close reading of the correspondence encourages readers to consider the letters in relation to the age-old question, "Does distance make the heart grow stronger?" and to the digital world whose technologies have reconfigured the ways for couples and significant others to remain in touch.

A Meeting between Sources: Textual Memories and Oral Memories

In an interview filmed in 2011, Antonietta discussed with me the letters that she and her late husband Loris had exchanged in the late 1940s, when they were *fidanzati* (engaged to be married). In her reflections on the memories in the letters, she recalled,

Those memories, let's say, were blurry, they were, really so distant from me, it's almost as though this period did not exist, instead, ah, no, no, that's not the way it is, that's not the way things are ... it's clear, and it became even more clear to me when I read it, when I reread the letter because these first ones, especially, I had never [re]read, and when I [re]read the letter, there, in that instant, I saw once again that moment, I saw again, I felt again the sorrow that I experienced sixty-three years ago: the pain, the emotion, and ... the distance ... yes, you know. It wasn't easy, however, you see ... we pushed forward with determination, with the desire to move ahead and reach our goal, and we did it! But, it cost us dearly. We spent very happy days together, but they were so short, so few, you know. At the time, we were always afraid, afraid of not ..., of losing each other, because when two people are far apart, that too can happen. Instead, everything has passed, and now all that remains are memories, memories that are much more vivid when I read these letters, the first letters that Loris and I wrote to each other.[101]

Letters, particularly love letters and migrant letters, are, in the words of historians Mary Jo Maynes, Jennifer Pierce, and Barbara Laslett, revealing in myriad, complex ways. Not only do they memorialize a single performance of the self, but also they reveal the terms that made that performance intelligible, the cultural register of the roles upon which their authors drew as they sat down to write.[102] Oral histories, by contrast, are mediated and re/constructed in contexts that involve more than the narrating self, and the researcher and/or interviewer who brings their own experiences, knowledge, and concerns to the interview. Oral histories and letters share other points in common. Both, for instance, are products of "an active process of the creation of meanings,"[103] and both sources originate in cultural processes in which relationships and their overt or covert experiences, not to mention the meanings embedded in a past, present, and future can be explored. Both sources elucidate individual and collective memories, and the memories in between.[104]

As oral historians have argued since at least the 1980s, oral histories, similar to other historical sources that recount human experiences (including a statement obtained at a government inquiry, a newspaper

Introduction

43

report, a diary, a memoir, a letter), are "an artificial, partial, and subjective representation, and all involve some degree of retrospectivity and thus variability over time," both of the narrators and the narratives themselves.[105] Given the parallels between the two sources, whereby "all remembering – involves a dialectical relationship between these different selves at different times,"[106] I explore the kind of knowledge that can be gleaned from the process of re/collecting memories when the letters and oral histories come together for a researcher's interpretation. In this next section, I discuss the triangulate epistemological enterprise of working with the letters, the interviews, and the collapsing of the two sources together; I examine the intersecting lives of the letters and their authors' experiences and memories in conjunction with inquiries about the letters with Antonietta.

From our first meetings, Antonietta greeted me with a smile and a readiness to get to work on the letters. Often, letters were placed on the dining table prior to my arrival, and no sooner had she prepared a cup of coffee for us than she picked up a letter and began to read it. Sometimes, she read a sentence, and then reflected on the memories that surfaced from the reading. Other times, she marvelled at the extraordinary emotional attachment she and Loris had expressed in their letters. When she came across a particularly compelling line, she often stopped in awe of the depth of their emotionality and the imaginary leap imbued in the letters. Other times, she appeared amazed at her own emotional journey, noting one day, "My God, I fell in love via correspondence!" Candid moments of light humour also surfaced as we came across uncommon lexicon or analogy that she or Loris had deployed in their letters. Nostalgia for a lost time and place infused Antonietta's rereading of the letters as well. Regret also emerged as she wondered aloud why she and Loris had never reread the letters together over the course of their lives.

During our meetings, we discussed her childhood and formative years and her family in her native town of Ampezzo. Her father's immigration to Canada and his twenty-year absence followed by his return to Ampezzo in 1947–48 were significant life markers. The summer of 1946 was a turning point as she began to enjoy the dance hall and the movies that her town offered. After meeting Loris, Antonietta also began to imagine living her life outside of Ampezzo, in Venice, where she dreamed of attending with Loris their favourite operas at the Teatro La Fenice and plays at the Teatro Goldoni, among other cultural events.

But what about the Second World War? Antonietta was barely twelve years of age when the war had started in Italy. In Antonietta's and Loris's letters, there is hardly any mention of war and its toll. When I asked her about why she believed this was so, Antonietta replied that the desire to forget the war once it was finally over was overwhelming. In one of our meetings in late 2011, Antonietta mused, "During the war, death was in our face. Once the war was over, all of us wanted to forget the sufferings, the anguish of the war."[107] Antonietta was a young girl when the war had started in 1939, yet even in her nineties, she recalls parts of the horrors that took place in her hometown while the German and Italian armies, the Cossacks and the Partisans waged war. Silence on the subject of war in the letters, however, underscores what was said and what was not said in the letters, not because the war was insignificant to her and Loris, but more probably because it was a reality that both were all too well acquainted with. Writing soon after the war required that memories of the war be preserved in silence in order to give way to the couple's earnest desire for peace and hope.

Other silences in the letters shaped their conversations – silences relating to desire and socially acceptable forms of expression. Family tensions and their repercussions represent other silences that surfaced in the transatlantic letters following Antonietta's arrival in Montreal. This silence concerns the experiences of Antonietta's parents. Antonietta, in fact, reveals very little about how her mother and father coped with living with each other after a twenty-year separation. Vittorio Petris did everything he could to please his daughter, not only by providing for her but also in supporting her wish for Loris to join her in Montreal. About Antonietta's mother, Lucia Martinis, scant details emerge in the letters about how she adapted to her new life alongside her husband in Montreal. One event evinces some of the challenges she faced in her migration from Ampezzo to Montreal, the day she suddenly fell ill – as described by Antonietta in a letter to Loris on 16 January 1949. On this day, Lucia suffered a nervous breakdown. The reasons for the sudden onset of the breakdown remain unclear in the letter to Loris. When I inquired about the incident, Antonietta briefly elaborated on the circumstances that had triggered it with the understanding that the information would remain confidential.

The letters, as I discussed earlier, describe feelings, events, activities, and everyday occurrences, with an intensification of emotive hyperboles, declarations, and reflections on the love the separated couple shared. But what happened to Antonietta's and Loris's affective bond once they were reunited? The couple grew together, and their love for each other flourished over six decades. In the words of Antonietta, "He adored me ... [H]e had a strong personality, at the same time, he loved me immensely."[108]

Meeting with Antonietta was instrumental in the transcription and translation phases of the project. Often, Antonietta would read the letters as I checked the accuracy of the transcriptions. The exercise of reading and cross-reading was especially important. This was not so much the case for Antonietta's calligraphy which appeared mostly legible, but rather for clarifying the meanings of words or expressions related to the local dialect. In the case of Loris's letters, Antonietta's reading of his letters proved beneficial especially because his calligraphy was markedly more intricate and illegible in part because of his penmanship but also because the pen's ink had bled through the paper. Reading his letters was further complicated by his writing style and language, which are more convoluted. At times, they left us both asking ourselves what it was that he had intended to say.

Loris wrote his letters through a language he was familiar with, a language whose poetic and religious character provided him with the tools to declare his love – in a way akin, perhaps, to Dante declaring his love for Beatrice. Loris wrote to Antonietta in a language that more closely preserved his masculinity while providing an emotional élan to the subject of his adoration. By contrast, for Antonietta writing was simpler, unequivocal, and serious. Her writing flowed with ease and lucidity as she candidly described her fears, her concerns and her affections for Loris. She appears to have written with less fanfare, not because she cared less, but rather because she was less hindered by language in declaring her love for Loris. She wrote with complete clarity. Rereading the letters together brought enjoyment and satisfaction to both of us, particularly to Antonietta, who showed grit, determination, and good humour in advancing with the project, despite never imagining her letters being part of a book.

Antonietta's participation in the recovery of the voices of the letters provided an important opportunity to reflect on two sources of memory coming together. The co-relation between sensory history and memory appears particularly relevant. Senses like touch, Paula Hamilton argues, can serve as an effective "mnemonic device or trigger to remembering."[109] If this is the case, in what ways did holding the letters over sixty years after they were written affect Antonietta's recollection of the letters and her transatlantic relationship with Loris? The excerpt that appears in the introduction of this section[110] evokes notions of time and distance, and the couple's determination to stay the course, as Antonietta held the letter in her hands. The memories of the experience and the challenges they faced are voiced quite strongly. Similarly, their resilience and steadfastness are highlighted in the narrative, as she notes: "we pushed forward with determination, with the desire to move ahead and reach our goal, and we did it!" With these words, the impulse remained to say more about their love at a distance, urging Antonietta to reflect on the difficulties the couple faced: "But, it cost us dearly. We spent very happy days together, but they were so short, so few, you know. At the time, we were always afraid, afraid of not ..., of losing each other, because when two people are far apart, that too can happen."

The awareness that their relationship could have been ruptured in the wake of distance gives way to resignation and reflection about the memories with the words, "Instead, everything has passed, and now all that remains are memories, memories that are much more vivid when I read these letters, the first letters that Loris and I wrote to each other." The sentence refers to the oft-cited perception of "I remember it as though it happened yesterday" that is associated with Proust's notion of "involuntary memory," signalling the obliteration of the passage of time between the original event and its re-experience in memory.[111] Through touch, time no longer stood between Antonietta and her memories. Touching the letters while reflecting on her love story with Loris helped her not only to recall the past but also it gave her a sense of the past in the present.[112] In doing this, past memories appear to have become more vivid and more tangible.

Self-narration and agency are two concepts inter-related in the juxtaposition of Antonietta's oral and textual memories related to the letters. Agency, in this case, is "embodied in persons who evolve in context; people's stories build upon their lived experiences over time and in particular interpersonal, social, cultural, and historical settings that they in turn continue to work through and transform in their present."[113] Examining Antonietta's narrative through the lens of agency underscores her voice and the reconstruction of the past as she views it today, perhaps no differently than when Loris had first shown me his letters and offered to discuss them for an earlier study. However, in Antonietta's case, there is an additional factor to consider. When Antonietta and I began the journey with the letters in 2011, nearly four years had passed since Loris's death, and Antonietta was still mourning. Yet, her decision to collaborate on this project remained undaunted. Perhaps revisiting the letters gave Antonietta an opportunity to be heard on her own terms. She understood that it afforded her space to engage with her life's accomplishments, amid the increasing isolation she felt following Loris's death and her move to a retirement home. The process of talking about the past became a form of therapy and a means of holding on to her memories, her identity, and her sense of place and belonging.[114] In actively collaborating with me, Antonietta contributed to making sense of history for her, her family, and others; she became an "active maker of history."[115]

Diving into Translation and Transcreation: [116]
Reflections on Translating the Letters

The letters of Antonietta and Loris have been translated from Italian to English to provide access to English-speaking audiences interested in international migration and intimate letters of the twentieth century. Advances in translation studies over the twentieth century have shown that translation, "far from being a dilettante pursuit accessible to anyone with a minimal knowledge of another language, is 'one of the most difficult tasks that a writer can take upon himself.'"[117] In the words of literary theoretician J. Levý, "A translation is not a monistic composition, but an interpenetration and conglomerate of two structures. On the one hand, there are the semantic content and the formal contour of the original, on the other hand the entire system of aesthetic features bound up with the language of the translation."[118]

For guidance in the process of translating the letters, I turned to the field of literary translation. The letters' literariness required that I draw more closely from approaches used in literary translation rather than in commercial or other areas of translation, even though the letters were not written for literary or publication purposes as is frequently the case of novelists, essayists, poets, and other educated writers. Overwhelmingly, the letters were originally intended for one reader, the absent lover. Translating the letters into English would change that. While the letters would need to reflect a lexicon, structure, punctuation, and style similar to the original texts, they would need to be translated for a broad audience. Inevitably, this would influence how I translated the letters.

A translation of the letters would offer a reading in another language. It would also breathe new life and continuity to the letters themselves, and give new impetus to the writings of migrants and their families and other mobile individuals in the twentieth century. According to literary translator Edith Grossman, a translation of this nature "expand[s] our ability to explore through literature [and other works] the thoughts and feelings of people from another society or another time ... It expands and deepens our world, our consciousness in countless, indescribable ways."[119] But what form must a translation take in order to be felt so deeply? Should it adhere more closely to the original text's language, form, and structure? Or should it reflect varying degrees of liberties from the original text in order to achieve, as Walter Benjamin suggests, "that intended effect [intention] upon the language into which he/she was translating which produced in it the echo of the original"?[120]

While these questions lead us to other questions, a point raised by Mark Polizzotti in his book *Sympathy for the Traitor* perhaps best responds to a translator's dilemma. He notes that "translation ... far from being a rote exercise, is a constantly shifting evaluation of priorities, in which the translator combs through the available resources and draws ... upon his own experience in order to voice the original author's utterances credibly."[121] As I journeyed through endless hours of back and forth reading, translating and editing the letters, I endeavoured to reconcile the issue of literal versus liberal translation.[122] The process required constant negotiation and renegotiation between ideas, language, and style. I drew inspiration from Sherry Simon's point that "translators are *flâneurs* of a special sort, adding language as another layer of dissonance to the clash of histories and narratives on offer in the streets and passageways. Their trajectories across the city and the circulation of language traffic become the material of cultural history."[123]

I strived to translate the letters while making every attempt to be faithful to the original authors' utterances meanings, intentions, as well as the letters' characteristics, vagaries, and quirks.[124] This included making choices that would help discern the English text as "emotionally and artistically"[125] close to the original text and, as much as possible, to the intention of the letters' first readers. As I read the letters, I thought of Antonietta's and Loris's voices, and I imagined their younger selves, sitting in a quiet space at home with a pen or pencil in hand, composing a letter for one another. In the process, I aimed to keep the text "emotionally and artistically" close to the original text. Hence, readers can expect to meet inconsistencies reflective of the intimacy and immediacy true to the nature of this personal correspondence. For instance, in a number of letters, the upper case is employed in the closing salutation, as in "Your Loris"; in other letters, the lower case is adopted. The irregularity in the letters is thus preserved.

In the following section, I highlight some of the more salient difficulties or dilemmas I faced as I translated the letters and made choices. At the outset, the language in the letters required multiple close readings of the texts for the tasks of initial understanding, researching, and identifying equivalent terms in English. The problem, as Grossman notes, is that the languages that are spoken and written are too sprawling and too unruly to be contained, and any attempt to grasp a language in the process of creating a translation is intensely complex to an alarming, almost schizophrenic degree, because the second language is just as elusive, dynamic, and recalcitrant as the first.[126] One of the issues I encountered in the Italian text is the frequent use of words like *pensiero*, literally meaning thought, or *grande*, meaning big. The common use of words like *bella*, the adjective in the feminine gender, or *bello*, in the masculine gender, meaning beautiful, is another example. In one of Antonietta's first transatlantic letters (30 September 1948), *bella/bello* is used six times. The questions here were two-fold: should I have endeavoured to use the English equivalent first used in this particular letter and later, throughout all of the collections, or should I have used instead synonyms that captured the nuanced meanings of *bella/bello* in the original text? I identified a solution in a compromise. I used "beautiful" in three of the six *bella* or *bello* instances in which the term seemed more appropriate and stylistically reflective of the authors' lexicon and likely intention to repeat certain words for an intended effect. In the other cases where the term *beautiful* seemed inadequate, I used other words like *special*, *better*, and *marvellous* that more aptly conveyed the action or event in question.

Local, dialectical, or regional terms also presented a problem, especially if the associated meaning was unclear. In a number of cases, I inquired of Antonietta about the meaning of the terms or expressions. One example was the occasional use of the term *vecio*, as in *mio vecio*, in reference to Loris, and *mia vecia* in reference to Antonietta. While *vecio* is an adjective that describes something old, in the regional languages of Friulano and Veneto, the term evokes a form of endearment that has little to do with the notion of old or a person's advanced age. In this case, I resolved to translate the affective appellation *vecio* as *darling* or *sweetheart* in the letters.

Issues around style and structure were also challenging in the process of translating the letters. Loris and Antonietta adopted remarkably different writing styles. As mentioned earlier, Antonietta wrote using an exceptionally candid, emphatic tone, articulating her thoughts clearly and fluidly to Loris. Her writing style is reflective of her cheerful and thoughtful personality. On the other hand, Loris adopted convoluted, complex, and lengthy phrases in his letters. His style has elements of pragmaticism and instruction with layers of religious and poetic overtones. In a small number of Loris's letters, the phrases and sentences, let alone the meaning, of Loris's messages were extremely difficult to decipher. When Antonietta and I met to discuss these excerpts, both of us proved unable to decode them. Following numerous attempts to understand and translate the excerpts, while committed to remaining as faithful as possible to the original text and capturing the aesthetic emotionality, due to their fundamental untranslatability, I opted to exclude them from the English text.

The opening salutations directed to Loris and Antonietta, as well as words associated with immediate family members or other individuals – *mamma* (mother), *papà* (father), *sorella* (sister), *fratello* (brother), *Signora* (Mrs), *Signore* (Mr) – were kept in the original Italian language. For greater clarity, the English equivalent of the salutation is offered in a footnote. In this way, I sought to highlight the artistic and the emotional in the letters' original language. By contrast, many of the greetings and salutations at the closing of the letters that were directed to the families of Loris and Antonietta were left out of the English text. Given the aim of this edition to underscore the constellation of ties between the migrant couple and the need to conceal the identities of the couple's extended family members, it made sense to leave these out.

Among the features that enrich this collection are the references to material culture, including Italian opera and specific lyrics drawn from the music of Verdi, Puccini, Mascagni, Rossini, and other composers of the Italian nineteenth and early twentieth centuries. In select cases, excerpts of arias were replicated in the letters with some modifications from the original. These replications in the texts may have been based on the authors' memory. In other moments, operatic lyrics were appropriated in the form of a dedication to the absent lover. Relatedly, the letters point to a writing style inspired by the melodrama, a literary genre that is referred to in Peter Brooks's classic *The Melodramatic Imagination* as "a drama accompanied by music."[127] The origins of the term point to a number of historical moments from Jean-Jacques Rousseau, who sought "a new emotional expressivity through the mixture of spoken soliloquy, pantomime, and orchestral accomplishment,"[128] and the French Revolution and its aftermath[129] to the Italian Baroque period.[130] Regardless of its exact historical origins, melodrama is closely associated with the modern, and it is "perhaps unique in its attention to both the affective and corporeal dimensions of modern experience."[131] From the cultural practices of *la bella figura* to the evening walks through the centre of town, John Champagne notes, the Italian cultural production of everyday life is steeped in melodrama.[132] Not incidentally, a melodramatic impulse undergirds the letters of Antonietta and Loris, and it seemed important to try to replicate this impulse in the English text.

A READING OF THE LOVE LETTERS of Antonietta Petris and Loris Palma leads us to discover the myriad ways in which romantic love was instrumental in a migration project shared by two individuals and their families. The emotional and affective discourses that run through the letters underscore the resilience and agency, among other aspects, in romantic love and migration in the postwar period. Antonietta Petris and Loris Palma managed to sustain close ties across the Atlantic Ocean with affection, imagination, humour, and presence, despite the echoes of longing, uncertainty, and absence. These letters also underscore the point that the language of love in a context of migration is not limited to longing and desire; it is entangled with other emotions and states of mind that derive from worries, insecurities, melancholy, joys, gratification, and empathy.

The letters, moreover, point to how migration was viewed and acted upon, moment by moment, by women and men involved in long-distance relationships leading to marriage in the mid-twentieth century. They reveal a world of intimacy that perhaps few can imagine inhabiting today. During this, perhaps last postal age, the letter was the most important communication vehicle available to transnational lovers. To stay in touch by letter was fundamental to the survival of their relationship, and it propelled the writers' imagination toward a positive outcome. As anthropologist Jack Goody notes, the expression on paper is unique not only for its range of emotionalities but also for its ability to create and expand those feelings through a process of reflexivity.[133] Writing fosters self-awareness, reflection, and creativity. It makes the implicit explicit.[134] How Loris and Antonietta assigned to their letters the task of transmitting – in socially, morally, and culturally appropriate language – their affection and desire for one another while waiting, reading, responding, and posting letters for what felt like an endless period, and how each correspondent managed the complicity and trust they shared throughout their long-distance love are highlighted in the letters.

Despite the sacrifice that separation engendered, most of the time each correspondent appeared to have coped with the limited communication while ensuring an even rhythm to the frequency of the letters and immeasurable patience. At other times, the strain of the distance appeared to be too much, as Antonietta wrote in one letter to Loris on 6 November 1948: "Do I deserve this kind of punishment? Loris, I beg you, please, as soon as you receive this letter, let me know something so that I may put my heart at peace. Oh! What a life. How tired I am of thinking of one situation over another. I cannot take this anymore." Despite feeling intimately bound to one another, there were moments in which each correspondent appeared uncertain about what to write, especially after a long day's work, such as this from Loris: "I am here with the pen in my hand, and I don't know what else to write, if you were here, then of course, I would know what beautiful words to tell you, I would know how to hold you tight to my heart, I would know how to kiss you" (3 March 1949).

The letters of Antonietta and Loris tell the story of a couple who defied many of the challenges of their migration and separation. What led this couple to believe in their relationship and stay the course during continued periods of separation within Italy and later, between Italy and Canada? What kind of mechanisms did they consciously and unconsciously use in their letters to pull the absent lover closer, and ensure constant complicity throughout their separation? In what ways did the process of migration underpin their correspondence? The answers to these and other questions are found in the evocative letters of Antonietta Petris and Loris Palma.

A Note on the Presentation of the Letters

This book presents the letters of Antonietta Petris and Loris Palma written in their entirety between 21 September 1948 and 7 July 1949. They are presented in chronological sequence in ten chapters, with brief commentaries introducing the letters by way of interpretation. A reminder on anonymity is in order. To respect the privacy of the friends and family members of the corresponding couple, the identities of all persons except Antonietta Petris and Loris Palma and their respective parents remain undisclosed.

Notes

1 Ramirez, "Sonia Cancian interviewing Antonietta Petris," http://purl.umn.edu/119661.

2 Gerber, *Authors of their Lives*, 107–8.

3 "*Approffitto* [*sic*] *dell'occasione per mandarti due righe, che ti dirranno* [*sic*] *che costantemente ti penso con sincero affetto.*"

4 Willcox and Ferenczi, *International Migrations*, 811. Cited in Gabaccia, *Italy's Many Diasporas*, 1.

5 Borges, Cancian, and Reeder, *Emotional Landscapes*, 2.

6 Braidotti, *Nomadic Subjects*, 35.

7 Nelia Palma and Wanda Palma, email interview with the author, 17 May 2018.

8 Nelia Palma and Wanda Palma, interview, 17 May 2018.

9 Loris Palma notes in a letter to Antonietta that he had found a photograph of the family when they were residing in Marghera, and his father had been drafted into the war. Letter from Loris to Antonietta, 8 February 1948.

10 Grondin, *The Art and Passion of Guido Nincheri*, 176–8.

11 Gabaccia, *Italy's Many Diasporas*, 11.

12 The project, Digitizing Immigrant Letters, is accessible at https://ihrca.dash.umn.edu/dil/. Four letters belonging to the Antonietta Petris and Loris Palma collection have been integrated into the project along with a short film of an interview I held with Antonietta in 2011.

13 Stanley, "The Epistolarium," 208.

14 Ibid., 208.

15 Ibid., 208. On time and the letter, see also, Altman, *Epistolarity*.

16 As the recent Italian historiography shows, many women had also joined the resistance and worked for wages. See for instance, Slaughter, *Women and the Italian Resistance 1943–1945*; chapter 6 in Willson, *Women in Twentieth-Century Italy*; Gobetti, *Diario partigiano*; Viganò, *L'Agnese va a Morire*.

17 Reeder, *Italy in the Modern World*, chapter 12.

18 Gabrielli, *Il 1946, le donne, la Repubblica*, 11.

19 ISTAT, *Serie Storiche, Istruzione e Lavoro*, Tavola 7.1. Current literacy rates are available through the UNESCO Institute for Statistics, http://uis.unesco.org/en/country/it.

20 Willson, *Women in Twentieth-Century Italy*, 112.

21 On *fotoromanzi*, see Morris, "The Harem Exposed."; and chapter 2 in Cullen, *Love, Honour, and Jealousy*.

Introduction

22 Langhamer, *The English in Love*. See also Coontz, *Marriage, a History*; Gillis, *For Better, For Worse*; Hammerton, *Migrants of the British Diaspora since the 1960s*; Passerini, *Europe in Love, Love in Europe*; and Stone, *The Family, Sex and Marriage In England*. Specific to Italian migration, see Cancian, *Transatlantic Correspondents*; Cancian, *Families, Lovers, and their Letters*; Cancian, "Love in the Time of Migration"; Cancian, "'My Dearest Love ...'"; Cancian, "The Language of Gender in Lovers' Correspondence"; Cancian, "From Montreal and Venice with Love"; Cancian, "'My Love, How Different Life Is Here ...'"; Baldassar and Gabaccia, eds. *Intimacy and Italian Migration*; and Francesco Ricatti, *Embodying Migrants*; and from a philosophical perspective, see Singer, *The Pursuit of Love*.

23 Langhamer, *The English in Love*, 6.

24 Beck and Beck-Gernsheim, *Distant Love*, 45.

25 Ibid., 48.

26 Petris, "Foreword," in this volume, xiii.

27 Burelli, "1940–1950 E in dieci anni la storia travolse un Friuli millenario," 23. The resistance on behalf of the partisans in Ampezzo Carnico and its surroundings was monumental. Within one and a half years after Italy signed the Armistice in 8 September 1943 Ampezzo became the capital of the Free Republic of Carnia for a few months in the summer of 1944. Magni, "Carlo Sgorlon," 235–51.

28 Burelli, "1940–1950 E in dieci anni la storia travolse un Friuli millenario," 22.

29 Ibid., 23.

30 The private hydroelectric firm founded in 1905, which became today's national electricity provider, ENEL, Ente Nazionale per l'Energia Elettrica.

31 Gabaccia, *Italy's Many Diasporas*, 133.

32 Loris Palma, taped interview by filmmaker Nicola Zavaglia, ca. 1997–98.

33 In 1948, commercial air transportation was not commonly used by Italians for transatlantic destinations. It became more popular in the 1960s.

34 Barthes, *A Lover's Discourse*, 112.

35 Baldassar, "Missing Kin and Longing to be Together," 252.

36 "May 4, 1949: The Tragedy of Superga," Torino FC, http://torinofc.it/en/contenuto-storia/may-4-1949-tragedy-superga; and Valeria Catalano, "4 Maggio, l'anniversario di Superga. Così scomparve il Grande Torino," *Il Corriere della Sera*, Accessed 5 April 2019, https://torino.corriere.it/sport/cards/4-maggio-l-anniversario-superga-cosi-scomparve-grande-torino/fiat-g212_principale.shtml.

37 Hammerton, *Migrants of the British Diaspora since the 1960s*, 7. British postwar migration up to about the late 1950s, Hammerton notes, was a movement driven overwhelmingly by an awareness of the forces of postwar austerity, by the shortages, chronic housing deficiencies, and for many, a sense that escape to the "new world," together with higher average incomes and living standards, was the only positive alternative to a dismal future in Britain, or in this case, Italy (*Migrants of the British Diaspora since the 1960s*, 27). As Hammerton and other migration historians have observed, the desire to migrate was grounded in the self-improvement ethos and ideals, which had motivated men and women to migrate a century earlier. This motivation was linked not just to escaping from poverty, but as Hammerton suggests, to improving a family's welfare, to guaranteeing its respectability and social advancement (*Migrants of the British Diaspora since the 1960s*, 27). For Italian postwar migrants, the motivations were not so different.

38 Hammerton, *Migrants of the British Diaspora since the 1960s*, 161.

39 Pozzetta, "Such Hardworking People," 645–6.

40 Italian Statistics report that 419,842 Italians left Italy for Canada between 1946 and 1971. ISTAT, *Serie Storiche. Popolazione. Emigrazione italiani e rimpatri. Espatriati per alcuni paesi di destinazione. Anni 1869–2014.* See also, Iacovetta, "Scrivere le donne nella storia dell'immigrazione"; Iacovetta, *Such Hardworking People*; Jansen, *Italians in a Multicultural Canada*; Ramirez, *The Italians in Canada*.

41 Ramirez, "In Canada," 94.

42 Linteau, *Histoire de Montréal depuis la confédération*, 464.

43 Iacovetta, "Scrivere le donne nella storia dell'immigrazione," 26. See also, Ramirez, *The Italians in Canada*.

44 Ramirez, "Montreal's Italians and the Socio-Economy of Settlement," 39–48.

45 Gabaccia, "Global Geography of 'Little Italy,'" 12.

46 Thanks to the work of the Société de diffusion du patrimoine artistique et culturel des Italo-Canadiens, co-founded by Loris Palma, this church was designated a National Historic Site of Canada in 2002.

47 Montreal's Casa d'Italia was formerly sequestered by the Canadian government as a result of suspicious Fascist activity during the war. In the postwar years, it became a social centre for the Italian community offering a dance hall, a restaurant, a tavern, and meeting rooms and offices to Italians in Montreal. Boissevain, *The Italians of Montreal*. Since then, it has become an Italian cultural community centre and increasingly,

Introduction

a "public demonstration of the Italian presence in Montreal." Linteau, *Histoire de Montréal depuis la Confédération*, 332.

48 Iacovetta, "Scrivere le donne nella storia dell'immigrazione," 27.

49 Iacovetta, "Ordering in Bulk," 51.

50 King, "Canada's Postwar Immigration Policy," 58.

51 Ibid., 61.

52 Fahrni, *Household Politics*, 8. See also Linteau, *Brève histoire de Montréal*; and Kuplowsky, *A Captivating "Open City."*

53 The government directive in question is PC (Privy Council), 1743. Cited in Iacovetta, "Ordering in Bulk," fn9, 76.

54 Ramirez, *The Italians in Canada*, 7.

55 See Cancian, *Families, Lovers, and their Letters.*

56 Febvre, "La sensibilité et l'histoire," 5–20. See also the work of American philosopher and psychologist William James, "What Is an Emotion?"

57 Stearns and Stearns, *Emotion and Social Change*; Stearns and Lewis, *An Emotional History of the United States*; Matt and Stearns, *Doing Emotions History*; Frevert, *Emotions in History*; Reddy, *The Navigation of Feeling*; Rosenwein, *Generations of Feeling*; Dixon, *From Passions to Emotions*; Plamper, *The History of Emotions*; Pernau et al., *Civilizing Emotions*; and the recent volumes: Rosenwein and Cristiani, *What Is the History of Emotions?*; and Boddice, *The History of Emotions*. See also, Plamper, "The History of Emotions."

58 Boddice, "The History of Emotions," 12.

59 Ibid., 11.

60 Passerini, *Europe in Love, Love in Europe* 295.

61 Redford, *The Converse of the Pen*, 9.

62 Studies that have examined emotions and migration include Hirsch and Wardlow, eds, *Modern Loves*; and Svašek, *Emotions and Human Mobility.* Theoretical perspectives can be gleaned from: Boccagni and Baldassar, "Emotions on the Move"; and Mai and King, "Love, Sexuality and Migration." Specific to migrant correspondence, see Cancian, *Families, Lovers, and their Letters*; and the chapters in the book, Borges and Cancian, eds, *Migrant Letters.* See also, Borges, Cancian, and Reeder, eds. *Emotional Landscapes.*

63 Goody, *Food and Love*, 122.

64 Refer to Borges, Cancian, and Reeder, eds, *Emotional Landscapes.*

65 See for instance, Hochschild, *The Managed Heart.*

66 Baldassar, "Missing Kin and Longing to be Together," 250.

67 Dror, "Creating the Emotional Body"; and Scheer, "Are Emotions a Kind of Practice?"

68 See Grassi, "Des lettres qui parlent d'amour."

69 Moscoso, *Pain: A Cultural History*, 55.

70 Ibid., 55.

71 Ibid., 58.

72 Ibid.

73 Sullivan, "The Art of Medicine," 884.

74 Bourke, *The Story of Pain*, 46.

75 Mai and King, "Love, Sexuality and Migration," 297–300.

76 Borges, Cancian, and Reeder, eds, *Emotional Landscapes*, 8. For an excellent historiographical overview of gender and migration in interdisciplinary studies among a plethora of superb studies, see Donato et al., eds, "Gender and Migration Revisited."

77 Simon, "Introduction: Cultural Expressions," 406.

78 Lorber, *Paradoxes of Gender*, 100. For a discussion on gender and language, see also the work of Cameron, *The Feminist Critique of Language*; Coates, *Language and Gender*; Lakoff, *Language and Woman's Place*; Hall and Bucholtz, *Gender Articulated*; Tannen, *You Just Don't Understand*.

79 Hondagneu-Sotelo, *Gendered Transitions*, cited in Mahler, "Transnational Relationships," 586–7.

80 Based on the short story by John Luther Long and later elaborated into the libretto by Luigi Illica and Giuseppe Giacosa, the three-act opera *Madama Butterfly* was composed by Italian opera composer Puccini (1858–1924). It premiered at La Scala in Milan in 1904. *Madama Butterfly* is the story of a young Japanese woman who marries Pinkerton, an American officer, and awaits his return to Japan only to discover upon his return that he has remarried. In Puccini's opera, the protagonist Cio-Cio San is arguably "the apotheosis of the frail suffering heroine" often encountered in Puccini's work, and whose genuine figure of tragedy is transformed "during the action from child-like innocence to an adult understanding and a calm acceptance of the destiny which her code of honour enjoins upon her." Budden, "Madama Butterfly," 139.

The two-act romantic comedy opera, *L'elisir d'amore*, was written by Felice Romani (1788–1865) and composed by Donizetti (1797–1848). It premiered in Milan in 1832. This love story tells the tale of a young wealthy farm owner (Adina), a young peasant in love with Adina (Nemorino), a flirtatious sergeant (Belcore), and a travelling salesman (Doctor Dulcamara) and his love potion. *L'elisir d'amore*'s continuing appeal is linked to the appropriateness of Donizetti's music to the variant of the "male Cinderella" myth, represented through Nemorino's good-

Introduction

59

heartedness and singleness of purpose winning out in spite of potions and unforeseen inheritances. Ashbrook, *"Elisir d'amore, L',"* 40.

81 Bauman, "Essay Reviews," 420.

82 McClary, "Foreword: The Undoing of Opera," xviii.

83 Reeder, *Widows in White,* 19.

84 See chapter 2 in Cancian, *Families, Lovers, and their Letters.*

85 Cancian, *Families, Lovers, and their Letters,* 61.

86 Rosenwein, "Worrying about Emotions in History," 842.

87 Baldassar and Gabaccia, "Home, Family, and the Italian Nation in a Mobile World," 5.

88 Ibid.

89 See for instance, the letters of Dante del Moro and Sara Franceschetti and Ester di Leonardi and Giordano Rossini in Cancian, *Families, Lovers, and their Letters.* Other excellent examples include: Caffarena, *Lettere dalla Grande Guerra;* Gabrielli, *Col Freddo nel Cuore;* and Gibelli, *L'officina della Guerra;* Hanna, *Your Death Would be Mine.*

90 Gerber, *Authors of their Lives,* 286.

91 Bossis, "Table ronde: la lettre d'amour," 39.

92 Gerber, *Authors of their Lives,* 155. See also, Baldassar and Gabaccia, "Home, Family, and the Italian Nation in a Mobile World"; and Glick Schiller, Basch, and Szanton Blanc, "From Immigrant to Transmigrant."

93 Gerber, "The Immigrant Letter between Positivism and Populism," 3.

94 On the economic and commercial worlds created by and for migrant consumption, see for example, Zanoni, *Migrant Marketplaces.* On the connections between international affairs and global migrant communities, see Gabaccia, *Foreign Relations.*

95 Anthropologists Nina Glick Schiller, Linda Basch, and Cristina Szanton Blanc also note in "From Immigrant to Transmigrant," page 48, "In identifying a new process of migration, scholars of transnational migration emphasize the ongoing and continuing ways in which current-day immigrants construct and reconstitute their simultaneous embeddedness in more than one society."

96 For a discussion on the combination of simplicity and creative ingenuity in ordinary individuals and the work of Antonio Gramsci, see Catalano and Fina, "Simple Does Not Mean Easy."

97 Catalano and Fina, "Simple Does Not Mean Easy," 33. Among the works of Stephenson, Hansen, and Blegen, see: Hansen, "The History of American Immigration as a Field for Research"; Stephenson, "Typical 'America Letters'"; Blegen, "Early 'America Letters'"; Hansen, *The Atlantic Migration, 1607–1860;* Stephenson, *Letters Relating to Gustaf Unonius*

and the Early Swedish Settlers in Wisconsin; and Blegen, *Land of their Choice*. Over the years, the scholarship on migrant correspondence has burgeoned. Among the more significant volumes, see: Baily and Ramella, *One Family, Two Worlds*; Barton, *Letters from the Promised Land*; Borges and Cancian, *Migrant Letters*; Cameron, Haines, and Maude, *English Immigrant Voices*; Cancian, *Families, Lovers, and their Letters*; Chávez-García, *Migrant Longing*; Conway, *The Welsh in America*; D'Agostin and Grossutti, *Ti ho spedito lire cento*; De Haan, "'He Looks Like a Yankee in His New Suit'"; Elliott, Gerber, and Sinke, *Letters across Borders*; Erickson, *Invisible Immigrants*; Franzina, *Merica! Merica!*; Frenette, Martel, and Willis, *Envoyer et recevoir*; Hoerder, *Creating Societies*; Jaroszynska-Kirchmann, *The Polish Hearst*; Kamphoefner, Helbich, and Sommer, *News from the Land of Freedom*; Liu, *The Transnational History of a Chinese Family*; Miller, *Emigrants and Exiles*; Miller et al., *Irish Immigrants in the Land of Canaan*; Sbolci, *Amore di terra lontana*; Sinke, *Dutch Immigrant Women in the United States, 1880–1920*; and Templeton, *From the Mountains to the Bush*.

98 Gerber, *Authors of their Lives*, 55.

99 For notable exceptions, see Fitzpatrick, *Oceans of Consolation*; Seymour, "Emotional arenas"; Seymour, *Emotional Arenas*; Gerber, *Authors of their Lives*; and Cancian, *Families, Lovers, and Their Letters*. For a sociolinguistc perspective, see also Cancian, "Una raccolta di lettere italiane inviate agli emigrati in Canada."

100 See for instance, the articles in the special issue, Borges and Cancian, *Migrant Letters*, and in Borges, Cancian, and Reeder, *Emotional Landscapes*. For an example of a digital project on migrant letters, see The Digitizing Immigrant Letters Project. https://ihrca.dash.umn.edu/dil/letters/.

101 *"Devo dire che quei ricordi adesso che me lo chiedi, quei ricordi diciamo, erano sfocati erano, erano così lontani da me e proprio è come se questo periodo non avesse esistito, invece, eh no, no non è così, non è così ... certo è chiaro, e mi è venuto ancora più chiaro quando ho letto, ho riletto la lettera perché queste prime soprattutto non le avevo mai lette, e quando l'ho letta, ecco, è stato un attimo, ho rivisto quel momento, ho rivisto, ho sentito la pena che ho provato 63 anni fa: il dolore, l'emozione e ... e quella, la distanza, si, lo sai. Non è stato facile però vedi, abbiamo ugualmente ..., siamo andati avanti con costanza con la voglia di continuare di arrivare veramente al nostro traguardo, e ci siamo riusciti! Ma, ci è costato caro. Abbiamo passato dei giorni felicissimi insieme, ma erano così brevi, erano pochi, sai, allora c'era sempre la paura, la paura non ...,*

Introduction   61

di perderci, perché quando si è tanto lontani può succedere anche quello. Invece, tutto è passato, e rimangono solo i ricordi, ricordi che sono più vivi da quando ho letto queste lettere, le prime lettere che ci siamo scritti io e Loris." The Digitizing Immigrant Letters Project, https://www.lib.umn.edu/ihrca/antonietta-petris-letters.

102 Maynes, Pierce, and Laslett, *Telling Stories*, 87.
103 Portelli, "What Makes Oral History Different."
104 Beard, "Re-thinking Oral History," 531.
105 Thomson, "Memory and Remembering in Oral History," 91.
106 Portelli, *The Battle of Valle Giulia*, 185.
107 Antonietta Petris, interview with author, 7 July 2011. Montreal, Canada.
108 Antonietta Petris, interview with author, 2013. Montreal, Canada.
109 Hamilton, "The Proust Effect," 220.
110 See also the short film, Ramirez, "Sonia Cancian interviewing Antonietta Petris."
111 Hamilton, "The Proust Effect," 222.
112 Ramirez, "Sonia Cancian interviewing Antonietta Petris."
113 Maynes, Pierce, and Laslett, *Telling Stories*, 33.
114 See Bornat, "Remembering in Later Life."
115 Maynes, Pierce, and Laslett, *Telling Stories*, 113.
116 Thanks to Michel Peterson for introducing me to the concept of *transcreation* developed by H. de Campos. Personal communication, 14 June 2020.
117 Quirk, *The Linguist and the English Language*, cited in Bassnett, *Translation Studies*, 16.
118 Levý, *Umeni prekladu, (The Art of Translation)* (Prague, 1963), cited in Holmes, *The Nature of Translation*, cited in Susan Bassnett, *Translation Studies*, 16. See also Levý's complete volume in English, The *Art of Translation*.
119 Grossman, *Why Translation Matters*, 14.
120 Benjamin, "The Task of the Translator," 76.
121 Polizzotti, *Sympathy for the Traitor*, 2–3.
122 Ibid., 3.
123 Simon, *Cities in Translation*, 6.
124 Grossman, *Why Translation Matters*, 10.
125 Ibid., 7.
126 Ibid., 68.
127 Brooks, *The Melodramatic Imagination*, 14.
128 Ibid., 14.
129 Ibid.

130 Champagne, *Italian Masculinity as Queer Melodrama*, 13.
131 Ibid., 12.
132 Ibid., 15.
133 Goody, *Food and Love*, 107.
134 Ibid., 121.

— Part One —

"Neither Here nor There"

*The Letters from
September 1948
to December 1948*

— 1 —

"That day an abyss opened under my feet"
Mobility in the Immediate Postwar Era

WHEN ANTONIETTA PETRIS boarded the British European Airways flight with her mother at Rome's Ciampino International Airport on 21 September 1948, she was among the 50,000 Italians arriving in Canada between 1947 and 1951.[1] Canada and other countries, including Brazil, Argentina, the United States, and Australia, and those in northern Europe, welcomed Italian migrants for economic expansion in the nineteenth and twentieth centuries. To Italian men and women emigrating after the end of the Second World War, *L'America* was a place in which the incorporation of foreigners symbolized what Gabaccia calls "the promise and accomplishments of American democracy."[2] Already in the first transoceanic letters between Antonietta and Loris, there is evidence of new work opportunities available. In one letter, for instance, Antonietta finds herself facing first-hand this new world of work for everyone, good wages, and abundance everywhere.

The myth of America dates back to at least the nineteenth century, following the visit of Europeans like Alexis de Tocqueville to the United States.[3] The military presence of American and Canadian soldiers among the Allied Forces in Italy after the Italian armistice announced on 8 September 1943 brought *L'America* one step closer to Italians' doorstep. As the Allied armies advanced on the peninsula liberating its people from Nazi occupation, the Allied tanks distributed to the crowds a mix

---

1 De Clementi, *Il Prezzo della ricostruzione*, 84.
2 Gabaccia, "Is Everywhere Nowhere?" 1115.
3 Paul, "Expressive Individualism and the Myth of the Self-Made Man," 367.

of the necessary and the excessive – American chewing gum, chocolate bars, cigarettes, and canned meat. These food items (along with earlier screenings of Charlie Chaplin films and old Westerns) renewed contact between the old world and the new world of consumption.[4] In Italian migrant households, this contact had already been in place with the return of Italian labour migrants, also known as *i ritornati* (returnees) in the decades before the war, and the missives exchanged between Italian kin who had migrated overseas and their family members who had remained behind, as in the case of Antonietta and her family.

The year 1948 brought significant changes to the worlds of Antonietta and Loris. In Italy, 18 April marked the general elections for the first Republican parliament with the Christian Democratic Party supported by the church and favoured by the United States in a fierce battle against the Democratic Popular Front.[5] The turnout was impressive. Over 90 per cent of the eligible population had gone to the polls.[6] With the Christian Democrats winning 48.7 per cent of the vote, they governed Italy for another decade and a half (until the 1960s) by forming centrist coalitions with the Republicans and Social Democrats.[7] Barely two years earlier, on 2 June 1946, the first free general elections in over twenty years were held. This landmark election was significant not only because Italians needed to elect their representatives to the Constituent Assembly and decide by referendum between the monarchy and a republic, it marked the first time in Italian history in which women had the right to vote.[8] Despite these political advancements that sought to secure equal representation for all Italians, the country remained in ruins, and famine continued to haunt millions of families. As Gabaccia remarks, the main challenge in these first postwar years was "to find enough to eat, not to puzzle over the future of the nation."[9] The long tradition of transnationalism became once again a way of life among Italian families.[10] With the

---

4 Isnenghi, *Breve storia d'Italia*, 117.
5 Reeder, *Italy in the Modern World*, 198.
6 Ibid., 198.
7 Ibid.
8 Ginsborg, *A History of Contemporary Italy*, 98.
9 Gabaccia, *Italy's Many Diasporas*, 153.
10 Ibid., 153–4.

Mobility in the immediate postwar era signalled a return to normalcy for the millions of families who, like the family of Antonietta Petris, had witnessed loved ones migrating to other lands beginning in the 1880s until the start of the Second World War, when the numbers dwindled to just about zero.[12] Kinship ties with family members who had emigrated in the decades before the war were reactivated shortly after the war was over. While this kind of migration involved a more central role on behalf of the state and its representatives in organizing and administering the migration of Italians, the number of migrants points to the war's failure to break the pattern of migration of previous generations.[13] Postwar migration did not occur in isolation. Rather, it was part of the reconstruction of deeper family patterns that involved mobility, as in the case of Vittorio Petris who travelled with his father to Germany and the former Czechoslovakia in search of work in the 1920s. As Vittorio's migration exemplifies, extended absences were part of these preceding migrations. The wives who stayed behind became what Linda Reeder terms "white widows."[14]

In contrast, migrations in the postwar period ushered in a period of greater contact and shorter absences. Advice about whether to immigrate, formal immigration procedures, and economic support coupled with the reassurance of family members who would help prospective migrants settle in abound in the letters exchanged between migrants and their loved ones at home. The devastation during and after the war, and the famine and precariousness that ensued reinforced the importance of the family and its well-being. Migration became a resource that many turned to in the mapping of new boundaries and new opportunities for family. Yet, leaving was far from an effortless venture. From many perspectives – familial, economic, political, and emotional – it came at a cost. It signalled leaving behind one's *patria* (homeland), one's childhood home, close

---

11 Ibid.
12 Ibid., 134.
13 Gabaccia, *Italy's Many Diasporas*, 156–8; Linda Reeder, in personal conversation with the author, 13 March 2019.
14 See Reeder, *Widows in White*.

friends and neighbours, immediate and extended family members, and one's love, with no immediate date of return in sight. For many, like Loris and Antonietta, migration was often experienced as a profound loss that brought despair, grief, as well as a glimmer of hope.

— Venice 23-9-48 —

Indimenticabile mia Nietta,[15]
It was as though I had died and come back to life, and an unambiguous joy inebriated me affecting me more than is humanly possible. While I compose these thoughts for you, I recall my transformation once I learned of your safe and sound arrival. I appealed to our Protector for our happiness not from superstitious ideologies or chance but simply out of faith. I lit a candle a few hours after your departure, and there, I whispered the words of our credo. In all of this, I prayed for his Grace. My prayers were answered not for my sake, nor for my tribute to Him, but solely out of mercy. Nothing, not the approval of a highly deserved victory, nor the forces of an extraordinary miracle could have transformed my comatose state into euphoria. By then, an atrocious anxiety had caused my senseless downfall. It's not that I was pessimistic, for I can rationalize the moment, but I worried about unforeseen events that could have ensued from such a journey.

The silence after your departure and the arrival of the radiogram did not last 48 hours for me, it lasted the time of an entire existence, as is usually the case when anxiety tightens at our throats. I had memorized all the details of your trip, from your departure to your arrival, but I could not understand the reasons for any eventual delays or incidents. This is the reason I was waiting for your telegram from London, but I received none. Fortunately, I had a little bit of life left in me, and I was able to obtain information about your flight from the BEA airline's offices at seven in the evening when I went to see them. With this news, I refrained from collapsing, and truth be told, I was pleased to see *Signora* E … in a good mood. She eagerly inquired about you,

---

15 My unforgettable Nietta.

Venezia 23-9-48

Imdimenticabile mia Nietta,

come se la morte fosse tornato a vita la gioia più sicura m'inebriò con un effetto più che umano e alla pari di quella riflessione posso valutare la trasformazione che operò in me la notizia del tuo arrivo sana e salva. Non per ideologie superstiziose, ne per scaramanzia, ma semplicemente per fede votai al mio protettore la nostra felicità e un cero che le offersi poche ore dopo la vostra partenza nel quale raffigurai il nostro credo e tutto in questo chiedevo grazia. Non per merito mio ne per i meriti che avessi nei suoi riguardi, ma ugualmente e solo per la sua misericordia fui esaudito. Il plauso di una vittoria più merita ta la potenza d'un miracolo non avrebbe sconvolto in me lo stato comatoso in uno stato felice, ormai il pensiero di una ansia ahora aveva creato in me uno scempio immaginario le non il pessimismo perché so valutare il momento ma un comune per gli imprevisti che un tuo viaggio può avere il ricordo che durò dalla vostra partenza all'arrivo del radiogramma, non ha avuto per me proporzioni di 48 ore ma di un intero esistenza come è solito a succedersi quando l'ansia stringe la gola. Tutto era chiaro il vostro viaggio, dalla partenza all'arrivo ma non per l'uguale motivo mi erano chiari gli eventuali ritardi o eventuali incidenti. Ecco perché a Londra aspettavo un tuo telegramma ma purtroppo non fui alie tato ma però ho sempre un po' di spirito che mi salva, e ho patito

Letter from Loris Palma, 23 September 1948.

as she too was saddened by your departure. I certainly could not have endured travelling home on that same day, absolutely not. My distress would have only worsened. That day an abyss opened under my feet, and I had to pay careful attention not to plunge inside, yes, my spirit and my heart were not normal, my body had never before felt a similar fatigue, my legs failed to hold me steady, rather they were there to vacillate my body back and forth, every part of me experienced the symptoms of total exhaustion, and I remained standing more out of courage, than out of willpower and strength.

If the emotions and sorrow are clearly presented to you here – together with the torment of not knowing when we will see each other again (something I had already reflected on during our separations) – you must know that the heaviest blow came in those final moments. There I was, trying to be strong, I wanted to give you the impression that I was a man of fortitude, but those moments proved to be too much for me, our powerful separation overwhelmed me, and I was crestfallen and devastatingly weakened by this condition of human frailty to which we are subject. I was already well aware of the sorrow I had felt many times before in our past separations, already my heart swelled and my throat tightened from the tears that I tried hard to suppress. When I glanced at the tears in your eyes, many times I tried to distract you so you would stop, but this time, the wine in the chalice from which I drank overflowed with bitterness. I am sorry about this, but we must recover so we don't feel worse. To have you back after a long and hard separation will take enormous effort but that is the direction we must take. Were we not the ones to wish this upon ourselves? All of this will be the harbinger of a happy day, a joyful hour, the thought of our reunion must energize us with courage and strength, our joy will be so extraordinary on that day that all of our sadness will vanish into nothing.

No longer are we separated by a few hundred kilometres and a mountain chain. Now, nearly half a world stands between us, but our thoughts and our promises will be preserved, they will be delivered, renewed, and channelled into our hearts across the tides of an ocean that knows no boundaries for our willpower. We won't be needing proof for our love to be nurtured, the most precious evidence will shine in our eyes, it already is there and sustains us. Our last kiss was the seal of our pledge which

Mobility in the Immediate Postwar Era 71

cannot be denied by the boundless lands and oceans. We are strong if we have the will. Everything is up to us, if we are sincere and pure, our every sacrifice will be rewarded. These promises will not be new to you, of course, on many occasions I called upon them to convince you that an opportunity would open for us, an opportunity that would not subvert our entire worlds, for this reason, my Tetina you acquiesced to my persistence and you nurtured the dream with me. Let Fate guide us, even if we must suffer to reach our objective, but for me, the thought of melding my ideal to yours one day, to possess your thoughts, your heart, and your person touches me with a happiness that is not only a pledge but a reality for us even though we are immersed in sorrow.

Yesterday on the 22nd of this month, I left Rome, alone, and I returned to my family in Venice, once again, I had completed my task in assisting you with your departure. Duty called on my return home and with much bitterness I left the Capital at 13:05, and with me, every memory of Rome, the city that witnessed us giddy with joy for several days, while now, I am steeped in sorrow. *Signor* D ... and *Signora* D ... who kindly hosted me on that last day stayed with me as they too empathized with my sadness, and through all of this, I left Rome in a highly emotional, bitter, disconsolate state, and in my heart, I revisited that street in which we walked together, and every corner, every detail was reignited in my memory. Overcome by bleak, disconsolate thoughts, I travelled across Italy to my home; I could never have imagined a more forlorn return: I extended your greetings to everything around me, they all reminded me of you, this is the reason why my return home was so bitter. My home, a place that on many occasions witnessed your presence and welcomed you, will not be able to embrace you now, and my thoughts were lost as they envisioned you in all the moments that you were here in my home, a poor and simple home that brimmed with the affection that my family, I hope, has offered to you. This poor Italy misses you, your person – which is the tangible part – but you left me your heart and your affections; I will need to preserve them well, cherish them, and replenish them with your love, I will keep them in their beautiful state until I will be with you again.

Be strong, I will never abandon you, you can be certain of this; never will my memory fade of you, my heart is yours not out of self-interest but out of love, you who wept at our moment of separation, my heart is yours for your absolute faith and your enthusiasm. I eagerly wait for your next letter where you will describe your trip, your arrival, and your most vivid impressions of the country that is hosting you, and that hopefully will welcome me soon as well. Tell me about your father's happiness, which I imagine to be immense, and the overall feeling of being in your new home. To you I leave the most beautiful description, only in this way will I be comforted.

If you will not have received my letter in the envelope of documents that your *mamma* had stored in her leather purse, try to find it now and remember that it was the last letter that I wrote to you before your departure, it was written on the evening in which you came to see me in the kitchen. I hope it is a keepsake of me for all of you, as I will remember each of you every day of my life. That short letter contains all of my affections for all of you, this is why I ask you to cherish it, for you especially, the letter is inscribed with everything for you to remember that you are the most vital part of my heart. It is so you can remember me during your American days in the same way that you remembered me, with the same affection, when you lived in the small town of Ampezzo. On the 21st I wrote to D ... and to your *nonni* [grandparents], advising them of your departure. I will now reply to *Signora* L ... and to your dear ones. Did your *papà* receive the radiogram I sent you on the 21st? To close this first letter of mine that has crossed the oceans, I will allow all of my sentiments of love to fold inside, the love that sustained me until today while I was immersed in sorrow, the letter from which you will receive all of my most ardent kisses, just like the last kiss I gave to you while in anguish. your Loris

— Venice 25-9-48 —

[A letter addressed to Antonietta and her parents in Montreal][16]
Miei tanto cari,[17]
In my utter sorrow, which is immense, and the tumultuous circumstances that today make me a prisoner of my thoughts, thinking of

16 Affectionate greetings and other articulations of love included in this letter, and more commonly, at the closing of the couple's letters, served as lasting reminders of bonds that united family members across the distance, as folklorist Joseph Sciorra notes in "'Don't Forget You Have Relatives Here,'" 55.
17 My darling dear ones.

Mobility in the Immediate Postwar Era 73

you so far away fuels my painful conviction. In the depths of my heart and my sadness, however, I find a joy that caresses your dream and brings light in the midst of such sorrow that is, the heart of your Nietta. I unite my heart to hers, a heart that is touched by bitterness, as it clings to a personal sorrow that negates the voice of reason for the detachment that could not be avoided. It was only human and only right to consider your reunion, even if I knew that it would bring a cloud of bitterness to the idyll of our Love.

It was easy for me to understand. I did not disapprove of losing Tetina temporarily. In fact, *Mamma*, it was always clear to you, I am sure, because it was true, my hope for you, *Mamma* and Nietta was a reunion with her *papà*, whom I understand needed to have you near him across the ocean. Therefore, I never denied consent; rather, I gave my consent. I gave it willingly and without prejudice. May God punish me if it might appear that I have a vested interest in all of this. Nietta knows me well and she is aware of the depth of my feelings. She can assure you that my intentions are in no way material.

So, if consent was attained, it was due to a clear reflection that I usually engage in when faced with life's dilemmas in order to understand the pros and cons. It led me to a decision that is clear to both Nietta and me. It mirrors an earnest desire to change our lives under a different sky, not because it's Canadà but because I aspire to live with dignity through my work and realize the dreams that each of us endeavours to realize when we love. I believe you are human, and thus, you are able to understand that my feelings and my expression will not change. I think of you walking in my footsteps while you could still see my love for Antonietta in my eyes. Our continuing youthful years often deceive the young foal of a radiant future. The unforeseen did not appear early in our lives, something that your path too has realized following a similar reflection, this path that has closed the door to time. My case is very different and you are at the root of this, you who love my Antonietta as dearly as I do, you who are aware of how much one can suffer and how much can be done. It is not necessary for me to describe to you the breadth and depth of my love for Antonietta. Surely, you won't be surprised if I confess my love for her with such ease. It is so beautiful to be completely yourself, and not someone you are not. This is why I can express myself freely.

My conscience is clear and I can tell you wholeheartedly that I wish for even more, to see my Tetina smile again, to join you as soon as possible, and to bring to an end – if divine light will guide me – the distances and separations we have always struggled against.

May my feelings be clear to you both. Your well-deserved trust in me will confirm it to you, as you trust me with my Antonietta with whom I have frequently shared my joys and hardships.

As I think of you so far away, so distant from me, that my thoughts are bitterly lost in joyful memories knowing that you are all together again. Just one thing is missing in your home, the beautiful smile of my Tetina. Tell her to smile because my thoughts will never abandon her. There is no doubt that I love her, and that I keep her close to my heart. My dear parents, please do not read this letter like a trial but more like a memory of me whom you have left terribly desolate as a result of your departure. May my affection and my faith in your happiness be always with you, even though a kiss for all of you is imbued with sorrow.

Affectionately,

Loris Palma

— Montreal 26-9-48 —

Mio adorato Loris,[18]
Today is Sunday, a Sunday that is imbued with memories and nostalgia, the first Sunday that I am in Canadà, I have everything I need here, even today when I went to visit a friend of my *papà*'s I was given the red carpet treatment, the table was adorned with all of God's blessings, every kind of delicacy was mine, but never, not even for a moment did I stop thinking of you, every passing minute reminded me of last Sunday, where we were, your face, still smiling and radiating with joy, a joy that imbues us only when we are together. When I thought of the distance that divides us, as I think of it now, I feel my heart tightening into a knot, I become breathless, completely breathless! Oh! How much I love you, even here, yes, my darling, maybe even more so than when I was in Italy, because now I can more deeply appreciate your attributes, I know the treasure that is mine, and what a loss it would be for me if I lost you; always be worthy, not of me, no, because I am no different from any

18 My adored Loris.

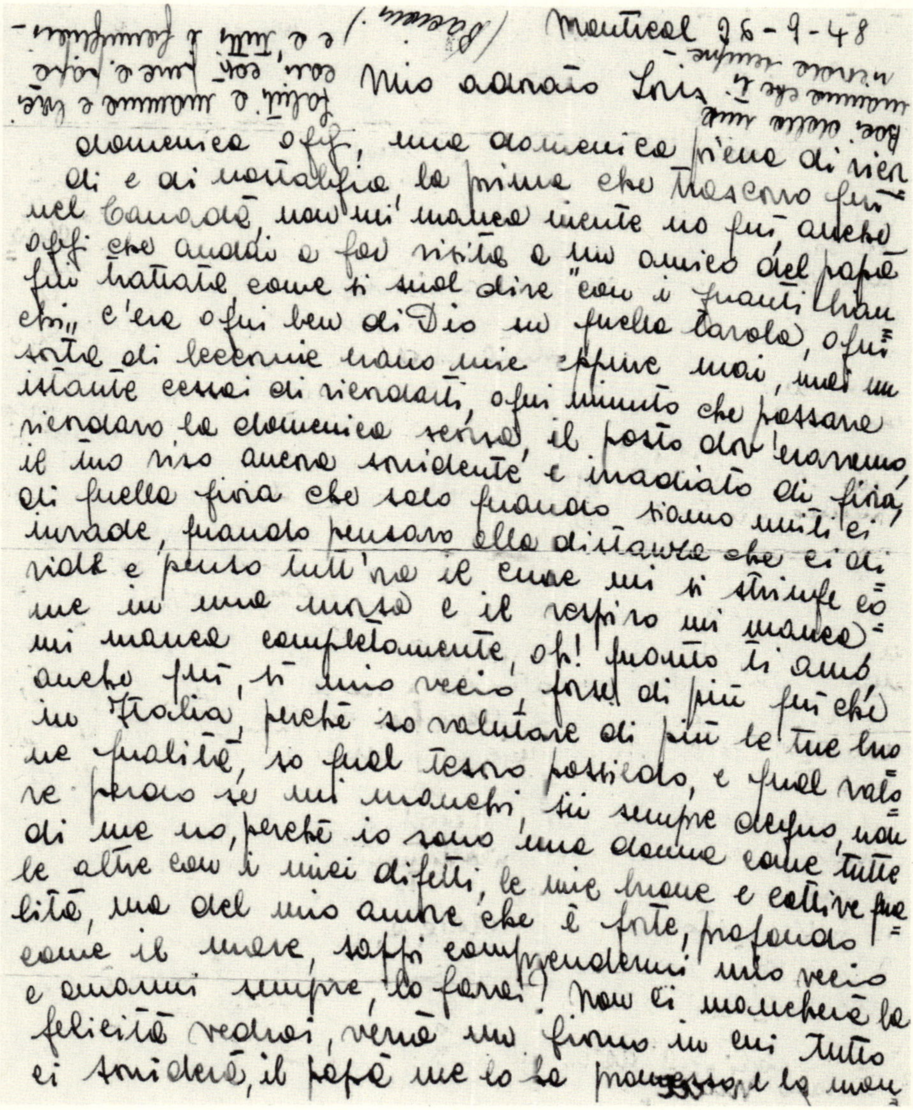

Montreal 26-9-48

Mio adorato Luis

domenica oggi, una domenica piena di ricordi e di nostalgia la prima che trascorro qui nel Canadà, non mi manca niente no qui, anche oggi che andai a far visita a un amico del papà fui trattata come si suol dire "con i guanti bianchi" c'era oggi ben di Dio su quella tavola, oggi sorte di leccornie viste mai eppure mai, ma in istante cessai di ricordarti, oggi minuto che passava ricordavo la domenica scorsa, il posto dove eravamo il tuo viso ancora sorridente e irradiato di quella gioia che solo quando siamo uniti ci invade, quando pensavo alla distanza che ci divide e penso tutt'ora il cuore mi si stringe come in una morsa e il respiro mi manca completamente, oh! quanto ti amo anche qui, mio vecio, forse di più qui che in Italia, perché so valutare di più le tue buone qualità, so quel tesoro possiedo, e quel valore perciò se mi manchi sei sempre degno, non di me no, perché io sono una donna come tutte le altre con i miei difetti, le mie buone e cattive qualità, ma del mio amore che è forte, profondo come il mare, saprai comprendermi mio vecio e amami sempre, lo farai? Non ci mancherà la felicità vedrai, verrà un giorno in cui tutto ci sorriderà, il papà me lo ha promesso la man

Letter from Antonietta Petris, 26 September 1948.

other woman, I have weaknesses and strengths, good and bad traits, be worthy of my love that is as strong and as deep as the ocean, try to understand me, my darling, and love me forever, will you do this?

Our world will be complete with happiness, you will see, there will be a day in which everything will smile upon us, my *papà* has promised me this, he will keep his promise you will see, he is always talking about you, even a few minutes ago, he told me that he will do everything possible to help you come here because he knows you are a good man and that you deserve our respect, you will see that in one way or another, you will come here. This week we will be paying a visit to his agent and we will see what he says, if it wasn't for the military service you could be here in six months – just think how different life is here in America, my Loris, you will realize this when you come, they live in comfort and abundance, we have everything, there is even too much and plenty of sweets. I have already visited different places with my *papà*, including the large department stores, and yesterday we toured the city in the car of one of his friends. With a lady I visited the English-language school that her daughters attend, she introduced me to the principal and to various teachers, they treated me with exquisite friendliness, and they wanted me to stay with them; everyone I know looks at me with admiration, they tell me that they are in love with me (don't misunderstand this!!). There are many Italian families here and lots of Italian stores as well, but when I run into Canadian people I feel very uneasy, you have no idea.

In another letter I will describe my impressions but first I will wait for one of your letters that will bring me, I am sure, both sorrow and joy. How are you, my beloved? I ask you to take care of yourself, regain your strength because you need it, and rest now that you don't have to run around so much for me; go to bed early, and don't go to *Sant'Elena's*[19] when it rains. Speaking of which, how is the Venezia team doing? Keep me posted on news and developments in Italy, I am in the dark here. All day long, the radio mumbles, but I don't understand a thing. Many affectionate kisses from your, now, "Madam N ..."

---

19 Sant'Elena is an island situated on the southeastern tip of the city of Venice. It is home to the second oldest stadium in Italy, Stadio Pierluigi Penzo, which opened in 1913.

Mobility in the Immediate Postwar Era

[On the bottom right side of the letter:] Kisses from my *mamma* who remembers you always. Greetings to your *mamma* and dear kisses, also to your *papà* and your family. Kisses

— Montreal 28-9-48 —

[Happy Birthday greeting card for Loris and postcard of St Joseph's Oratory, Montreal]

[Back side of the card]:

Mio adorato Loris,[20]
Perhaps these greetings will not arrive in time for your birthday, nonetheless I am certain that this little keepsake will be equally appreciated. Not even this year am I with you on this special day, actually, I am very far away, further away than I have been in the past years. Do not be discouraged. Remember that my heart and my thoughts yearn for you and they desire only to be with you. Only one single objective gives me the strength to accept this suffering, the hope that one day you will join me in this country, a country that smiles solely to me for now. You will be here, Loris, you will, because this is my wish. Without you my life is so empty! I hope that you will have few other birthdays without me (I wouldn't want anyone else), I wish for this birthday to be delightful and beautiful for you. Kisses from your Nietta
[From Antonietta's parents] Our best wishes from me and Vittorio. Greetings to everyone in your family.

— Montreal 30-9-1948 —

Amore mio,[21]
Last night *papà* arrived home wearing a big smile, he said he had something special for me if I gave him a kiss on the cheek. I did not hesitate for a second, and a moment later he handed me your letter. I don't know if something more beautiful in the world would have made me happier, I jumped for joy and with unprecedented eagerness and excitement, I started to read it. Of course the first time, I didn't read

20 My adored Loris.
21 My Love.

it, I devoured it, I understood just a few sentences—the most beautiful ones that made my heart throb – and I cried, I cried so hard that tears rolled down and my chest heaved in desperate sobs. That cry brought me serenity, it melted the knot that had been constantly tightening at my throat, and when I got up from my bed to go into the kitchen, I was smiling. It's useless to despair, you need to be strong, they say, but that is easier said than done. Sure we are strong, but when the heart is overflowing with sadness and sorrow, nothing can keep us quiet, and no one knows how to diminish the pain.

Please don't think that I am always like this, and that I am like this with others. Never! I especially am not like this with *papà* who has done so much for me, and he continues to do so much. These are the first days and it's logical that they are going to be tough; if it were otherwise I would need to admit that I don't love you, nor do I want you to see me depressed either, but how can I do this? How can I be silent with you, my confidante, my Life, my Love? I cannot, I just cannot. You must forgive me if my letters make you sad and intensify your sorrow, but isn't it better perhaps if we suffer together? Everything will pass, I will learn to accept this new torment and wait with patience as we continue to hope that fate will smile upon us so that we can soar with joy to the heights of our suffering.

I feel good here, I have a comfortable life, *papà* and *mamma* provide me with everything I need, everywhere I turn there is kindness and grace, even too much of it. And everywhere I go, you are always with me, continuously, anything and everything reminds me of you, a song, a postcard, a word, last night, I went to see an Italian film, *Un americano a Roma*.[22] I leave it up to you to imagine what it was like for me to watch on screen those places so dear to me, the places we had visited and admired together. It is absolutely true that you need to move away from your homeland to long for it, to regret everything that previously seemed ugly and boring. I remember the evening I arrived in Montreal, I sat in a chair in the waiting room, the radio was playing American songs, and suddenly

22 Antonietta mentions here that she went to see an Italian film entitled *An American in Rome*. There is perhaps some confusion with the title, since the Italian film *An American in Rome*, starring comedian Alberto Sordi and directed by Steno, was only released in 1954.

Mobility in the Immediate Postwar Era 79

I heard the first notes of a song that I know, "Dove sta Zazà."[23] I listened to it and relished it to the point that it seemed they were playing the most beautiful romantic melody by the best musicians ever, and then suddenly two giant tears began rolling down my cheeks. Oh! When you will be here everything will be different, everything will be more marvellous, I have no doubt. Now I live and wait for you, I live to see you again and forever, I plan to work until you arrive, in that way time will pass more quickly, I too want to contribute to our happiness, a happiness that is assured. Tomorrow I will go to visit the factory with *papà* and I will start working on Monday. I am sure that work will be more satisfying here than in Ampezzo; my *papà* says they will give me at least 2000 lire per day, I don't know, it seems impossible to me! The wait will be hard but the joy, immeasurable. Let's wait. Our day will come! It will come! You see I constantly talk about this, I don't know what else to talk about, and all day I do nothing but think about these things Often, I whisper words to your photo that I keep on my dressing table, I whisper words to you pretending you can hear me, I do this every single night and day, I kiss you. This is the way it is until you are here, then, things will be different.

I don't know if in my previous letters I described to you the airplane ride, I think so, we had marvellous weather, thank God and thanks to my Protector to whom you prayed, you were worried, weren't you? My poor darling, how wonderful you are, but you see, everything went well. On Wednesday at 5:30 we arrived safe and sound in Montreal. Now is your chance to take care of yourself and to rest as much as possible. I thank you for the letter you wrote to my *nonni* and to D ... Please write to our elders once in a while! In another letter I will describe to you my new home, that is, our new home, which we will make more beautiful once we will be married. I remember all the promises that I made to you, and I will do my best to keep them. I will now write to your *mamma* and to your *papà* Gigio whom I hope is feeling better. My precious dear, to you I send my most ardent and passionate kisses and my affectionate greetings from yours always, Tetina.

23 The song "Dove sta Zazà" ["Where is Zazà"] was a widely popular Neapolitan song that tells the story of the mysterious disappearance of a woman during the Feast of San Gennaro. It was composed in 1944 by Raffaele Cutolo (lyrics) and Giuseppe Cioffi (music). See Caselli, *Storia della canzone italiana*, 30.

— Venice 2-10-48 —

Nietta mia adorata,[24]

Even more precious than a treasure, I safely keep to myself this first letter of yours that I received last night on the 1st of October, 10 days after your departure. These ten days of silence have been nothing short of a bleak agony, even though I was aware of the enormous distance that divides us. Everything was as we had anticipated, this was clear to me, but my innate human spirit overwhelmed me with an avalanche of mood swings and questions — constantly fluctuating and causing my poor heart to carry the harshest, the heaviest of crosses. During these ten wretched days, I felt something I had never felt before, I came to realize what truth is, that love is immortal to the point that while it was conceived under the guise of humanity, it can endure distances from one end of the Earth to the other. The will that guides us and sustains our fate is leading us onto an atrocious path that we ourselves chose, so we could reach our goal more easily, the goal we agreed to on that immortal day of our first kiss. Unfortunately, the thorny and tortuous road ahead will require that we keep our earnest smiles hidden, our spontaneous, thriving passionate love, it is a portrait of a dream that reaps bitterness for now so that our smiles may glow in the future. Everything will appear bitter in this transition, even more so if a thorn or two of our fate will show droplets of blood [?].[25] Because of this, your writing brought me enormous joy. Those words that skidded across the ocean waves delivered your thoughts as they travelled toward me, one metre at a time. They have dispatched your sorrow, your agony, your discouragement, and yes, as I read them, the words became more real to me. Your well-written and profoundly truthful thoughts are something that I keep preciously to myself, they are thoughts that confirm and guarantee the truth. If I respond so spontaneously it is because I believe you and because I do not doubt your words, oh no, my dear Tetina, I have read and understood your sorrow and your love in the same way that you have spoken so truthfully. For this reason, I place myself before God for

24 Nietta, my beloved.
25 Throughout the letters, a question mark in brackets represents words or phrases that were not legible in the original letters.

Mobility in the Immediate Postwar Era 81

this force that you so generously offer me, I humbly bow to your love. And so, after endless days of harrowing anxiety and haunting trepidation, tonight my heart can dream of you, beautiful you, and mine, next to an affection and a memory that renew my first and last feeling until you are with me, the feeling that in your eyes [?] all my life. My feeling is an invisible thread searching for and conversing with nature, which, like now, and like never before, ties me to your thoughts, to your movements and to your person, which now belongs to me in a spiritual, sacred way. Yes, I feel it, and your principles confirm to me that you are mine, mine in spirit for now, with the hope that in the future – obfuscated at the moment, though its path will be crystallized – that you will be mine, mine in body and soul, so that we will meld our joy and bitterness into smiles and erase the lines of worry that now appear on our brows. May this be [?] now in the harshest moment of our exile.

And now, as I hinted a few lines ago, as though this torment were not enough, I have some bad news for you. Be strong and think of the day of my arrival. After trying to find the gentlest of ways to tell you, I chose the simplest. On the day after you left, I began to inquire about my status in the military so that I could be aware of the time that I still need to serve. Imagine, I was so sure of my transfer from the navy to the army that I went to the military district office requesting an unrestricted licence for the permission to leave the country. Unfortunately, fate was not on my side. The day after, I received a notice requesting my presence at the naval office (meaning I am still part of the navy) [?]. I cannot tell you how distraught I was after receiving this terrible blow and how much it made my dizziness worse, even if it was already in full swing after you left. Unfortunately, my Nietta, it is I who am to blame for this terrible incident because, not willing to give in to fate, last year I tried everything [?]. To be a fatalist is a good thing. This is why, right now, I cannot do anything against fate, all I can do is hope for a drop of luck. I really don't know when I can leave, but it will need to be next year.

This is horrible, it delays all of our plans, everything. Yes, Nietta, if all of this acerbates you, it is my fault, because while I thought I was doing something good, I ended up hurting you. In the end, the responsibility however is not entirely mine because it was the ministry who reached this decision a few months ago. It looks like I am an expert at giving you only bad news as though the rest were not enough, but I beg you, Nietta my dear love, do not judge me, do not believe for one minute that I would do this for my own ends, God can always punish me if everything that I tell you, if all of this, is not true. What guides me in reaching our goal is my eagerness [?]. Please don't think this setback was my doing, for the love of God, no, because I truly wish to join you. I would be vile if I had done this myself. Instead, my Tetina, you must believe inside the deep tremor of my heart, which finds itself torn in two, a large part is bitter, and a small part is happy. I have little hope that my attempt will generate positive results, if that doesn't work, oh my Nietta, everything will be delayed by one year and several months, yes, Nietta I speak to you openly about this so there will be no misunderstanding. Please be strong when you receive this news, everything is according to God's will and so, as a fatalist, I believe we should follow God's wishes. This delay weighs on my soul, this experience will make a man out of me, and I will come to you with greater maturity in my duties and responsibilities. There, everything delays our wedding, but I will move ahead anyway in this period, not now because it's too early, but definitely when I will be in the army and you will have initiated the paperwork for me. This bitter experience will make you love me much like it will make me love you more. Oh, yes! my Nietta.

[Top of the letter:]

Can you use a pencil when you write, the ink makes it difficult to read the letter. Thank you. More kisses, Loris.

— Montreal 5-10-48 —

Mio adorato Loris,[26]

It is useless for me to hide from you my troubles and my worries. It's been a few days now, actually, several days since I have heard from you, and I cannot imagine the reason for this silence. When this happens, the ugliest thoughts appear in our minds, especially when one is so far away from the other, like we are; I just don't know what to think. Is it a postal delay (and this might very well be the case) if … Oh! If I told you all the reasons, there would be a hundred! But all of these come to

26 My adored Loris.

nothing, that is, I think of you, and at the same time, I cannot believe what I am writing. Are you ill? If this were the case, you would have asked your *mamma* or someone else in the family to write to me. Lazy? No, I have never known you to be lazy, your letters have always been punctual, the last letter looked a little scribbled from fatigue and sleepiness, but you have never been late. So, what is it? Maybe it's a postal delay, let's hope that I will receive news this afternoon and all of this will be behind me. In the past two days, I have done nothing else but look at the letter box, even at 11:30 last night when I returned home from a visit to a fellow Friulano, a friend of my *papà*'s, with my *mamma* and *papà*. Imagine if at that hour I would have found something!

Instead, in these days I received news from my dear ones back home. They tell me that you wrote to them and that you might be visiting them in Ampezzo at Christmastime. If you can, please visit them. You can just imagine how delighted they will be to see you, even though your presence will renew their sorrow as it will inevitably remind them of their Antonietta. Please write to me and tell me how my loved ones and the others appear to you. You must provide a detailed summary of everything you see for me, even if it will bring pain to my ears. In the past few years, I was already counting the days that separated us and I eagerly awaited Christmas only because you were coming up to visit. Now everything has changed. This year will be a year of memories and nostalgia for me. So much nostalgia!! I never thought I would feel it so intensely, if you were here, things would be different. I miss you terribly, my few distractions and leisure activities do not fill the emptiness that I feel from missing you.

Still a few days remain before you will undergo the military examination. It's on the 11th of November, if I am not mistaken. It's still not clear to me for how long you must serve in the army, is it two years? And when do you leave in April? As soon as your term is over, will you come right away to America? Yes, yes, you will join me immediately after, right? I want to put an end to this torment as soon as possible, not because we are far away from each other, because I still love you despite this, but rather because I am afraid of losing you, or that you might get sick, or that another war is coming. I am telling you ...[27]

27 The remaining part of the letter is missing from the collection.

— 2 —

"I will know how to wait knowing this is the last time"
Writing and Waiting across National Boundaries

AS ANTONIETTA AND LORIS wrote to one another between the cities of Montreal and Venice, the boundaries of the private sphere gave way and their individual private spheres became anchored in a space beyond that of a single nation, and in a transnational social sphere.[1] Writing letters across national boundaries affected them in other significant ways as well. It extended the couple's psychological and emotional boundaries. In penning letters over long distances, a reflective process takes shape both in the practice of writing and in the emotional and reflective discourse that emerges from the letters. Writing, Jack Goody notes, comprises reflexivity. This reflexivity may then lead to an elaboration or heightening of emotions.[2] The impact of writing extends to the point that consciousness itself is transformed by the technology of writing.[3]

As Walter Ong suggests, "writing heightens consciousness."[4] By extension, distance, a source of frustration and sorrow for Antonietta and Loris, which they continuously sought to bridge in their letters, pushed them perhaps to reflect more about themselves and their relationship and the tenacity with which they endeavoured to stay connected. Certainly, writing was no easy task for either of them. It

---

1 Baldassar and Gabaccia, "Home, Family, and the Italian Nation in a Mobile World," 5. See also, Glick Schiller, Basch, and Szanton Blanc, "From Immigrant to Transmigrant."
2 Goody, *Food and Love,* 122.
3 Ong, *Orality and Literacy,* 81.
4 Ibid., 81.

Writing and Waiting across National Boundaries 85

was not easy to write and make clear one's message, without gesture, without facial expression, without intonation, without a real hearer.[5] As Ong notes, readers endeavour to foresee circumspectly all possible meanings a statement may have for them in a situation, and they need to make the language work so as to be clear all by itself, with little or no existential context. It is, of course, no wonder that writing is commonly agonizing work.[6] Despite these challenges, writing was vital to migrants and their loved ones. In the case of Antonietta and Loris, staying in touch and conforming to the exigencies of the correspondents' *pacte épistolaire* effectively pushed the couple to dig deep within themselves, understand their feelings, and discuss them in relation to themselves and the events around them.

The practice of writing served also as a form of therapy for managing their sorrow. It was at once a means of self-preservation and a galvanizer of creativity, order, and resilience.[7] In the words of Louise DeSalvo, writing "permits the construction of a cohesive, elaborate, thoughtful personal narrative in the way that simply speaking about our experiences doesn't."[8] What emerges from this kind of intimate discourse is creativity.[9] The letters of Antonietta and Loris provide a window onto an epistolary creativity, not only in their use of words and style but also in the myriad ways they way endeavour to mimic and reference cultural productions – from film to opera, from popular songs to plays – to exude a creative sensibility and highlight further their affective attachment for one another.

Writing intimate letters, perhaps no different from other forms of biographical writing, promotes a sense of order, and relatedly, an "emotive organization of memory."[10] Writing requires composing a thought or reflection and putting it down on paper in a structure that is at once coherent, relevant, and socially and emotionally appropriate,

---

5 Ibid., 102.

6 Ibid., 102–3.

7 On letter writing as a form of therapy in migration, see Cancian, *Families, Lovers, and their Letters*, "Introduction," 3–20. For a discussion on letter writing in other contexts, such as war, see especially, Gibelli, *L'Officina della Guerra*.

8 DeSalvo, *Writing as a Way of Healing*, 41.

9 Ibid., 41.

10 Ricatti, "First Love and Italian Postwar Migration Stories," 170.

and in the case of intimate letters, emotionally compelling, as in Antonietta's and Loris's collection. While writing cultivates the qualities of absorption, encouraging focus and engaging letter writers at the same time,[11] it also compels them to create structure in their minds and memory about the form and content their narrative requires in order to be best understood. In designing an order in the missives, their feelings became coherent rather than chaotic, solutions and acceptance were on hand, rather than puzzlement or despair.[12]

Writing also brought hope, sometimes in the same letter where melancholy prevailed. As the writers composed their thoughts, they became observers of themselves and the world around them.[13] In doing so, they sometimes developed resilience. Louise DeSalvo explains: "We regard our lives with a certain detachment and distance when we view it as a subject to describe and interpret. We reframe the problems in our life as challenges as we ask ourselves how to articulate what is on our mind in a way that will make sense."[14] Finally, writing letters helped to make letter writers' life stories come alive, both to themselves and to their corresponding confidantes.

— Montreal 8-10-48 —

Mio unico bene,[15]
Here I am to you, for you, as always, heart, soul, and all of me. It's exactly 15 minutes to 11. In Italy, it must be about 5 o'clock, if my calculation is correct. You are still at work perhaps, while I have finished my day long ago. Yes, my darling, since Tuesday I have been working in a large factory. I wanted to try it even though *mamma* and *papà* did not agree with me. I hoped to succeed, to feel happy and gratified to be working and receive the praises of my department supervisor, a French-speaking lady. I wanted to do this, and excel at it so that I

---

11 DeSalvo, *Writing as a Way of Healing*, 73.
12 Ibid., 45.
13 Ibid., 73.
14 Ibid.
15 My only treasure.

Writing and Waiting across National Boundaries   87

would feel I am contributing to our future together, but I am just not able to, the work agitates me far too much. I am not so strong. The work requires that I remain all day at the machine, sewing constantly with no break in between. I am so discouraged and disheartened, but what can I do? I was hoping I would adjust to the deafening noise of the machines, to the arduous work, but I returned home more and more tired with each passing day. This evening *papà* scolded me for not quitting. I just cannot do it any longer. Perhaps it's better that I work from home with *mamma*. Tomorrow, *papà* will go out and buy a sewing machine for me so I can begin to work at home.

My precious love, I have so many things to tell you, things that happen during my days here, but I don't know where to begin. I think of you, I remember you *constantly*, as I remember the days we spent together, every detail returns to mind, I remember everything. I reread your letters the minute I have a little free time because this is all I have of you now. Only in the letters can I read your thoughts, can I hear your voice. How many times do I need to look away from your photograph when I enter my room, so as not to cry, so as not to suffer. My darling, do you know what this separation does to us? Nothing but make us love each other more and fuel the flame that lights up our hearts.

What does it matter if I need to wait two years to see you again, don't be discouraged. I will know how to wait patiently, I have waited for so long, how many times I awaited your arrival, cried when you left. I have proven myself, I will know how to wait knowing this is the last time. I think that from then on, our long-awaited prize will be well deserved, what do you think, my darling? I will be ready for that long-awaited day, and the days that follow will be days of preparation and anticipation.

Do not despair, my precious darling. I was the one who asked you to stay home and away from military duty. Believe me I don't regret it because in one year, I learned to love you more, to know you and understand you more deeply and more intimately. You know why that is, if you remember well while we were in Rome we declared to each other that we are made for one another, during this time, my love has deepened for you. It has grown strong roots that no one can overturn, don't you remember the beautiful days we spent together? How can we forget them? If you had reported to duty, we would not have lived these days together, don't you see? I recall the Butterfly's words, "and I wait a long time, and does not weigh on me the long waiting."[16]

Only one thing frightens me, the thought that there will be another war in Europe. Oh, my God! I am so afraid, my darling. What do you think? What are they saying in Italy? Here, we hear so little news about politics, and on the radio, they only speak in French or English, it's terrible not to be able to understand the language. I hear *papà* and his friends discuss politics from time to time, but even then, they are only their ideas. Talk to me, tell me something, tell me when you think you will be reporting to the army, and how long you think you will be there. In this way, I will have an idea about when I can expect you. I started an English-language night class, it is held three times per week, I hope to learn something, but it's so hard! I have become friends with two young Italian women, and we call each other often. This evening, one of the girls took me to school, and we returned home in the car of *papà*'s business partner who came to pick me up.

I leave you now because I am exhausted. Please excuse my bad writing. I could not write any better. Big kisses and greetings to everyone in your family, and to you, one single, long and passionate kiss together with a huge and tight embrace, forever your Nietta

[On a separate note:] If you don't receive news from me often, don't worry. As you know, I am in Canadà and letters take a long time to arrive. One thing should keep your spirits up: I am yours, yours alone, and I love you forever. After tomorrow is your birthday, I sent you a special card, did you receive it? Perhaps you didn't because I sent it by ship. Once again, my best wishes to you, I will be thinking of you on Sunday and I will pray that God may help us reach our goal.

Kisses, your Nietta

— Montreal 10-10-48 —

Loris mio adorato,[17]
Today I cannot tell you that I remember you more than any other day because yesterday too, and the days before, you were constantly in my

16 Castel, *The Complete Puccini Libretti*, 334.
17 My adored Loris.

heart. I think of you today with such profound intensity to the point that in my mind I am following your every move in everything that you are doing. Today is your birthday (I have just interrupted my writing in this minute to listen to a program of Italian songs. They are now playing "Mamma Rosa,"[18] oh, what nostalgia!!) They are still playing songs, now they are playing a Neapolitan song, and I don't care to listen to it. Every Sunday from 1300 to 1330 they play half an hour of Italian melodies and songs. I wait for this program on the radio with indescribable eagerness. As I was saying, it's your birthday and since I have known you, I have never had the pleasure of being near you on this day. To be honest never before have I thought of you as intensely as I have this year, never have I prayed as fervidly to God asking Him to reunite us, or at the very least, that our hearts and spirits feel united until the day we will be together.

This is what I prayed to God this morning at church, an Italian church, and tomorrow I will do the same, the Holy Day of Our Lady of Graces, I will pray for one grace, just that one. My darling, I can imagine how much you too must be thinking of me today, a day that should be a joyful one for you, but it's not, I know this because the person who gives you joy is not with you, be happy nonetheless knowing that I love you, I love you so very much. I wanted to send you a gift for this special day but it was not possible this time, I will send you a gift at a later date, I know you will appreciate it just the same. Now, my darling, I send you again my sincerest wishes along with the most affectionate kisses and one passionate kiss that is for you on the day of your twenty-first year.

your Nietta

Big kisses to your *mamma* and your loved ones, and your *papà* Gigio along with all your loved ones.

[Top of first page:] Many best wishes and greetings from Vittorio. Many best wishes and greetings also from your *mamma*.

---

18 The song "Mamma Rosa" (music by M. Schisa, lyrics by B. Cherubini) was first released in 1943 by Luciano Tajoli (1920–96), a very popular singer and actor in Italy and across Italian migrant communities after the Second World War. See Giannotti, *L'enciclopedia di Sanremo*, 203.

— Venice 10-10-48 —

Nietta mia amatissima,[19]

Twenty-one years ago, today, I opened my eyes to life, I was at the beginning of my existence, an innocent creature who perhaps came to this world with the single objective to love you. And, so my era, my epoch began, of course, I was not thinking then what I am thinking now, that is, my duty to love you. If I were to draw you a sketch, it would be like this: a tiny baby with a big heart, a heart made to love, of course, no one knew what kind of love, and who this love would be assigned to, but I hope that my heart is only for you so that I may love you profoundly, and offer you a love that is whole and limitless, a love that nourishes your talents and the virtues in your conscience, aware of tomorrow, without doubts or biases. It looks ahead with perfect clarity, dignified of the power of the heart — which has waited endlessly to possess your heart, a heart that agrees to reside in mine.

Twenty-one years ago, I certainly did not know who would have refused a love born from me, I did not know that I would meet you, and love you, nonetheless, I did not believe in appearances, rather I looked for remote mysteries with the hope of discovering a new phenomenon. Perhaps for this reason, perhaps as a result of my education, I reserved the best part of me, as though a victory were already on course. To carefully observe the work of a good soul is innate in me, especially in someone who is as modest as me though skilled at distinguishing opportunistic conveniences, for the fear of losing one's soul or risk encumbering one's spirit. For this reason, I began to love you, only in this way is it easy for me to love you spiritually, and not just physically.

Love is the most arduous enterprise because love blinds you, you are transported by the passion of being loved, love is the fruit of self-analysis so that you will not commit any wrongs. Love is the virtue of human strength, the virtue that withstands pain and gives life to sorrow; love is the weapon that defends you and your good principles, love is tied to your happiness. Oh, my dear Nietta, if my love for you were not great, it would not make it this far. While it has run into obstacles along the way, it knows how to overcome them, it has

---

19 Nietta, my dearest love.

charted a course to cross the oceans and reach you, it knows how to ride across the waves like a ship, a large, majestic ship with everyone and everything on-board, but the heart is a heart and for this reason, it only knows how to love you.

With the first twenty years behind me, plus one, few think of my age because they see me as a man, but you alone are capable, I am sure, to understand me, to understand my weaknesses, to understand my wishes! By now, you are far away, but I hope that despite this, you will not change in the way you understand me, in the way you love me. I hope my letters delight you, I hope that they are always a reflection of me, and that they remind you of your Lorissin, who has chosen to spend the final hours of his day remembering you, with profound sadness, because you were much more near to me in the past years.

This is the first birthday that I spend alone here in Italy, perhaps there will be others, not many I am sure, and so, we must wait and trust that this temporal watershed will pass, and we will reach the day that will enclose our expectations, our disappointments – transforming them into a monumental joy. Believe in my heart, believe completely in my heart which I have given to you in the past and in the present; believe in my love that I have nurtured only for you. For this reason, should discouragement reach your spirit, immediately free yourself from it, and reignite in you the faith you have always had in loving me.

Last Thursday I received your third letter. I was almost certain I would have received news from you on that day. And so, it was, I read the letter numerous times, avidly and carefully. In reading it, I understood how difficult life is there for you, I realized that your sadness has done nothing to change your state of mind. Trust yourself, oh my Tetina, you must be strong to withstand these difficulties, keep your spirit strong, a spirit that I hope resides inside of you as it is conceived by love. Today Sunday, I went to watch the game at Sant'Elena's, and with dimmed satisfaction, I returned home; nonetheless the Venezia team is very strong, and their best players will certainly delight their fans. In the past few days, the weather has returned to normal temperatures with a splendid, bright sun lighting up the blue sky. Every kind of cloud has passed and everything smiles with enthusiasm, even though cold temperatures have started to set in for everyone, but not in my heart, it remains warm always from the sun of your love. Kisses and hugs, most affectionately your Loris

[At top of first page:] Kisses to my *papà* and *mamma*. Tell them I am waiting to hear from them

From all of my family, infinite, dear kisses

— Venice 17-10-48 —

Nietta mia amatissima,[20]

I have been waiting for this hour to be alone with you, free of obligations so that I may remember you today with the same affection I felt exactly one month ago, the last Sunday we spent together in Rome. It's 5 o'clock in the afternoon this Sunday, 17 October. I have not been out since 10 o'clock last night. I finished working at 5, after which I went to my evening class. I returned home at 10 and from then, I did not move. I wanted to write to you this morning with a fresh mind, but I was waiting for the barber, a friend of my *papà*'s, who usually drops by at this time. Once that was done, *papà* arrived with a truckload of fire wood, and I alone unloaded it and stacked it against the front door. I could not carry out my plan; because of these tasks, I also missed this morning's Mass. When I finished with everything, it was 12:45, it was too late for Mass, and I still had some cleaning to do.

Once all was completed, I had lunch and napped for a couple of hours, and feeling rested, I listened to the soccer[21] match on the radio for 15 minutes, and now, with no other delays, I am writing to you. This endeavour — so easily understood by you — fills me with much gratification. A month has passed since we said goodbye, my dearest love, Tetina, since then, one month has passed since this tribulation began, one month since we were together in Rome, walking side by side, happily, cheerfully, and all too conscious of what awaited us in a few short days. On that Sunday, we knew how to conceal our bleak feelings with a smile, so that we would not be miserable, we were happy, we were fulfilled because we were together. We were happy because we could hear our hearts sing. On that day, everything was new

20 Nietta, my dearest love.
21 The term *calcio* is commonly known as "football," except in Canada and the United States, where the term *soccer* is more commonly adopted.

Writing and Waiting across National Boundaries   93

to us, perhaps it was the wait of the previous days until I arrived in Udine that the desire to remain side by side culminated. Everything seemed to be going our way that day, but in reality, the day was an omen of sadness, a distorted presentation of news, a dark sunset clouded by listless rays of sunshine appeared, and we were unable to do anything to clear the sombre skies. Every day that sky reappears, as it does now, I watch it and long for nothing, it is dark and grey. Perhaps the rain of these days has turned the sky ugly. Not true. The sun shines behind the clouds, the same happens to me, to us, we are not the sky, but children of the sky. Perhaps it will help us to keep us linked together, we should try to mimic it; to mimic the sky is not difficult, it might help us to imitate it as the sky mirrors always the sun of our strength.

May the sun of love continue to be with us even when the downpour of our human bitterness clouds and darkens our faces, even when our smiles and our gazes betray the beauty of our spirit tested by our sorrow. May the sun continue to brighten our days in everything that we do. The sun is more powerful than sorrow and it will light up our faces again. Should it not return, for us too it will be over. After a life tried and consumed by the trials of love, there would be no point, it would be like something that has wilted around beautiful things. On this, I have some experience, I created an alibi, a pretext for me to love you more, the pretext is anchored in the way I do things, at times arrogantly, but hidden inside is a precious treasure that no one knows about, that is your heart. Your heart is as vital to me as the blood that runs through my veins. In this way, I have known you better, I can love you more, and in this way, I can convey to you how much I have loved you, how much I love you still. There is only one reward for my work, your heart, your understanding.

In reading your last letters, I realized how pragmatic you are about things, how right you are in your judgments. For this, I adore you more. The words in your letters lift my spirit, placate my sorrow. You are aware of the mistake that I made last year, and now, you share my blame, you were and you are a good person. With constant fervour, you think of me, by now I am resigned, this too will pass, this storm as well will pass, and you will wait for me always, won't you? Yes, I am certain of this. The time that divides us was supposed to be two years, now it's been extended by a few more months. Patience, it's God's will, and everything will pass. You are strong, and so am I, together we will overcome even this struggle, hoping that, as far as I know, there will not be another war. No, my Tetina, with regards to your question, unfortunately the international situation is not one of the calmest, but before a war occurs … Stay calm, my Tetina, and you will see that everything will pass. Do not be alarmed, there is no reason.

I read that you started working, and have now stopped, it was hard for you especially because you are not physically strong. I could not understand your willingness to keep working against the will of your *papà* and your *mamma*. I understand very well your desire and your need to work, but health comes first, oh my precious darling. The sewing machine is likely now at your home, and if you wish, you can continue to work. Please, don't strain yourself as you are continuously wearing yourself down. In fact, I hope this letter of mine finds you in excellent health, as the same is for me. For fifteen days, my knee has been painfully swollen, no matter how I position it. I will go next week to have it examined. I was not able to do so these past few days because there was too much work at the Central Office. Tomorrow, Monday, [?] and for this, I too was scheduled for shift work but because I have my classes, they are giving me some time off.

Last Tuesday I wrote a nice long letter to your *nonni*, I am telling you in confidence, I hope to visit them at Christmastime, I am not sure but I will try to head up there. About my military duty, I have an appointment on 12 November and in March, I believe, I will be leaving. I pray to God that I can resign myself to this new ordeal, trusting that time is assisting us to plan everything that we dream of, agonize over, and aspire to. My family remembers you and your family always with great affection. They often speak of you and your dear ones, you are all in our hearts, and we remember you always, between W … and my *mamma*, between [?] and *mamma*, between myself and everyone else. You must remember that we are constantly thinking of you, and especially me who cannot forget your profound desire to be loved and remembered, I am sending you thousands and thousands of kisses as you constantly reside in my heart's memory of our love.

Infinite kisses,
your Loris

PS I would love to have a recent photo of you, one taken in Canada. Tell me where you live, what you're doing. I am very pleased to hear that you are learning to speak English. Try to make the most of it. I know that it's not easy, but you can do it.

Give many kisses and remember me in a special way to your *papà* and *mamma*, as I hope to receive a letter from them. Kisses to you again, your Loris.

— Montreal 19-10-48 —

Mio adorato Loris,[22]

Tonight, I am determined to write to you despite the late hour and the fact that my body demands rest. It's 11:30 p.m. and the family of a fellow-villager was here for a visit until now. *Papà* had invited them to dinner, a delectable dinner with wildfowl and polenta. On Saturday, we went hunting and they caught 14 huge birds, and so for supper tonight, we feasted on them. I received your letter three days ago. I wanted to write to you upon receiving it, but between one thing and another, I postponed it to later. For the past 4 or 5 days, I have been travelling from one place to another as I am always being invited to people's homes. I am tired of wandering. I hope that all of these visits are over (after being here for nearly one month, don't you agree?). It's never been as busy as it has been in the past few days; you would think they conspired together. Last night, I even missed my class so that I could visit a friend of *papà*'s with my parents, the truth is I had a great time, you know, nothing exceptional, just talking, having a few laughs, playing a few songs on the gramophone, and that's it, but you know me, you know how much I enjoy these familiar, simple get-to-gethers, much more than pompous parties. I felt happy last night, so much so that I had almost forgotten the worries that have been nagging at me for the past month. I spent two, three hours of utter peace, I don't know if it was the glass of wine they had offered me that had put me in a good mood – it's the second glass that I drank since I have been here. The wine was strong, one hundred times strong, as L … says.

22 My beloved Loris.

Wine is not usually available here, almost everyone drinks beer or soft drinks, I was also surprised about something else, people always add a drop of milk in their black coffee, they offer coffee with the sugar bowl and a little pitcher of milk. I have already become accustomed to their way of life; I am even happy to take my coffee in the same way that they do. I find it very interesting too – (I ask you to please forgive me, my darling, if I did not write to you last night or today, because we are the 20th today, I wanted to finish my letter this afternoon, instead at 1400 hrs, a lady came to pick me up to take me to the hospital where one of her sons is staying because he is sick, so here I am writing to you this evening, not at the same hour as last night as it's nearly 11 o'clock. At 7:30, I went to school and my two friends came over, you know the girls I talked to you about. I am free now; last night I just could not continue and almost fell asleep on the paper.)

I realized this evening that I wrote some silly things to you, how we drink tea, coffee, etc. etc., forgive me, my darling, it will certainly be useful to you to know about the customs of these places. In this way, you won't be surprised when you come here. How much I enjoy talking with you like this, it almost seems certain that you will be joining me, the words that I say give me faith and trust, yes, I must see you again. I must see those splendid eyes that light up like stars, your beautiful mouth that I kissed so little, that face I caressed so seldom because we were always separated and away from each other, I am yours, my love, yours in spirit. I belong to you, and nothing and no one in this world will keep me away from you, fate will not agree otherwise, because we are the makers of our destiny, we create our destiny with our own hands. There, determination and patience – two things that must never separate us. Will they always be with us? Yes, do you agree my darling? Until now, we have always walked along, as they say, a straight path, and we have reasoned with our brains. Though we are young, we know how to weigh the pros and cons, if we succeed in our plans, we can consider ourselves lucky and smart. We should not be the ones to say it, but if you think about it, it's true, this is the way it will be, because we want it to work out and we ardently wish for it.

A few days ago, we received news about the trunk we had sent on October 1st. I hope to have it in our possession in the next few days.

I am excited because at least I will have something else that is yours and that reminds me intensely of you, it contains my winter clothes, of which I have none now, I had my blue coat dyed and it looks new again. I bought a new green hat with brown trimmings, for Sunday; I will buy a green purse and gloves too. I will take a picture dressed like this, though I don't know when, honestly, I dare not ask *papà* for anything else, he has spent so much money on us in this period, he just bought us an electric machine with lighting. I need to be a little patient, a bit at a time everything will come, as my poor *papà* says, he is so good to me, Loris.

Here, we already had our first snowfall. On Monday night, it was a light snowfall that lasted half an hour. Did your *sorella* [sister] W ... change house? Is baby M ... growing? It's been one month since I saw you and it feels like I have been here for a century. How much I think of you all, and I remember all the kindness that everyone has shown me, I have forgotten nothing. Everyone at home was so friendly, so affectionate with me, and this made me happy. You too have done so much for me, so much that you cannot imagine; you drew me a little away from the world I lived in, you took me to a world I dreamed of knowing. You set out to teach me the most marvellous and admirable of things – things that raise the spirit above all else, music, for instance, that I now love deeply because I know more about it, and many other things. You introduced me to your city, the most beautiful city, the most enchanting city in the world, and, ... yes, you helped me to change the way I felt, because your ideas are right and sound, your gifts – are they not beautiful and fine? Never before did I receive similar gifts. Yours were the first and the most appreciated. Do you believe it? You see, now it almost seems like I am talking with you. It's the first letter I write that discusses different topics, the others described only pain and suffering, I am beginning to feel better a little at a time. You see now we are becoming more resigned and more hopeful for a joyful tomorrow.

Now my precious, before I leave you I want to tell you one phrase, one short phrase in English so you can see the progress that I am making. I love you (*Ti amo tanto*). Isn't that good? Good night (*Buona notte*) my darling.

Many many kisses from your Tetina.

98 September 1948 to December 1948

Kisses to your *mamma* and everyone else. Send me the address of your *zio* [uncle] M ... Thank you.

Kisses from my *papà* and my *mamma* who are lazy writers.

Many greetings.

[Best regards from the S ... C ... family]

— Venice 20-10-48 —

Nietta mia amatissima,[23]

I chose this moment to dedicate to you every drop of my joy that will be melded with this treasure as I recall tomorrow's date, the date that marks precisely one month since your departure. In this minute, I combine and fuse all of my passion tied to this feeling, to the feeling of Verdi's music, which inspires me as I write to you now; certainly they are not poems, but simple phrases that speak of our love.

I turn to the purest spirit that galvanized Verdi in his struggles for victory, so that he could create the Italic music that remains unparalleled, so that in his sorrow, he could love more, and submit to the ideal of eternalizing the voice of the spirit, to love the family and *la Patria* [the homeland] both spiritually and musically. With this premise and with his genius, he set to music the most beautiful things that touched his heart, the kindness of his soul guided and protected Verdi wherever his thoughts took him, with sentiment, Verdi loved and created with simplicity a single style that mirrors the philosophy of many generations who draw the most honest inspiration from music to express the purest of feelings.

How beautiful the music is, how magnificent our music is, how much it illuminates and embraces every marvellous thing, how much every single note is a gift for our heart confused by human and material sounds. [?] This means that common sense must take over, and that through our spirituality, facts will be constructed. It is exactly like this, oh my beloved Nietta, may the Holy Spirit lead us and our fate, may our feelings be kind-hearted and build the foundation for our new life. Egoism and materialism must not serve as our guides. If the moral spirit, the Christian spirit is lacking in our hearts, we can compare ourselves to slaves, slaves of our own selves. The consciousness

23 Nietta my dearest love.

Writing and Waiting across National Boundaries   99

of our actions is always subordinate to our objectives, always tied to the spirit with which we act. I don't think that my explanation is new to you, no, I'm well aware of this, but I wish it to compel you to reflect further now that you are acquainted with a new world so far away. How could I doubt such a thing? This is the question that looms over me most often. Oh no, I have no doubts and no biased notions. Often, I know the truth, it envelops me and sheds light on my ideas. In this way I can love you more! It was last night that I thought about this. The idea came to me at the time I received with total and singular affection your greetings for me (sent to me by ship on 28 September). You cannot imagine, and I cannot fully convey my joy in receiving them, how much they strengthened my conviction. Here is where my conscience takes over my determination. Never did I enjoy a more gratifying gift and your greetings on this day The lovely and fine image on the greeting card compelled me to search for a meaning. The drawing envelopes your utter faith, my utter hope in our Love. A protective mantle that will without a doubt encourage us, it is a medium of affections that emanates a fragrance from your heart. (I continue tonight from where I left off 24 hours ago, given that I could not continue writing for reasons you can well imagine since I was exhausted and very sleepy), and now that I return to yesterday's words, here I am moved by your delightful gift, yes, my darling, I am so excited. You are extremely perceptive in making the perfect choice for us [?]

This is the way things are, my beloved Tetina, if we had wings, or better yet, if I had wings, I would have by now crossed the seas, and reached your nest [?], to greet the new day with you. Until now, nothing is working for us. The wings are not for us. It is not the right moment for me to join you. That day will come, I am sure, depending on God's mercy, I will be able to join you, and I too will be able to fly to a new world, so that I can find you always with open arms, ready to embrace me and possess me. Your letter that I received this evening reassured me of the concern I expressed earlier. that is, my faith in you as I think of you in anticipation of my arrival, even if the wait is long, it will not change our thoughts or our plans, it will serve as a pledge for withstanding our long suffering. Your nightmare that frequently awakens you at night [?], when memories more easily return to our thoughts is a sign of the reality, that is, this is proof that you are avidly thinking of me, and it is for this reason that I believe in your love, it is for this reason that I believe in your struggle. You must be strong to persevere this rugged path, light will follow this darkness. You must be strong to think of me still in your homeland, in your country. I am here because circumstances force me to be here, I am however, always yours, oh Tetina, yours in your soul, yours in your country. Every morning since our first morning, I sent you my greetings in the sacred mountains. Tell your dear parents, convey that to them in my memory, I offer my affection, my love for you. I travel to work every day with these thoughts, without much care for anything else, now I cannot share my hardships with you any longer, like I used to.

A few days ago, I wrote a long letter to your *nonni* and I received replies first from D ..., then from your *zio* O ..., D ... asked me to scold you for not keeping your promise to write to her. She says that she has not received a single line. Knowing that you never wished to forget her, I ask you to please write to her as soon as possible. She especially deserves to hear from you, much like A ..., O ... wrote a lovely letter, reaffirming once again a unanimous affection on your family's behalf. He told me how your *nonni* are doing, while one of them sings every day, your *nonna* stays in the backyard, like usual. Even L ... and A ... wrote to me, and I will respond as soon as possible. I always try to reply first to your letters so I can be close to you and send you always many kisses, as many as I have.

your Loris

— 3 —

"This is America for the crazy!"
Linguistic Currents in Postwar Montreal

"IT'S A REAL MINESTRONE," remarked Antonietta in a letter to Loris on 25 October 1948 citing a metaphor her father employed in describing his impressions of a multilingual Montreal. To Antonietta, who had just emigrated from a place characterized by one national language (Italian) alongside regional and local variants like Friulano and Veneziano (Venetian dialect), Montreal appeared to have a cacophony of languages. However, in no time at all, Antonietta quickly apprehended Montreal's linguistic divide and the significance of the "economics of language"[1] that were at play for her and Loris. In examining Montreal's linguistic stage, Sherry Simon notes that "like Brussels and Barcelona today, like Prague and Trieste in the late nineteenth century, the linguistic divisions of Montreal are the product of an internal colonialism, reflecting the shifting power relations that shaped the development of the city."[2] A product of double colonization – first by the French and then by the British – Montreal experienced a change in language at every act of appropriation in its history, from the early days of Jacques Cartier's first encounter with the Iroquois inhabitants of Hochelaga to the foundation of the French colony's Ville Marie and the appropriation of the English language in 1759 by British conquerors.[3]

---

1 Chiswick and Miller, "International Migration and the Economics of Language," 1–95.
2 Simon, *Translating Montreal*, 21.
3 Ibid.

In the 1940s up to the 1960s, while dominated by a French-speaking majority, Montreal remained, "an English city containing many French-speaking workers and inhabitants."[4] A veritable linguistic division of labour characterized the City of Montreal in the 1940s and 1950s, when a large concentration of Italians settled in the city. While the anglophone community tended to occupy most of the city's well-paying managerial positions, members of the francophone community occupied the lower-paid positions. This reflected a significant income gap between the two linguistic communities.[5] Up until at least the early 1960s, English was the language of upward mobility in Montreal, and immigrants like Antonietta and her family navigated the "economics of language" both locally and transnationally.

From a local perspective, shortly upon arriving in Montreal – a city immersed in rapid economic growth – Antonietta began taking English-language classes, much like other immigrant groups arriving in these years.[6] While taking evening classes, she worked in a garment-making factory under the supervision of a French-speaking section manager. With her parents, co-workers, and friends, she spoke in Italian or Friulano. Given the linguistic proximity between Italian and French, we can imagine how much more at ease Antonietta felt in appropriating French over English as she endeavoured to make Montreal her new home. Still, the human capital of the English language and its hegemony over French was discussed and negotiated by immigrants with a majority of Italian immigrants working for more English-speaking employers than French-speaking, and working alongside more French-speaking co-workers than English-speaking.[7]

Language negotiation among Italian immigrants extended beyond the local. As "a transnational social field,"[8] letters served as a powerful tool for migrants to advise their kin, prospective migrants, about the socio-economic and cultural conditions they could expect to find once

---

4 Jacobs, *The Question of Separatism*, cited in Levine, *The Reconquest of Montreal*, 1.
5 Levine, *The Reconquest of Montreal*, 3.
6 This includes Holocaust survivors. See the article by Shefiel and Zembrzycki, "We Started Over Again, We Were Young."
7 Boissevain, *The Italians of Montreal*.
8 Gerber, *Authors of their Lives*, 155. See also, Glick Schiller, Basch, and Szanton Blanc, "From Immigrant to Transmigrant."

they decided to migrate. By advising Loris to take an English-language class while in Italy, Antonietta underscored the economic benefits for him in becoming proficient in English. This proficiency would translate, she alluded, into more successful labour market outcomes in his field of interest, and higher earnings.[9] Implicit in Antonietta's advice was the conviction that English-language acquisition would lead him (and her and their family) to greater economic well-being while ensuring wider access to social and cultural networks beyond the Italian migrant community in Montreal. As Chiswick and Miller also note, language learning – in this case, both English and French particularly after 1961 – also held the promise of opening opportunities of civic engagement to immigrants.[10] Loris's eventual linguistic proficiency in French and English led him to many years of employment with the City of Montreal and later, in civic engagement for his work in the preservation and recognition of Guido Nincheri's artwork.

— Montreal 25-10-48 —

Mio adorato Loris,[11]
I do not want to delay any longer in replying to your last letter, as I have done for the other letter. I know how much my silence worries you, but sometimes, even though I am aware of this, I am late in responding to you, always for different reasons, of course. I ask you to forgive me, to sympathize and bear with my faults, which are not so serious I think. I received your letter like all the others, I read it over again a thousand times, even last night in bed, I don't know how many times I gazed at your writing, and I fell asleep with your words in my hands. This morning, I found the letter crumpled up beneath the blankets, you write well, very well; unfortunately, I will never be able to match your writing skills, even less so now that I find myself mangling the Italian language in a pitiful way, my poor dear language! Even real

---

9 Chiswick and Miller, "International Migration and the Economics of Language," 7.
10 Ibid., 8.
11 My beloved Loris.

Italians speak it incorrectly and they add French or English words here and there. It's a "real minestrone" my *papà* says. This morning a French lady called me. She is the director of the factory where I worked. I must tell you that in order for us to understand each other, it took some time. As I mixed in some Italian words with French words, she managed to understand me. "This is America for the crazy!" says my classmate. Here we speak every possible language, all the races of the world are here, black, red, white, and if there would be people of green colour, they would be here too. But, the language spoken by most people is English, actually *papà* tells me that if you could learn a little English, it would be a great benefit for you, you would have better chances in finding work that is more suitable to you, or work in your trade. Isn't there an evening course you could take in Venice? I do not mean now, because you have your other classes, but later. Would you like to do this? Could you look into it, Loris? It would be good for you and for me, it's another sacrifice, I know, but what does it matter if one day we can have the joy of well-being and serenity?

You asked me to describe what I do during the day. You might not believe me, but I do more or less what I was doing in Ampezzo; however, now I also need to worry about the groceries, because my *mamma* will not leave the house since she does not speak the language. Sometimes, I go out with a few married women. When my *papà* returns from work in the evening, we go out for a visit with friends or acquaintances who invite us. Sometimes, I visit a few of my girlfriends at their homes where we listen to some wonderful Italian music albums. On Saturday afternoons, my *papà* does not work and so, we too take the day off. For example, on Saturday, we went out to a nice place, and yesterday afternoon we were out all day. We went to visit the magnificent Saint Joseph's Oratory, and other sites. As you can see, I spend most of my days with my parents, I am not complaining, I feel content because I know that it makes you happy and it cheers you up. I will have those photos made for you soon, and I will send them to you. We received news the other day that our travel trunk has arrived in Montreal. We will be going to reclaim it today.

My adored love, what else can I tell you, other than what I have already told you a million times? I adore you, my darling, I love you so very much, remember me and love me forever, tell me over and over

Linguistic Currents in Postwar Montreal   105

again for me to be sure that you have not changed, and that you have not changed your mind. Oh, if the opposite were true, what disillusionment it would be for me, the most terrible, the most bitter of all. You will love me forever, won't you, my Loris? Forever. I leave you now as I must meet with the director of the factory who has asked to meet with me. I wonder what she wants, maybe that I return to work? I will let you know in my next letter. You too, write to me, like in your previous letter, tell me what you are doing, where you are going, so that I can have the feeling of you being close to me. Kisses to your *mamma* and *papà* Gigio, and everyone, especially W ..., her husband and the children. Tell her I will write to her soon. To you, a thousand kisses and the biggest possible embrace, your Nietta.

— Montreal 30-10-48 —

Mio amatissimo vecio,[12]
The clock in my parents' bedroom indicates it is exactly 4:15. I can see the time perfectly from here. I chose to write to you in the living room today, and from this angle, I can see their bedroom as two thin columns separate the rooms, we are planning to divide the rooms with two sets of curtains. I want to describe to you our home, where we live, I don't think it's easy but I will do my best so that you can have an idea and imagine me more vividly in my new home, the street (that is, "the street") as the English say, is very long and quite crowded at all hours, the bus passes at every hour, there are countless stores that line the street. Once you arrive at the address number 7090, you will see a door like all the others, you look up and you will see several small terraces. We live on the third floor, you then climb the stairs, open a door, and you immediately will find yourself in a long hallway. On either side, there are several doors, at one door, you will find the kitchen, at another, my bedroom, at another, the bathroom, then there is the dining room — not quite furnished — the bedroom of my *papà* and *mamma*, beautiful large windows and a balcony that leads to a terrace. In the hallway, there is a huge oil heater, and on the wall between two doors is the telephone.

12 My most beloved sweetheart.

Imagine me talking to my friends often or talking with a French- or English-speaking man asking for my *papà*. Can you imagine me in this way? My *mamma* refuses to even take the receiver in her hand, so it's up to me. I don't say "pronto" anymore, but rather, "allo?" then, with an Italian word or two mixed in to the other languages, I manage to make them understand me. If you think about it, it is quite funny, and many times I laugh about it, but it's not that carefree laughter I once had, no, it's no longer like that. It will come back, I hope, though, I think that it will be back when you will be here with me. Believe me, even in moments of distraction and amusement, I cannot forget you, actually you are present more than ever because I would like for you too to be part of our lives here. The day before yesterday we were invited by the wife of G ..., they were very kind in the way they welcomed us, there were several other guests. There were many pleasant conversations around us, and we even talked about you, you see, even though you are not here physically, you are here in spirit, it felt like you were near me, just like when we used to visit together *Signora* M ... (ah, bless those days).

Last night, my *mamma* and *papà* and I went to see the Italian film, *La Traviata* starring Maria Cebotari and Giovanni Malipiero.[13] Oh, what a film, my Loris! Just beautiful, and that music, how much it brought me back to you! Have you seen it? If you haven't, it's worth seeing. I reread your last two letters, in them I find so much true love, so much affection, I draw so much comfort from your words, you cannot imagine, they bring me everything that I need to continue to live, to love, and to hope like thousands and thousands of other girls.

13 Among the best loved, if not the most acclaimed operas by Giuseppe Verdi (1813–1901), *La Traviata* (libretto by Francesco Maria Piave, 1810–1876), was originally premiered at the Teatro La Fenice in Venice on 6 March 1853. In Montreal, in the years 1948–49, *La Traviata* was performed in February 1948 at the Mont-Royal Theatre, starring celebrated soprano Moldovian-born Maria Cebotari (1910–1949), Italian tenor Giovanni Malipiero (1906–1970), and baritone Mariano Stabile (1888–1968), and featuring the chorus, ballet, and orchestra of the Royal Opera House of Rome. Advertisement for tickets appeared in the francophone newspaper *La Patrie* on 7 February 1948. Interestingly, Antonietta is referring here to the film version of *La Traviata* featuring Maria Cebotari and Giovanni Malipiero.

Linguistic Currents in Postwar Montreal   107

What is life without love? Nothing! You know very well that it is
nothing. And, you are my love, you are my life, and if you should go,
what would I do? How could I continue to believe in tomorrow,
in the future? You are everything to me. You are in my heart, in my
soul, inside all of me, and you will be with me forever. You are the
flame that burns constantly in my chest, it is alight until it will flare
up one day, more radiant than ever when we will be able to hold each
other in a long, eternal embrace.

I understand you received my letter of best wishes, I am pleased
that you liked it; I wanted to do more for you, but that will be for
another time, you will wait, won't you? Your last letter is well written.
I very much liked your description of, let's say, Verdi's life, his was a
life of sacrifice for the completion of his work, may his perseverance
be an example and model for us, only in this way will we be able to
reach the summit of our glory and our joy. My *papà* has just returned
home with the idea of going to the mountains. We will stay there
until tomorrow evening. You see? He too wrote to you, the last sentence being, "V.[?] is always angry because you are not here with her."
I wrote to D ... some time ago. What can I tell you, Loris? In the first
days I didn't feel like writing. Now, I have started to write to everyone.
I must leave you. Greetings and kisses to all of your family, and a
thousand kisses to you and a warm embrace. Forever yours, Nietta.

[Antonietta's mother and father write:]

From me as well, to you and your family – whom I think of often –
my best wishes and greetings, *Mamma*.

Hello old man, how are you? We are all well, I wish the same for
you and your family. Greetings and best wishes to you. The old lady is
always angry because you are not here with her, Vittorio.

[on a separate sheet with no date; circa 30-10-48]

My heart is always in suspense, I will be content only when you
will be here, unfortunately, in this world, nothing comes without
sacrifice, be strong, our struggle has begun and we must bring it
to an end, we will do it, won't we, my darling? In these days, I also
received news from M ... and A ... I was very pleased to read their
letters. Did you hear what happened to poor A ...? We were so very
sorry to hear about the death of her *papà*, she did not need this!
We can expect anything in this world, I think about this more and

more. Certainly, not everything is rosy, as we often think it is when our young hearts begin to bloom. Here too there is no lack of pain and sorrow, every family, every individual wears a cross that is more or less heavy. Finally, after running between one office and another, our travel trunk was returned to us with everything intact. We were required to leave only four or five bottles of grappa at customs, I now have all of your letters and your gifts for me; my *papà* told me I could have used another trunk for all those letters. He is always joking, you know him, don't you? I now leave you with the immeasurable hope to receive news from you this afternoon. Many kisses and an enormous embrace from the person who cannot forget you.

Forever yours, Nietta.

— Montreal 6-11-48 —

10:30 evening

Mio amore,[14]

No peace. There is no place for me to find peace. You can imagine why, can't you? Not even today did I receive news from you. I am devastated and disheartened in a way I cannot describe. Why, tell me, why do you do this? Do I deserve this kind of punishment? Loris, I beg you, please, as soon as you receive this letter, let me know something so that I may put my heart at peace. Oh! What a life. How tired I am of thinking of one situation over another. I cannot take this anymore. Tonight, I am thoroughly discouraged, and I ask myself if happiness actually exists in this world. Maybe it does, but it lasts for such a short time that we barely notice it. And what does it take to find it? And when we do find it, how hard we must fight for it and what sacrifice it requires. You see, tonight I am anything but optimistic, believe me it feels like everything is against me, and there is no other reason for this but your silence, your prolonged silence. Don't do this my darling, write to me, you know that I suffer immensely from your being far away. Why then add these moments of trepidation to me? I admit that your silence might be due to a postal delay, but to me this reason is only a remote possibility. Nothing but horrible thoughts come to mind.

14 My love.

Linguistic Currents in Postwar Montreal

To distract me a little, I went to the movies tonight; just my luck, the movie made me feel worse, a moving film with a tragic ending. The woman leaves on an airplane, and the man is left alone in his sorrow. As the airplane is about to take off, the propeller approaches him and kills him. As I watched the woman sitting by the window and the man in terrible pain at the airport, I did not know what to think … It's just horrible. It reminds me of when I left you at the airport of Ciampino. There, you see. When things start off badly, they end even worse. I left the theatre with tears streaming down my cheeks, and a terrible wound in my heart. I await your news, my Loris. Write to me, write to me, tell me what has kept you away, and if you are to blame. I love you, my precious. I beg you, love me always, just as you loved me when we were near to each other. Infinite kisses from the woman who remembers you and adores you.

Your Nietta

Kisses to your loved ones, especially to *mamma* and *papà*.

— Venice 6-11-48 —

Nietta mia piccola,[15]

I still needed to finish writing the letter I had started on November 4th – a day I wanted to make the most of since I was off work. I had started writing it after lunch, I was nearly half way into the letter, but … but I couldn't finish it, because I had not written it properly. It begins with a description of my state of my mind and it conveys to you how I was affected by that strange conversation of mine. I recopied the letter to let you know how stupid those words had been, I will now tell you in a few words: On that day (November 4) as I sat at the table at noon, I drank one glass of wine (a little too large), and this made me a little cheerful, and it helped me to get over a little of the melancholy I was feeling. For this reason, as I was leaving the table, I wanted to start writing to you, but you can imagine how such a letter would turn out when we are this way. Once I got halfway into the letter, I realized I had not written as I usually do, you can see this as I wrote even: I hope, actually I am sure, I didn't confuse Jews for Samaritans; but instead, I wrote a jumble of words in which everything from rocks

---

15 Nietta my girl.

and earth to herbs is mixed in together. I ended up leaving it for the next day, regretting that I had not been up to the task of finishing it. Heavens, I thought, I will explain my reasons to her. Now that I should be doing this, I don't remember them ... yes, I was a little merry from the wine, I was writing poorly, making many mistakes, my thoughts were not right, and I was ashamed to send you the letter, which would leave you with an impression of me as half-drunk.

I am pleased I decided to write a letter like this, only in this way will we both be content, because in this way while I know you did not imagine me staggering near you, I think you would have been happy to see me, even for just a second, even if I had drunk wine up to my eyeballs. I say this because I believe we would do anything to reach the impossible. I certainly would not do it in this moment, with a clear mind, oh no, appearance and formality are too important to me. I don't like it because it would mean contaminating – even just by appearance – who I am. I continue this letter a few days after starting it on Saturday, when I left it to attend class until today, Monday, upon my return from work. And now, I begin again my conversation with you, now, and I am so very sorry.

I felt an incredible, an immeasurable sadness because I know how much I may have hurt you. A set of things prevented me, no! I was the one who stopped myself from continuing. Unfortunately, today's hours passed heavily and bitterly. [?] I write to you now, even though I know that my letter will arrive to you late. If my letters are a balm for your heart, I know how bitterly long waiting for a letter must have been for you. Unfortunately, I found myself feeling morally disapproving yesterday and today, condemning and forgiving myself at the same time, I thought I had been extremely careless and managed to eventually calm myself thinking that I had in fact committed nothing bad or dishonest. This regret that I felt, has beaten at my heart, yesterday when I was partially happy, today, instead, everything is dark and grey. I carefully pondered over the truth, something I have never denied to you, regarding this regret, I understood and realized that I love you. If I did not love you, I would not have suffered. I suffered because in my conscience I could not lie to you, I suffered because I could not find an excuse to justify my behaviour, ah no, this has always been the amulet of my conscience, that is, honesty, and I did not

Linguistic Currents in Postwar Montreal   111

want to sin against my own principles. I suffered because as I thought of ways of torturing the body, you were thinking of my spirit, and left without a compelling reason, I felt defeated.

Courage lifts the spirit to the point of exaltation, just as its absence leads to exasperation; I did not reach that point because our souls were not stolen. In truth, now that I am forgiven, I have returned to you as always, I think you too would forgive me, actually, I am certain that you will forgive me. The evidence does not point to a crime. If I am guilty, one word alone is my defence: Sunday, and so, I begin my story on 28 September during which I worked like a slave from 7 in the morning until 9 in the evening. Because of this, I missed the soccer match, you know how important the sport is to me, a distraction of my ordinary life. Still, I did not make a big deal of it, and on Monday I rested. I had nothing to write to you about since I had sent you a letter just the day before. It was a day of rest without much fuss. Actually, it was a very dismal day since it was All Saints' Day and the Day of the Dead, and I visited the cemetery where my dear ones have been laid to rest, I dedicated my afternoon to them.

On Tuesday, I started working at 6 and because it was a company holiday, I was home by the early afternoon. I still had the previous class work to recopy and study at the same time. This is how I spent half my day on Tuesday. On Wednesday, I went to work like usual, and on Thursday, November 4 it was a holiday. There was no game to watch because the Venezia team was playing at the S.P.A.L. Ferrara (Venezia won 3–1 in an unbelievable game).[16] That evening I had a class to attend, and I ended the evening by dropping by the Bar Campanile. It was on that day that I started the letter which I am describing to you.

On Saturday, I started to write this letter, but I had to stop for a moment since I needed to go to school. I promised myself I would continue the letter on Sunday. This is where the last part begins, that is, I felt awful about missing out on the great game played yesterday November 5 between the Venezia and Brescia teams. I felt equally bad about not travelling with the team, given there was a special train

16 The acronym S.P.A.L. stands for the professional soccer (football) club Società Polisportiva Ars et Labor based in Ferrara, Italy.

taking everyone to Brescia. It was at the last minute that I decided on Saturday midnight and so, yesterday morning I left for Brescia. This is what prevented me from writing to you. Still you cannot imagine how much I thought of you, especially as I travelled and my thoughts wandered into the distance, where I saw you and with all my strength I imagined you in front of me. How many times have I imagined you before my eyes, especially the way you looked on the last day. It is a memory that will not fade over time. There, these are the thoughts that accompanied me deep in my heart.

This is how I passed the day, my eyes alone focused on the game, even if it was a good and fortuitous day for the Venezia team. Everything for soccer, the prosecutors will declare, and in response, I will remark that I have always considered work first, and then, pleasure. I leave to you my case, and with you, my doubts. I hope you will be kind and fair in your judgment, Madam Justice; send me your response, free of prejudice. Do the right thing … hand me the sentence based on the wrong I have committed. All of this is done and written now, so that I could tell you what I do and how I spend my days. If you are surprised about yesterday's trip to Brescia, try to remember also the 14 hours I spent yesterday at work. Never did I forego on my duty in exchange for pleasure. This will have been the first time. It is not serious, because first of all, my truce and my prayers were only for you. Big, full kisses and a heart filled with love, your Loris.

— Montreal 14-11-48 —

Mio amore,[17]

My revenge? Oh no, don't mind that. You know how easily I forgive others, and especially you, whom I love so deeply, it is a joy. I don't know how I let so many days pass. Of course, on the 12th I started to write a letter, and then, I don't know why, I had to stop. During these days, I received two letters from you, one on Monday, and one yesterday. You cannot imagine how comforted I am by your letters and how much happiness they bring to me. For this I ask you, I beg you to write to me, to write to me once a week punctually, I will try to do the same so that neither of us needs to suffer. It does not matter that the

17 My love.

Linguistic Currents in Postwar Montreal 113

letters aren't filled with romance, one line, one short letter is all we need, it's the memories that matter, the memories that must be constant, lively, and continuous because if one day that disappears, it will be over. Our dreams will be lost without the chance of realizing them.

Nearly two months have passed since we left each other. I don't know how you feel, sometimes it feels like I arrived here only yesterday, other times, it feels like I have been here for many years. Oh, if only it were so, I would be much happier, just two years would need to pass, and I would have to wait for far less time. Well, I am aware that the path we have taken is steep and thorny, the sacrifice is tremendous, let's hope that the joy will remain the same, how many sighs await still! I am comforted when I speak with my *papà* about you and our future. He is generous and kind when he speaks with me. He will begin the first steps this winter when he will not be working because of the cold temperatures, we will be visiting the emigration [immigration] office together to find out about the application process and the required documentation, he says it's better to begin with the paperwork in this way, so that everything is ready at the right moment. They have now introduced a new law, the fiancée can sponsor her fiancé, provided the marriage takes place within 30 days of his arrival in Canada. So many Italians have arrived during this period, I realized this last night when I attended an event with my *mamma* and my *papà*, it was organized by a number of Italian soldiers. If you could only have seen how friendly everyone was, we sang the most beautiful and famous Italian melodies with indescribable enthusiasm. Among the songs we sang was, of course, "Evviva Venezia città delle belle donne."[18] Several Venetians were there, and maybe for this reason, everyone looked happy; oh, how I enjoyed listening to the Venetian dialect being spoken. It felt like you were here speaking, everything reminds me of you, even last night, as I prepared to go out, I thought of you a lot, as we were leaving, my *papà* even said, "If your old darling [V ...?] could see you now." Not to flatter myself, but I looked lovely. I had sewn the dress myself, a green, sky-blue taftà dress, tight at the waist, a square collar and a sparkly brooch, puffy sleeves, a full skirt with many ruffles and a big bow in the back. I wore

18 "Long Live Venice, the City of Beautiful Women."

a pair of small diamond earrings. How much more jubilant I would have been if you had seen me; the others' compliments irritated me instead of pleasing me, how much more I value one of your compliments. I will have a picture taken with that dress on, are you pleased? I have here before my eyes your last two letters, it feels very sweet to read those sentences written only for me and with so much feeling, love me always like this, never forget to think about your Tetina who remembers you and loves you from so far away.

I have now replied to your letter written on Monday, and have here your last letter. I need to reflect a little more before I reply. It seems the accused knows how to exonerate himself in surprising ways, the judge is undecided on what to do, the crimes are not too serious. She is willing to discharge him, however, with the assurance that nothing of the sort will recur again, otherwise he is unrelenting. To make amends on wrongdoings is good, it's even better to try to avoid falling in the same traps, this applies to both of us, right? The trip to Brescia did not surprise me, I know how much you enjoy soccer, and how much of a fan you are. I prefer you take part in these healthy forms of entertainment than others that set out to ruin young people and lead them down destructive paths. Actually, I want you to play soccer as much as possible so that it becomes your pastime, necessary and indispensable for men and women, if you go to the Bar Campanile, say hi and give my best greetings to *il Signor* V ... and *Signor* T ... (I believe this is his name). I am warning you, however, no more getting drunk, for this time you are forgiven, even if it came after an extraordinary win of the Venezia team; I hope that ... they don't win again! (Oh! what did I just say! Hey, if they win every once and awhile, you can drink to celebrate, but not more than that! In other words, it's better if the team does not always win.)

Today, D ... wrote to us telling us that *la nonna* is feeling very down. I am so sorry to hear this, Loris. If you can, please do your best to visit them at Christmastime so that you too can tell me how she is doing, and how she seems to you, I am very worried about her. I leave you now, my adored one, with the hope that this letter of mine reaches you soon. May the kisses that I ardently send to you serve as a pledge of my endless love for you,

your Nietta

Linguistic Currents in Postwar Montreal

— Montreal 17-11-48 —

Mio indimenticabile Loris,[19]

The hope and joy that breathe new life into me are as infinite and grand as our beautiful Italic sea. I received your letter of the 10th of this month, it's a gratifying letter pulsating with good news. I know I should not have any illusions for myself, I know that I should not allow myself to be excited about the news you just gave to me, but what can we do, my darling, I cannot do otherwise. Finally, I see some light after such bleak darkness, at least now there is hope that I will see you a little sooner! If nothing comes of it, it will not matter, it will be just another disappointment at the time of receiving the news, until then, I will live with the hope that you can make it happen, and this is wonderful to me, believe me. Since I have been here, I have never had a more magnificent day as the day I received your letter; I laughed, I jumped like a crazy girl. Now remember, my love, try not to make the same error as you did last year, try to have yourself permanently discharged, if you can, so that you don't have to go through another exam next year, at least if they enrolled you in the army, only one year would remain for you. Please Loris, do these things carefully so everything will proceed smoothly when you receive our call (that is, when I will be able to sponsor you). I have faith, my adored one, I have a lot of faith that everything will go well, and I will forever be grateful to God for being so generous and kind to us.

But, how did you manage to do all of this without my knowledge? Oh, yes, I can imagine! What a dear you are, Loris, how could I not love you? This sentence made me laugh: "I have never felt so good," followed by, "today at 3 I will be admitted at the hospital." Isn't it funny? How can they diagnose you as sick if you have never felt so good in your life? Where there's a will, there's a way for doctors! Let's hope so. I hope so. (Oh! Love! The things you make us do!) Sometimes we lose our minds over love! If all goes well, I will be the happiest person in Montreal, do you believe me? I will be thinking of you constantly these days, my Loris, certainly, more intensely than usual. What struggle you must endure, my darling, to reach our goals! How busy you must be during the day between work, school, and travelling to

19 My unforgettable Loris.

and fro, and, to say that I was so inconsiderate to reproach you for not sending me news, even then, it was not your fault. Do you forgive me, my love? Oh! I am sure that you will not hold a grudge against me. May my kiss tell you how sorry I am for having troubled you, may my affectionate embrace tell you how much I adore you.

your Nietta

Greetings to your *mamma* and everyone.

Kisses from my parents who send their best wishes for a joyful outcome. My friends thank you for your greetings. Actually, you sent them kisses. Don't you think that might be a bit much? I want those all for myself!!

— Montreal 23-11-48 —

2200 hours

Mio adorato Loris,[20]

It's 10 o'clock, these are my hours of bliss, the most serene hours, the hours in which I worry less, happy hours, hours imbued with a new light that brightens my gaze, and an enviable joy fills my heart, in these hours, my lips smile more often, they more easily turn into a smile, just like when I was a little girl, and I would play cheerfully with a new toy I had long wished for. The joy is similar, equal to the satisfaction of then, or perhaps even greater, yes, much more because I have grown up (not by much, I hope!! But it's the years that count, isn't that so, my darling?)

The news you have sent me has left me speechless, breathless, and utterly wobbly. I never thought you would be able to make so much progress; even now, it feels like a dream. I had resigned myself to a prolonged wait and this sudden news has stunned me and moved me beyond measure; those two long years have now been shortened, and by a lot. Now, I don't need to sigh with resignation at the thought that I will be spending such a long time without your affection, without your words, and ... yes, without your kisses, for two people who love each other like we do, it's horrible to be so far apart, and we are intensely aware of this, since we have tried it ourselves, we cannot describe all that happens inside of us, the degree with which we

20 My adored Loris.

Linguistic Currents in Postwar Montreal   117

suffer, in the tiniest of details, with our souls in agony especially when it seems everything is working against us. Each of us is aware of this depressive state in which we find ourselves, we understand each other, we can easily empathize and imagine what the other is going through but cannot express.

Now that our ordeal is almost over, I can honestly tell you that two years would have been terribly hard on me. How many times I surprised myself by thinking, "Oh, if it weren't for another year in the army, he could be here next to me!" I would remind myself, we cannot go against destiny, and resignation would inevitably take over, the thought of seeing you again one day – even if in the distant future – brought me serenity and tranquility. But now, all this aside, a new epoch is about to begin, as you too wrote, the past is now buried, it is the future that matters, my darling, the future is bright with blessings abounding for us; yes, I will do everything possible for everything to work out at the earliest! Oh, I am so happy, my precious, just thinking that nothing will keep us apart, nothing, everything is clear now, and it will be resolved shortly. To whom do we owe this joy? God has been so generous toward us. He has listened to our prayers, we will thank Him and never forget Him, not now, and not even when our happiness will be complete. It's almost 11:30. I will not deny that I'm feeling sleepy, my eyes are getting smaller, you can see it in my handwriting that is no longer legible, I will now go "a cuscé" as the French say. Think of me and imagine me more content than ever, I will fall asleep thinking of you and kissing you ardently as I do now so that my most affectionate and sincere kisses reach you in a few short days.

My parents also kiss you and are delighted to hear the news. Kisses again, and forgive my poor writing.

your Nietta

Please thank W ... and your *mamma* for their words. Tomorrow I will write to them. I would like to add an extra sheet here, but I'm afraid it will exceed the weight restrictions Please thank your *fratello* [brother] C ... for his thoughtfulness. Kisses to the nephews and to everyone in my family.

118 September 1948 to December 1948

— Montreal 29-11-48 —

Mio Tesoro,[21]

I was just looking at the calendar to include the date in my letter, it seems almost impossible that we are already the 29th of November, time is flying by, and this cheers me up because every hour that passes signifies one hour less of waiting for you, in this way, the days, the weeks pass. I am waiting for you, always, do you see that? I wait for you and I think of you everywhere I go, in every moment whether I am at home, crossing a street, whether I'm at school, talking to someone, taking a walk, always and everywhere. Lately, I have not been describing how and where I spend my days, the last piece of news had thrown me off balance, the letters I had written to you contained joyful, cheerful news (I wish I could always write to you like this). By now the excitement has subsided a little, things are returning to normal, however, with the hope that everything will move in the same direction as now.

In this short period, I have not always been at home savouring the sweet news. Oh! no, I took walks, I travelled, that's right, I even travelled, on Saturday, I visited a small town in the mountains with my *mamma* and *papà*, a place that is 3 and a half hours from Montreal. We were there on Saturday and all day Sunday at the home of my *papà*'s friend, even though we spent the night at a hotel, and there, *papà* and I experienced "extraordinary success," we danced together, and everyone admired us, everyone congratulated us, people shook my *papà*'s hand and bowed to me (can you imagine your Nietta in such a situation?). The next morning, I went hunting with my *papà* and two of his friends. What luck they had! They, that is, not me, because I did not do anything. I had a small rifle with no cartridges (don't laugh). Here's how it was, as *papà* was preparing to reload my rifle and I called out an expression that still makes him laugh ("*Nostra impiamilu*" in Friulano; in Italian, "Don't start loading it for me"). In the end, they caught a good-sized moose with small horns. It was a young moose, poor thing. The meat was delicious but frankly, I had had enough, as the proverb says, "all good things must come to an end." During this season nearly everyone goes hunting, and they

21 My precious.

Linguistic Currents in Postwar Montreal 119

almost always return empty-handed, they're already talking about turning you into a hunter of ... crabapples!? As *Signora C ...*, the wife of my *papà*'s partner, keeps telling me, "When your Lorenzo will be here, I urge you not to let him go with these two rascals, keep him home, make sure he stays with you, and he doesn't go hunting on Sundays." She is a very kind and thoughtful lady. I talk to her a lot about you, she listens carefully, and earnestly takes part in the conversations.

On Saturday I received the letter in which you tell me that you have not received news from me, I hope you have managed to allay your worries, I know how hard it is to be without news, however I believe I have written to you on a regular basis, if it were not the case, forgive me, my precious. The situations have been reversed, but you see, it's only out of fear, a stupid fear, are we not sure of each other's love? In that case, why think that something awful has happened when a letter is late? Oh! No, this must not happen again, we must wait patiently, and feel confident that that the letter will arrive, let's promise this to each other. I promise this to you. But ... don't make me wait a week, please!!! (I must now leave you my adored love, it's late, exactly one minute to one o'clock in the morning. I will continue tomorrow morning, good night my precious. Good night, until tomorrow!)

And here I am with you today, 30 November, more rested in mind and body. I have just finished a few household chores and I gave a bath to the little bird we have at home. If you could see how cute he is, just like a child he gives you sweet kisses if you rest your cheek on the cage, and when he wants something, he begins to chirp loudly, and he won't leave you in peace until you give in to him. (Oh, Heavens! I need to leave you again, *Signora C ...* called, she wants me to accompany her for some errands that she needs to run. I will continue later.) Here I am again, I have returned to this letter which apparently does not want to end, let's hope I can conclude it now. I lost my train of thought, I have no idea where to begin so that I can finish the letter. There is only one thing I can tell you, that is, I love you, I love you forever, these words are so easy to say, especially when they gush from the heart, they just cannot be stopped, no, they must not be stopped. When two people love each other like we do, there is no need to resort to plans (I am referring to the remark in your last letter). Each of them needs to express their love, to feel loved, a love that is reciprocated, and in that case, a love grows deeper and stronger, someone who does not feel loved enough behaves differently, the impact of love is extraordinary, someone who does not have a heart brings suffering to the person who has offered his or her heart. I adore you, my darling, I love you, I will tell you over and over again without fear that you will take advantage of my love because I know that you love me in the same way.

Many many affectionate kisses,
your Nietta

— Venice 30-11-48 —

Nietta mia indimenticabile,[22]
It is for this reason that the adjective "unforgettable," that I just wrote, induces me to think constantly about our lives, about everything that we remember looking back to our beautiful, yet fateful days together. You are my unforgettable, not only because of who you are generally, the feminine features from which spring your gentle thoughts of love, the naturalness with which you approach life, but also, and more importantly, in the way you love mystically. You are unforgettable to me more mystically than physically. This is especially because until now, you have belonged to me in spirit alone even though I have no preconceived notions about a physical union, this contrasts over a thousand times with male sentiments that by nature have generated necessary changes inside of me. This vitality is melded — mystically, spiritually, and it adorns and embraces our love with an overflow of happiness — and physically, humanly, as our love works to preserve our intentions. The joys of matrimony are not limited to the body. It is through the spirit that we create the happiness we yearn for.

With the hope of seeing you again, I draw from our courage the faith of seeing you again soon so that we may alter our misery and our burdens, because we cannot live on bread alone. Bread constitutes, sometimes, a sad bitterness, because those who have plenty of it generally lack spiritual antagonism. I value more being gratified than awarded, it serves always to convince me that every fleeting thing

22 My unforgettable Nietta.

Linguistic Currents in Postwar Montreal 121

belongs to the earth. Not everything that graces the spirit is identical, the heart loves and wishes to be loved, sacrifice is a pure expression of generosity, every disappointment silences a spirit's torment. All is spiritual, all is divine, all seek truth, appearances are not enough, all things are nourished by the heart's venting and from human resistance. This is the reason you surround my thoughts with your unforgettable self, this is why you are unforgettable, my Nietta. This is why my thoughts compel me to love you, to love you dearly, this is why I tell myself over and over again: that which the spirit creates cannot and must never be undone. A whole life surrounds us, a new life is beginning for us. This is the greatest achievement of our love story experienced these past few years, from my perspective, I cannot suppress the sincerity of my determination to tell you that I have always fought against myself to protect our love. It contains too much of my existence for me to abandon this love, it is as precious as gold because the preciousness of your person has disillusioned me many times; when disheartened, I searched for you like a miner in search of gold, but where were you? God determined that I would find you here in our land, here in our Italy. He wanted to offer me a little edelweiss, a resplendent Queen of the Alps, and there, exactly there, a sign emerged that we began with the treasure of your thoughts passing through me. All of this summarizes my highest love and my desire to love you, this love does not deny the force of our faith, from which every day we await new perspectives. Today's was the most gallant of all.

Yesterday-today-tomorrow, how eager I am as I wait for your news, how moved I am to receive your news, the jitters were not the same as usual, what misery these days. Tonight, as well, an enormous disappointment similar to the one of the past few days, the disappointment was as strong as the certainty of receiving a letter from you, as strong as my desire to read you jubilant and satisfied with the outcome I had assured you would be positive. The anxiety and uncertainty contrasted sharply inside of me, generating a feeling of alarm that led me very quickly into a state of hopelessness. By contrast, there is no way I can be sure of anything, I can only hope that the result was positive and that my reassurance did not disappoint you. If it were so for whoever and whatever reason, be sure that I have suffered, fought, and won. If the news brought you bitterness, it brought me the opposite, it generated in me utter joy, I had done everything to make you happy, to bring a smile to your face. You can be sure, my Nietta, that whatever is created in spirit cannot, must not be annihilated. To this I will add that my love for you is immortal, there will always be a place in my heart for you, it will be like this always and forever. These reflections emerge from the misery I am fighting against; however, I hope to feel differently tomorrow night, as I hope to have in my hands your news, as I hope not to be obliged to swallow another disappointment tomorrow night that brings to a halt my beating heart. If all of this has happened, there are reasons and considerations to think about.

I want you to know that the letter that confirmed the news about the military service was mailed to you on Sunday, November 14, I had not sent it by Registered Mail and I did not request a confirmation of receipt, since I expected a response within ten days or so, that's right, now that I think of it. I received a response to my first letter in which I write to you about my stay in the hospital, one week has passed already since I received your letter, and I am surprised that I have still not received a response to my second letter, the letter that discusses the decision. For now, and don't think of me as untroubled or pleased, I have faith in tomorrow and I am wishful that I will be able to read you, hopeful once again that you will have remembered your words written a few letters ago about the need to respond to each other's letters with greater punctuality. For a passionate kiss, I am not angry, actually I would give you many more kisses right now, in reproaching you I am ever more aware of loving you.

Your Loris.

[At top of first sheet]

W ..., L ..., M ..., A ..., *mamma* and *papà*, nephews and B ... together with C ... assign me to give their greetings and kisses to you and your parents. Give them a big kiss and greetings from me, for you, another *bussada* [kiss].[23] Loris, *tuo vecio*[24]

I hope to give you some good news with regard to the application.

23 In Friulano, meaning "kiss."
24 Your sweetheart.

— 4 —

"Christmas trees are everywhere"
Reconciling a New Christmas Celebration

WITHIN JUST A FEW MONTHS after stepping foot on Canadian territory, Antonietta was immersed in Montreal's Christmas celebrations. For Antonietta, Christmas signalled new traditions comprised of festive lights, Christmas trees, Santa Claus, and gift-giving, as well as screaming children and chaos in Montreal's main department stores. For Loris, Christmas remained a religious celebration, one that he shared with his family in Venice, and one that was overshadowed by melancholy and nostalgia for the years when Antonietta was still in Italy with him.

Christmas in Canada's bilingual cosmopolitan city was significantly different from the more sobering religious event that Antonietta and Loris experienced with their families in Italy. Since the 1920s, Christmas in the United States and Canada had become less a civic celebration and more a family celebration with gift-giving increasingly integral to the event. Abundance and materiality were becoming synonymous with Christmas. Antonietta became acquainted with the gift-giving tradition – beyond the nuts, fruit, and homemade traditional gifts she had received from her family in Italy – introduced by her father's friends in Montreal. The gifts that she received and later enumerated in a letter to Loris on 27 December are embedded with further meaning. Gift-giving helped to cope with relationships that were important but also insecure.[1] Theodore Caplow moreover notes that gifts were offered to persons whose goodwill was needed

---

1 Caplow, "Christmas Gifts and Kin Networks," 391.

but could not be taken for granted.[2] The gifts that Antonietta received at Christmas represented a form of gratitude by her father and mother and their friends in response to her efforts in making Montreal her home while her love and her extended family to whom she was affectionately attached remained an ocean away.

Christmas in Montreal was likely a culture shock for Antonietta. It brought her into close contact with Christmas traditions that were very different from her native Ampezzo. In a letter written nearly two weeks before Christmas, she describes on 10 December 1948 *Babbo Natale*, that is, Santa Claus, "a man dressed in red with a long beard," taking extra care in her letter, signalling the novelty to Loris about this seasonally popular figure whose ubiquitous presence appeared in department stores, shopping malls, and street corners in North American cities.[3] Antonietta's description, however, evinces other details as well, that is, the places, where Santa Claus often made an appearance amid the abundance of toys and screaming children on the toy floors of Montreal's main department stores.[4] To a young woman who had no former contact with this Christmas tradition, the visit proved to be more of "a celebration of consumption, materialism, and hedonism,"[5] that she rejected. It was an experience that affected her in ambivalent ways, overwhelming ways infused with chaos and confusion. The contrast between the Christmas celebrations she participated in as a child in her hometown of Ampezzo with those she first experienced in Montreal represented yet another difference from her life in Italy, and likely underscored a nostalgia for home.

Christmas holidays in the company of her parents' friends and acquaintances also represented a transnational Christmas for Antonietta. The holiday gatherings afforded Antonietta the opportunity to learn, and eventually emulate for the family she planned to have with Loris, the practice of kinwork, much like countless other Italian immigrant

2 Ibid.
3 Belk, "A Child's Christmas in America," 87.
4 The department store which Antonietta is referring to here was very likely Eaton's, since by the 1950s, Eaton's and Christmas had become synonymous, and as Braden Hutchinson notes, in large part due to their innovative approaches to retailing. Hutchinson, "Objects of Affection," 184.
5 Belk, "A Child's Christmas in America," 96.

women in Canada and the United States. Kinwork, in the words of Micaela Di Leonardo comprised "the conception, maintenance, and ritual celebration of cross-household kin ties, including visits, telephone calls, presents, and cards to kin; the organization of holiday gatherings; the creation and maintenance of quasi-kin relations; decisions to neglect or to intensify particular ties; the mental work of reflection about all these activities; and the creation and communication of altering images of family and kin vis-à-vis images of others, both folk and mass media."[6] In appropriating the practices of kinwork in the Italian immigrant community of Montreal, Antonietta would undoubtedly be an agent of change and support for Loris upon his arrival in Montreal.

— Montreal 7-12-48 —

Loris mio carissimo,[7]
I just got out of bed, and my first thought was about writing to you. I want to do it immediately so that I don't postpone it to the rest of the day or until tomorrow. This is how it's usually done, we remember to write, and then we put it off to another moment, in the meantime, the days pass, we don't receive news, and we let those who are waiting for news worry anxiously. Unfortunately, we remember to write only later, when we take the pen in our hands, and we are shocked at the date on the calendar; I have before my eyes your letter of the 25th of the previous month, it's a joy to receive your news and a pleasure to read your letters, so affectionate, so truthful, so beautiful, believe me, nothing gives me more joy than receiving your letters, the letters in which I find what I am seeking, love and fulfillment. You should see me when I read them, I stop at every word, and when I find a phrase that I especially like, I reread it, and smile with delight. I feel loved and I am happy. This is the way our love is, this is the way love should be, even though not everyone is capable of a love like ours. Oh no! This is why I believe in our love. We believe in the sacrifice, we

---

6 Di Leonardo, "The Female World of Cards and Holidays," 442–3.
7 Loris my dearest.

know how to be patient and how to fight for our love, and when it's the moment to rejoice, we are happy, so very happy, even if we have a few miserable satisfactions, for us who love each other so much, the feeling of fulfillment is immense because it is offered to us from the person who is the keeper of our heart.

The surprise news I received a little while ago has quietly brought tremendous joy to my heart; who would have thought that such news was possible? Of course, I was always hoping for a way out, fundamentally it is hope that lifts a person's spirit, if hope is lost, we feel disheartened and defeated, isn't that so? To wait for you for two years would have been very long and hard. I would have faithfully waited for you, of course, for your arrival because I love you, but what a sacrifice! You still don't know, or you're not sure if you will be exonerated from the army, let's hope it will work out, but were it not the case, at least it would not be as bad as before, isn't that true, darling? One year passes quickly, but two …! (An extra one.)

I can imagine you running around, eager to reach your objective, oh my poor dear! And to top it off, you kept me in the dark about all of this so that I would not worry and suffer with you, you decided to advise me only once you were certain that everything would work out, you are such a good person, my adored love, how could I not love you? Everything you do makes me love you more, nothing you do for the sake of my happiness escapes me, I remember every detail, and I will make it up to you one day when we will be together forever. Now my love, I leave you with the certainty that I love you as always, more than ever, and that I live only with the hope to see you again, here next to me. Dear and affectionate kisses from your Nietta.

[Top, right side of sheet one]

Kisses to your *mamma* and to all your loved ones. My *mamma* remembers you with affection, a thousand kisses from my *papà* as well.

— Montreal 10-12-48 —

Mio adorato Loris,[8]
I don't know if I will be able to write a long letter today given that I am not in the best state of health, it's nothing serious, a headache, and eyes

---

8 My adored Loris.

Reconciling a New Christmas Celebration   127

burning terribly. For these reasons, I don't think I can write for very long, if I feel this way today, I have myself to blame. Yesterday I was in bed all afternoon with this persistent headache, and then in the evening, I felt much better, but today, they invited me to visit Montreal's largest store where there are so many things to see, especially at this time of year. I won't tell you about the confusion that there was, especially on one floor, the toy floor, children screaming, trains taking children on rides around the store, babies crying to see *papà Natale* [Santa Claus], a man dressed in red with a long beard, it might have been fun for the children but for me, an enemy of confusion, I only grew increasingly tired and unnerved, so much so that I returned home, as I mentioned to you earlier, in the same state as yesterday, except that this time my eyes were burning badly from the blowing wind outside. I am here extremely distressed and anxious; I realize this was not the best moment for me to write to you, oh! No, you need other letters, my darling, not this letter that is badly written, letters that are affectionate and sweet, but how can I do that? I cannot, not at this moment. Can you wait a few minutes until I recover, my precious?

(I have now returned, four hours after writing to you, I rested a little and I feel much, much better, I took an Aspirin for the headache, and it worked.) I just reread the letter you wrote to me on the 30th of the past month, this letter helps me immensely to grasp the depth and constancy of your love for me, your reasoning is straight from your heart with no traces of lies, everything is written with transparent sincerity which has really overwhelmed me. You know how to love and you know how to make others love you, you are correct in your reasoning, however, a little … too quick to judge. You write, "If all of this has happened, there are reasons and considerations to think about," but how could you think that the news would bring me sorrow? If in my last letter you could see how delighted and hopeful I was that everything would work out! It made sense that a confirmation of your news would make me die of joy, this did not happen, because as you can see, I am still alive, nonetheless, your news brought me immeasurable joy and exhilaration. If you had been right, I would have done nothing but tell you lies until now, I would have filled the paper and pages with deceit and lies, but I am not accustomed to doing this. I love you so much that I would not be able to hide anything from you.

128   September 1948 to December 1948

I understand, however, that when we don't have news, we think of every possible scenario, the worst thoughts, the most unreasonable thoughts get into our heads; I am certain that by now all this has passed and that my letters have brought peace to your heart. Do not worry, my darling. You can be sure that I love you, and that I know how to cherish our love here, like I did in Ampezzo, my dear small town. My lifestyle has not changed much while I have been here. I am almost always spending time with my parents, at home, during leisure time, and when visiting people, even my *mamma* can confirm this too you. I am still taking English-language classes in the evening, and I am starting to understand quite a bit, the words of my teacher have been a source of encouragement, one evening she saw me looking ashen as I was leaving the classroom and she called out to me, "How are you Miss Petris?" "Oh! Miss, I am so discouraged, I don't understand a thing." It was the first classes. "Don't be discouraged," she replied, "come to class just the same, keep it up. Montreal was not built in a day, you know." And, she was right. Today, I am pleased that I am continuing the course, even if I am not learning very much, at least I am learning the more important things. I find the classes more interesting now, and I listen carefully. I hope to learn at least one language, which we need here. With the hope of receiving your good news regarding your time in the military so that we can begin to prepare the first set of papers, I send you my most ardent kisses and my most affectionate touch.

forever your Nietta

A kiss to your *mamma* and to your entire family, including your nephews. Dear greetings and kisses even from my *papà* and *mamma* Lucia.

Greetings to everyone.

— Venice 12-12-1948 —
(Sunday, 11 o'clock in the morning)

Nietta mia amata,[9]

A few days have passed while waiting for your letters. You can imagine what happened in the meanwhile and that it was something

9 Nietta my beloved.

Reconciling a New Christmas Celebration 129

unlike anything else in the past few years. The silence of these past twelve and more days was not your fault, as I checked the dates and stamps on the envelope. The dates correspond to a normal postal delivery of long-distance correspondence with only a few days in between. Once I realized this, it was much easier for me to calm down and come to my senses from ideas that at times make me reckless and rash in reaching conclusions. I think the most extenuating plausible reasons justify my misunderstanding, or compel me to convey my enthusiasm which sometimes pushes me to write too clearly what I can only imagine. In truth, those days were eternally long, I lacked interest, and as though it were not enough, other setbacks occurred, other disappointments compounded by my own. What bitter, dark days. My eyes lacked the bright light of hope, truth, and acceptance — all so I could understand better everything.

Soon after receiving the good news about the military, a small cloud hovered over me and my family again. Perhaps we are right to believe that everything is designed, peace had just been restored when as a result of the current situation, rather, the current general conditions of our country, my *papà* was laid off from work. This is not important, in the sense that there is a solution to everything, that is, I can bring a solution to everything. I say this because the burden of this new situation will be on my shoulders. This is not the reason that it felt like a dirty trick handed to me by fate, but rather because it came as a moral blow to me; given my troubled state of mind, I was not able to keep things calm. This additional burden, this new predicament did not affect my courage or resolution so much, it affected my heart, which was already feeling down and disappointed from the silence that I just mentioned. It felt like everything was against me, and here too I found a solution. And here I am resigned to all of this, here I am ready to organize my life in a more effective lifestyle. It is now up to me to bear the responsibility of the family, I will be the one who will consider as much as I possibly can their well-being, that is for the elders and two other people. I don't feel it's a burden or a sacrifice, I am conscious of this, and I remember everything that my parents have done for me. Unfortunately, I did not need this, but thanks to God, all is taken care of now. Think of me more attached to my home, more intent in the fulfillment of my duties.

The good thing is that I will learn how to manage my family, and I am confident I can do this, I feel responsible as the hoped-for role of head of the family. In this way, I will be training, dedicating myself to the sacrifices in order to benefit the most from my mission. All of this gives me a sense of contentment, satisfaction, not because of my new role but rather because I will learn to love you even more, to love you is my most ambitious dream, to reach you is a monumental mirage. The situations we have lived recently seem to be in our favour, and I hope it won't be long before they are over, since I should be receiving a definitive response in the next month. For this I ask myself what you will do afterwards. Will you begin the paperwork? I read in one of your first letters that it is possible to complete all the requirements in six months, is this true? Even if we need to marry before? What does your *papà* say about this new nuisance, that is, about this new bother? I would not want to be a hindrance to anyone, I don't want to be seen as indiscreet, I hope he has a lot of confidence in me, as I have in him as I recall him and his affection. May God help us now, that is, may God continue to help us, and wish for us to be together soon. You can begin the application documents when I will have given you the go-ahead.

In this moment, I look back to the days of last year where you were near me as we awaited the arrival of your *papà*, whom you worried about meeting because you did not know him, you were close to me to the point that I almost had to help you stand, everything has changed bitterly, people change. The fact remains that you are now with your *papà* who loves you, and you are eagerly waiting for my arrival. Wait for me with the generosity of your parents, wait for me as you are imbued with eagerness and excitement the way you were one year ago, only the kiss is different, before it spoke of blood ties, now it speaks from the heart. I remember that one year later tomorrow is your *mamma*'s namesake day. I hope that on this day you extended my wishes and greeting card. Remind her of that day, and tell her of the one and only days that you saw me dressed in a blue uniform decorated with stars [?]. Things are different now and have changed significantly from one year ago. Let's hope that things will be different again next year. Different in the sense that I will be close to you, we will be happily married, and experience the joys of married life and we will

Reconciling a New Christmas Celebration   131

delight in the affections of our children and our dreams. With these thoughts, I now close the year's activities, and I close this letter with the singular wish to love you, to kiss you, and to make you happy.

forever,

your Loris.

Before leaving for her new home, W ... asked me to extend her greetings to you, and to send you many kisses, like my *mamma* and *papà*. My best wishes once again to your *mamma* for *Santa Lucia*. C ... is in Ampezzo these days. He will be able to tell me how your elderlies are doing.

— Venice 13-12-48 —

Nietta mia piccola,[10]
AND, WHEN, THE PHOTO?
You might be happy to wonder the reason for which I am writing to you within 24 short hours of the last letter I mailed to you yesterday Sunday, 12 December. There is no reason for this other letter, if nothing else but to wisely use these two hours that remain with me before I go to bed, before I rest my body, tired even today, as always. Just two hours! It's a small slice of time that more than ever before reminds me of a time of joy and happiness of just one year ago. The 13th of December 1947, is a date that marks my memory, the highest point of our love, marking our love, the most resounding sign of our spiritual union that pushed each of us in the direction of the other, where we found mirrors of our thoughts under the same light on a single horizon. Just as it happened to our spirits, it happened to our souls and to our bodies, to the body that protects and agrees with our thoughts, it symbolizes our meeting, I as a sailor, you who had just arrived in Venice to wait for the arrival of your *papà*, Vittorio. Right in this instant the year tolls, a year that had started under good auspices, the year that will end in complete transparency, a year that has signalled the reality of many things, the value of constancy. The year started with good intentions, we expected it to be the year of events, in fact, it did not always bring sweet things, sometimes, it brought bitterness and trepidation, all to betray the prologue you presented one

10   Nietta my girl.

year ago tonight. You were next to me that evening, you radiated with joy, you were beautiful and loyal in your sincere ways, in your eyes, next to me, you wore a pure and moving happiness, you were moved by my return to you from the military, you awaited my return, this has not changed your gaze as you now await my arrival from so far away, you await the white ship which will transport me to you, oh my little Butterfly.

A furtive tear will wet your cheeks, or will appear in your eyes,[11] upon hearing you being called like this, the same thought moves me no less (this music that accompanies me transports me above my ability to sing, "Heaven! One could die; more I do not ask,"[12] can we die of love). Isn't this the greatest poem of all, because to love and to die calls for a tribute to joy and sorrow, both ripening and cultivating love. We cultivated our love willingly and passionately engendering, weaving together passion, fear, and love. Joy and sorrow interwoven until the end, until the light of day will absorb the demeanour in our eyes.

Today this is not all that I remember, your *mamma*, my *mamma* in the tiniest of details, with concern and sincere affection, this is her day, her celebration [?]. I dedicate to her my sincerest recollection, she who is away from her land. To her, I extend my wishes of the Italian saint, *Santa Lucia*, to her I dedicate renewed and sincerest wishes from someone who feels grateful to and loved by the bearer of her blood. For you, my Tetina, there is more for you in this letter, something else that will bring you the same joy of last year, soon I will provide more explanations so you won't worry and torment yourself. Well! Next Wednesday, I will be passing the last military exam in Venice. This exam is not for the navy but for the army. I want to explain to you that since I was released by the navy, most likely I will be exempted from the army (perhaps it's already confirmed). It is all I can say for the moment so as not to jinx myself.

11 These lines appear to be inspired by Gaetano Donizetti's aria "*Una furtiva lagrima*," in *L'elisir d'amore*, Act 2. See Castel, *Italian Belcanto Opera Libretti in Three Volumes*, 333.

12 "Cielo, si può morir, di più non chiedo." Excerpt drawn from the Italian opera by Gaetano Donizetti *L'elisir d'amore*. Act 2. English text drawn from Castel, *Italian Belcanto Opera Libretti in Three Volumes*, 333.

Surely, this news will bring a warm tear of joy to you. I will confirm all of this as soon as I can. Be happy but do not let it get to you, it will be as God wishes. I say this also because should the opposite occur, you would not be devastated. As for me, it is a question of luck. For you, I pray that all our saints keep you calm and optimistic. All of this will come to an end, and then we will really begin a life together for us, and everything will be more beautiful.

By now, you know the reasons for my writing to you between letters, my ideas will be clearer to you, and you will know that I am, of course, happy when I can offer my Nietta a few tiny joys and a few big kisses,

your Loris

I'm including my response to your letter of the 7th of this month.

Please don't praise my writing.

I assure you that I along with everyone else are in good health. W ... has already left Venice, everything is ready, she asked me to send you many kisses, along with kisses from M ... and L ... and greetings from B ... Kisses from me.

[at the top of the first sheet:]

Greetings and kisses for your *papà* whom I greatly respect

Your Loris

For you, your Loris

To your friends and the C ... family, dearest and distinguished greetings.

— Venice 16-12-48 —

Nietta mia carissima,[13]

The moment we and our loved ones have long agonized over seems to be finally here. I have finally received the good news that releases me from all obligations, the news that will give you the joy you have been waiting for, with this news you will receive the happiness that was formerly greedy with you in releasing good news. We have reached this point, with both resignation and much faith, neither of which were translated into distrust but rather in pessimism. Write to me immediately your reaction to this news. I cannot wait to hear from you.

---

13 Nietta, my dearest.

I hope this letter will reassure you and convince you that everything is going well, thanks to God's help and a good dose of luck which has always stuck by me. I will not discuss anything else in this letter because the main purpose of this letter is to advise you that you can start the paperwork. About this, I have much to tell you.

Therefore, every doubt and apprehension have now passed, you can now begin the application process for my departure, only one thing I would like to specify, that is (do this as quickly as possible) given that the process is long and we only have one year's time to complete it. That is, I must leave within one year, if I surpass that time limit, I will be subject to another exam ... If instead I leave when I can within the year, I will not be called for other interviews or exams ... This is the reason and here is my explanation, this should assure you of my willingness – and I hope it is so – even to your *papà*, to whom I owe everything and on whom everything depends. Therefore, in addition to the joy that accompanies this news, may you also have the energy and the strength to do whatever is required, and since everything depends on you, I hope I will not find a closed door.

Regarding the formalities, it remains to be seen which method is the simplest and most expedient (that is, for me to leave and get married) (or whether to marry before leaving). I am happy with whatever you and your *papà* decide. I remember reading in one of your letters that everything could be completed in six months, nothing would be better, for this reason I would arrange everything in a short period. At this point, I had to stop writing because they were waiting for me at the SADE office, and I wrote as quickly as ever, even to give you the last word, that is on the date when I will be holding in my hands the document that permits me to expatriate.

I am now utterly certain, and no less happy, with this, I can assure you that you can proceed as soon as possible with the application. I cannot believe the nightmare is over. Now, all we need for everything to be complete is your collaboration of which I have no doubt that you will do everything possible together with your *papà*, whom I remember especially tonight because one year ago at exactly this hour he arrived from America and he embraced you, and then he met me. It is the 16th of December and fate has decided that tonight it would be my turn to give you the good news at this hour, in the same way

Reconciling a New Christmas Celebration

you had received good news, perhaps the most extraordinary of news, one year ago, of course, many things have changed in one year; we too have changed, between us there has also been a change, one significant change, and that is, from last year to now, our love has been transformed, it has doubled, it has multiplied. I believe this is due to the three years that we have been engaged, which have allowed me to know you better even if we were apart, even in the midst of countless disappointments. Perhaps it is because of this that I have learned to know you better because you have sustained me, but now, may this news bring to you my joy and my willingness so that you may listen and follow me with a thousand kisses.

your Loris

They replaced my teeth, you can imagine how I am able to speak at this moment, but not for long

[at top of first page:]

For your *papà*, whom I remember with affection, I send my greetings and my hope, for your *mamma* with whom I hope is well, I send her a thousand kisses from her son Loris[14]

For you again and forever, a long passionate kiss until my arrival, Loris

— Venice 19-12-48 —

Piccola Nietta mia,[15]

And here is Christmas approaching very quickly, the Christmas of every year, the Christmas of one single memory, the celebration that brings, or at least should bring, peace for all of us, peace in every heart. A few days separate us from this day already, they are only a few days, even though in my heart I wish that special day would be many days away, so that I would not remember this Christmas from past Christmases. This year, nothing reminds me of Christmas, everything is missing in my [?], everything is missing from the habits I had adopted with the joy of seeing you. And this Christmas I will be missing the one dearest, beautiful thing that would have brought

---

14 A common tradition among Italian families required that a son-in-law or daughter-in-law refer to their spouse's parents as mother or father.

15 Nietta, my girl.

me peace, one thing will be missing, one person, one warmth, the warmth that is diffused in the middle of ice, a cradle that is home to a sweet baby. I will miss this because 1,948 years ago, this miracle happened, and in a small way it recurs every year and with it, a sense of peace is renewed in my heart, where the desire to hold you close germinates, in the same way that I have held you always in the past years. Everything is different now, and everything has changed; the possibility of seeing you has filled me with determination, strength, joy, faith, and even if things are different this year, I did not let my spirit collapse. The word Christmas was equal to emotion, and peace came to me this year bereft of interest because I think about everything that has distorted my happiness for this day.

What saves me and no less enlivens me is the prospect of being close to you on future Christmases, Christmas days in which I will remember my family, my homeland, my people, and the places in which I celebrated past Christmases, but none of this helps to make me feel better. With you away on this day, my thoughts are shattered against an invisible wall, a wall of solitude, a wall of distance — if I could overcome it I would not hesitate, but stubbornly, I realize I am exaggerating because the day will come and it will come soon, I hope, so that I will be holding you tight against me again in my affections, just as I had done when I found you nearly frozen to death waiting for the bus that would take us from Villa[16] to Ampezzo. You were the sweetest thing as you waited for me in these conditions with the greatest of courage, you were dear to my heart because I was aware of your deep feelings toward me, what I would do to see you now like this! Oh, I would definitely lose myself in the excitement, even if inside of me the most ebullient joy would remain.

In any case, may things go the way they are supposed to go, the same with the festivities, one thing is certain more than ever, that I will withdraw myself, the one you have known, the one who convinced you of his love, the one who made you smile at times, the one who lifted you so many times when you were down. May this Christmas imbue us with courage and determination, may it bring us

---

16 Loris is likely referring here to the commune of Villa Santina, just twelve kilometres from Ampezzo.

Reconciling a New Christmas Celebration 137

together again in our combined happiness, pleased with our sacrifices and content of our destiny. On this paper written in the evening of Sunday the 19th, I wanted not only to re-evoke some of the joys we have shared, but to be with you through these words as though they were a preamble to my departure – which now remains for you to proceed with, may this also be, in extraordinary ways, a wish, an omen for serenity, even if this letter may have saddened you, may it convey my sincerest greetings and an hosanna of peace.

To assure you of all that I have said, I want you to know that I needed to write to you this evening, because in effect I had forgotten to do so earlier – not out of habit but out of reality. May you receive with this letter the single, most important wish, and may my love for you be the only love evidenced to you. May this love that I nurture for you serve as a pledge of my wishes, a promise of monumental peace for you. With my sincerest wishes even for the new year, may my discouragement in being alone be redeemed with a long, passionate kiss at this cherished time.

Your Loris

Merry Christmas

For *mamma* and *papà*, my dearest feelings of gratitude and affection, and may this Christmas be for them the happiest and most beautiful ever. Kisses from that person who loves you and thinks of you always. Your Loris. To the C ... family and your friends, best wishes. Best wishes also to all Italians there. For you, once again kisses and Merry Christmas.

– Montreal 22-12-48 –

Mio amato vecio,[17]
a few days ago, I sent you a letter in response to your last one, I now respond to a letter written just 24 hours after the previous one. This makes me feel certain that you think of me constantly, and that you never forget your little Tetina who lives so far away. But distance does not matter, as a novelist correctly wrote: "Love is the truest bond between two people, not proximity." He also wrote some humbling words for humanity when he uttered the sad verdict: "Out of sight,

17 My beloved sweetheart.

out of mind." I read this expression a while ago in an Italian book that someone loaned me for reading, and it touched me to the point that it remained imprinted in my mind. These words are fiction and we are proof that though we are apart, we can protect our hearts. Christmas is just a few days away, and here, we are feeling it in full force, Christmas trees are everywhere, brightly lit windows are filled with toys, everything points to the holidays, while everywhere we feel an important holiday approaching, in my heart, so much melancholy, so much sadness; for me these days are filled with beautiful and indelible memories. Last year was for us a week overflowing with events, as I remember it, I was back in Ampezzo after having embraced my *papà* in Venice, I was not sad to leave you, I knew that within a few days I would have been in your arms again and near you. Oh! Marvellous days, when will you return?

I hope all will move in positive directions so that soon you will be with me again, again and forever, as I wrote in my previous letter I hope that you can be here in six months, of course, six months is the earliest. Now we need to see, after the holidays we will meet with the agent who prepared the application papers for me and my *mamma*, and he will be able to explain everything, and I will give you news, I will do everything to ensure that you can be here in the shortest time possible, always with the hope that your news is good, that is, that you can do something also for the land [?]. Here all the girls who have a boyfriend in Italy are sponsoring them without getting married first, I believe that is the easiest way to proceed, even though they must be married within one month. I think this is the best way, in any case, we will see what the agent says.

Since Monday, I have been back to work in another factory, here I am doing much better, the noise of the machines is less loud and the work is less laborious. I think I will keep it up, I wanted to try working outside again because I was terribly bored at home. There is also the fact that the money will be useful to us. You must forgive me if my writing is getting worse, but I feel a little tired, the first days at work are always the hardest, but I will adjust. I was just looking outside the window, it's snowing, for Christmas we will have quite a bit of snow, we will be spending Christmas with la *Signora* C ... who has invited us. What can you expect, we don't have our families with us

Christmas card from Antonietta Petris, Christmas 1948.

this year, and it would be awful to spend Christmas the three of us alone here ... (Oh! I can't even find the right word!) I will undoubtedly remember our Christmas of last year, a beautiful Christmas, no one was missing, absolutely no one, no relatives, not my *papà*, and not you, all my dear ones were there. Oh well! We cannot always be happy in this world. Please write to me and tell me how you spent that day, and do not forget me. Now I send you many, many kisses that show you how much I love you, and I embrace you affectionately.

your Nietta

Greetings and best wishes from *Signora* C ... and my friends.

Kisses from my *mamma* and *papà*. Kisses for your *mamma* and your family, including W ..., that is, especially her, and her husband. Send me her new address. Kisses to my nephews. Kisses again to you.

— Christmas 1948 —

[Christmas card with personalized text signed by Antonietta as: Antonietta Pétris]

[To Loris]

Remembering our Christmas of last year, I wish you a Christmas as cheerful as our Christmas of last year. With the hope that our next Christmases will witness us together forever. Many kisses and sincerest greetings from your

Nietta

— Christmas 1948 —

[Christmas card in a separate envelope addressed to Loris's family]

Miei cari,[18]

It's Christmas soon, but for me, it will not be a joyous time, someone who is dear to me will not be with me on that day, it is your son who in the past few years brought me bliss with his visit. You know very well how deeply I love him, and you can imagine how profoundly I will feel his absence especially during the holidays. This year, he is with you, I will not have him with me. I will remember him, and think of him often, as I think of you whom I also love. Sincere wishes

18 My dearests.

Reconciling a New Christmas Celebration   141

to M ... and A ..., to you dear *mamma* and *papà*, an affectionate kiss
and best wishes for a Merry Christmas and Happy New Year.
Your Nietta
[From the mother of Antonietta]
To all of you whom I fondly remember, together with Vittorio.
I send my best wishes and many greetings. Lucia Petris

— Venice 27-12-48 —

Nietta mia carissima,[19]
I have thought of a thousand ways to begin this letter, a thousand
memories have prepared me to start this letter, a thousand overlap-
ping thoughts compete to be heard, to be written to you, oh my little
Tetina. In the past few days, every word, every sentence melded into
disappointment, every action, every sight nostalgically reminded me
of past joys. All of this tormented me continuously, because I could
do nothing about it, and I could change nothing. My eyes hid then
and now, a grey deficiency of harmony, of light, the eyes are opaque,
lacking a flame's ardour, a flame that is lit but distant and silent.
Everything seemed destined to discourage me, the sacred celebration
of Christmas was itself disheartening; the days of past years are nothing but a pale resemblance of the days I live now. Those days were
beautiful, radiating with glory, the skies were clear, even though the
future appeared gloomier than now, this year my heart has missed all
things, everything, including your writings, even your words, never
would I have imagined this, never did I think it was possible, perhaps
or certainly it was due to a delay in the mail, I don't know. All I know
is how much this deepened the wound in the vault of my heart. How
much I dwelled on this, how much I waited, maybe I don't deserve
this, but I too am made of flesh and spirit, and I feel burdened by it
more than ever. All has passed, almost all.
Tomorrow we are just a few days away from New Year's Eve, and I
still cannot smile, that smile, along with the joy that each of us understand the peace and happiness are all still missing. And so, with bitter
joy and painful memories Holy Christmas has returned this year. It
lacked the enthusiasm that connected us to the past years, it came

19 Nietta my dearest love.

without the ideas that usually animate and characterize this sacred celebration. Even in my appearance, not to mention, my feelings, I lacked the reason to celebrate Christmas, the most sacred of holidays, the most mystical of all holidays, to everyone else it was without a doubt a call to love, as the holiday and tradition bring together all the children, dear brothers and sisters around the Christmas log to be blessed with the good news, the wish for renewed peace. Poor me, alone by that log, the coal nearly out, and I there dreaming of being forgotten and equally disheartened for needing to be strong; at the same time, I prayed that peace was with you. May the peace ringing in the Angel's ears come back to us, may it lift us, bless us, peace is not the expression of vile people, but the instrument of strength, may it guide us down our path, may it keep us good and calm in the passing of these days, may the spirituality of this peace lift us always toward truth, may this be the objective that ties us to our memories, truthful and limpid in our reciprocated love.

It was a silent and cold Christmas given the absence of one person, it was grey from the sadness and the ice; silent from the absent beating that turns the heart into a coffer, dark from the timid light of the sun whose rays shed no warmth. All of this was a bitter reality, and in my sorrow I felt a loss of life – a stark contrast from desire, everything was missing from me and from you, but perhaps more from me because I was not resigned to persuading myself otherwise, oh, it is not so easy to leave everything behind, or to postpone it at the very least; it was fate's brutal blow that kept me from leaving for Ampezzo because of work obligations. This new burden was enhanced by my misery already rife with disappointments. This was my Christmas gift, an abyss of uncertainties. At the same time, I do not wish to despair even if my only joy was taken away from me, even though this joy was my singular reason to cheerfully return to your home, for me, returning to your family and your dear *nonni* was the only moment of contentment for me. I was deprived of this too, and so Christmas Day was like any other day. Because I am certain beyond any doubt of loving you, this blow was even more painful as there was no way I could hold in my hands a real memory, I could not kiss the land of your home, it was a real disgrace, and I know this news will hurt you, but

Reconciling a New Christmas Celebration 143

you must be as strong as I was for not going, after all I am responsible for this predicament.

Though I was equally disheartened, my greetings for you for a merry Christmas remained the same, oh! You might show some contentment for your parents not to be disappointed, but in your heart, I alone know, I can imagine your disheartened state and I will not falter in giving you my answer. You must have followed me throughout the day, accompanying me with your thoughts to the end, you must have suffered, you must have remembered me, and in doing so, you must have suffocated the memory of our past joys as I did no less, to the point that in several instances my throat tightened as tears rolled down. You are dear to my memories, you are dear to my heart, more than anyone else, and you are dear to me for having reciprocated my love, for cherishing my love, and holding a special place for your Loris, the privilege of loving him and listening to him. Of this I am sure, everything tells me this, your ways show it, your affection assures it. But until now, our path has been an absolute march, you have made real progress in your apprenticeship, in a short time you have loved me, known me, and believed those few words I dared to voice.

I cannot imagine how Christmas is celebrated in the new world where you now spend your days, I don't know with whom and how you spent Christmas Day, traditions change as locations shift, and as a result, I cannot read your cheerfulness. I can, however, imagine you were beautiful standing next to your parents, content that their premonition of the past years was realized again, and that you can now live your lives together, enjoy their good health and your trust in them. Your little heart must feel gratified by this, the joy of your parents must make you smile, along with their fate and their reunion. Since I started reading your letter last night, I thought and hoped I would read some of your good news, but the reality was against my anticipation and I, feeling disappointed, resumed this letter today, the 28th, as joy commingled with sadness.

In my last letter, in which I include my best wishes to you, I also informed you of the good news regarding the military exam, and I gave you the authorization to begin the application process, as we had agreed. Do you agree with me? Will you do as I asked you in my last letter? The most extraordinary, joyful news will be this. My only solace is to hold you again in my arms. Do not take too long to reply to me, do not concern yourself of other uncertainties that may lead to additional difficulties. Listen to me, and always be certain of my affirmations. I await your news, hoping for a demonstration of your clear understanding and a decisive objective, that resolution that makes you clear-sighted and perceptive.

W ... has asked me to thank you on behalf of everyone for the greeting card you sent to us. My family also sends you their greetings even if their card was first sent to Ampezzo, A ..., or rather *Zia* A ... quickly sent it to them. For me, honestly, nothing has touched me in these days, not even the business card. Oh well, it will be for another day, the wishes always make me feel good.

As I close this letter, I send you my most sincere and propitious greetings with the wish to hold you close in my arms soon, may the new year bring joy and happiness to all.

Wishing you a good year's end, and a better start to the new year, especially to you my Tetina, I kiss you dearly and send you a thousand best wishes, your Loris

Greetings to your parents, infinite greetings always to your friends and acquaintances whom I dutifully bow to, and a thousand best wishes

Loris Palma

[Top, left side of page one:]

I am waiting for your prompt response concerning the documents.

— Montreal 27-12-48 —

Mio amore,[20]

Finally, I can devote myself completely to you, I can compose my thoughts for you and my actions without haste. It has been a long time since I sat down to write to you calmly, with work and running around these past few days, I had no time to think about what I wanted to write, and I am sure that you have come across badly written and awkward sentences in my last letters. You must excuse me and forgive me, my beloved, perhaps my writing has changed but not my thoughts, you always have the best part of me, for you my heart

20 My love.

Reconciling a New Christmas Celebration 145

beats always, I live for you, you are the one I love and dream of, my precious. These last few days have been leisure days, running errands in shops and visiting people, however, not to the point of making me forget you. Actually, you have been present more than ever, even if I have received many things (especially fun activities and gifts from my *papà*), I missed very much, you can imagine what I missed, your presence, your face, your gaze, your kisses which are everything to me, you were not here in these festive days and I felt your absence enormously and I was not happy. As I wrote to you already, I spent Christmas Day with *Signora C* ... together with her husband and her little girls, including naturally, my *papà* and my *mamma*, we had joyous moments, good conversations, laughter, and at some point, actually *Signora C* ... said, "Let's hope that for next Christmas another person will be joining our little group," and she added while looking at me, "your Lorenzo." In that moment, I ardently replied, "Oh *Signora*! I very much hope so!" Yes, my darling, everything is in our favour; it is now up to me to take action and I will definitely go ahead with things, you can be assured that you and I will be happy. Next year I will no longer be alone, you will be here warming my heart, you will be the one to bring a smile to my lips, the one who will bring a brilliant light to my eyes, you will no longer be far away, I will be able to look at you, touch your face with these hands and listen to your beating heart. Do not say anything, do not reproach me for expressing myself in this way, these are my thoughts and my wish for you, that is, to have you here with me, then this land that is so frozen and cold will be warm to me, and the grey and gloomy days will be clear, open skies to me; you are the one who will bring the magnificent Italian sun, our sun. My Loris, I think of you constantly, and the memory is alive, brilliant and without blemish just like the first day I arrived here; you too must love me always, and never forget me, you must never forget me.

After the holidays, as I wrote to you already, I will meet with the agent for information concerning your journey here. I can give you one piece of news, in one year we can absolutely apply for you to come here. Write to me, tell me how you spent Christmas, my darling, my relatives were eager to see you in Ampezzo, did you perhaps visit them? I have an inkling that you didn't, am I right? When you come down you will see how we celebrate Christmas here, gifts and

146   September 1948 to December 1948

greeting cards are exchanged, me too, while I arrived here not too long ago, I received numerous gifts, from my *papà* a gold necklace, from *Signora* C ... a box of three different perfumes, a lady gave me a box of chocolates, a man gave me a bigger box of chocolates, and my godfather gave me a makeup and hairbrush set. It is a lot, isn't it? Last year, I received a gift only from you, remember? I was so happy, much more than this year, even if I received more gifts. (I just took a break for several minutes, memories, memories, my darling, my mind lingered into the past and paused at a Christmas that is far away, the Christmas of one year ago, but that's enough, looking back brings me sadness, oh! My Loris, my Loris, I implore you, do you hear it? I am sighing!)

Yesterday, Sunday, I practically spent the entire day at home, I went to Mass in the morning, and after lunch, I went to bed, I was exhausted after staying up late on Christmas Eve. I was exhausted on Christmas Day, and wanted to write to you in the evening but at around eight o'clock, guests arrived so that not even last night did I go to bed before midnight. Today I woke up early to go to work but I came home shortly after because there was nothing to do, it's the holidays and it seems everyone is taking some time off. Then I cleaned the house and ended the day by writing to you, tonight I plan to go to sleep very early. I forgot to mention that my *papà* also gifted me a lovely coat, hat, and purse, he is a good man, isn't he? My poor *papà*. They are now calling me to supper, goodbye my beloved Lorissin, many, many kisses and an affectionate embrace, I love you.

your Nietta

Greetings to you and your family for the New Year on behalf of my parents. Kisses to all.

— Venice 28-12-48 —

Words are not enough in my wishes for you for a Happy New Year, I entrust this task to my heart and my affection for you. May this year be prosperous for us as I kneel with joy to kiss you.

Your Loris

Ampezzo, December 2013. PHOTO: SONIA CANCIAN.

Antonietta on her way to visiting family friends, Montreal, November 1949.

Antonietta on the balcony of her home in Montreal, 1948–49.

Antonietta, studio portrait prior to Loris's arrival, Montreal, 1949.

Antonietta and Loris on their wedding day, 17 December 1949.

Antonietta and Loris with their families and friends outside the Italian church Madonna della Difesa in Montreal, 17 December 1949.

Antonietta and Loris at their home in Montreal, early 1950s.

At their new home, Vittorio and Lucia Petris (left) and Antonietta and Loris (right), Montreal, early 1950s.

Antonietta and Loris many years later.

The collection of letters, Montreal, January 2011. PHOTO: SONIA CANCIAN.

Antonietta at her home in Saint-Léonard, Montreal, with her letters. September 2011. PHOTO: SONIA CANCIAN.

Sonia Cancian and Antonietta Petris at Antonietta's home, Saint-Léonard, Montreal, December 2018. PHOTO: SONIA CANCIAN.

— Part Two —

Letter from Loris Palma, 28 December 1948.

"Worlds
Apart,
and Near
to Heart" *The Letters from January 1949 to July 1949*

— 5 —

"A new year, a new life"
Optimism and Melancholy Gazing into the Future

IN THE LATE 1940S AND EARLY 1950S, Europeans were still reeling from "the dark years of the worst war in history,"[1] despite efforts for individuals and families to get on with their lives. In 1949, fear of a new war coming to Europe was in the air. This fear, discussed briefly in Antonietta's and Loris's letters (see the letters of 8-10-48 and 17-10-48), was not without cause. Historian Tony Judt describes this early period after the war as a time of "heightened insecurity and much talk of war"[2] in Europe. The Cold War did materialize, and with it emerged several striking legacies, notwithstanding the signing of the Universal Declaration of Human Rights in 1948 and the North Atlantic Treaty in 1949, and a concerted willingness between Western Europe and the United States and Canada in favour of co-operation and integration.[3] The Cold War marked a deeply divided Europe, the Korean War (1950–53), the Cuban Missile Crisis of 1962, and a nuclear age dominated by two superpowers, the United States and the Soviet Union, both in possession of weapons of mass destruction.[4] In Italy, funds from the Marshall Plan (1948–51) were directed to the importation of coal and grain, the assistance of struggling industries (for example, textile), and investments in engineering, energy, agriculture, and transportation

---

1 Kershaw, "Foreword," *Roller-Coaster*, 1.
2 Judt, *Postwar*, 149.
3 Ibid., 151.
4 Kershaw, "Foreword," *Roller-Coaster*, 1.

networks while consumer goods remained at pre-war levels.[5] The challenge of "finding enough to eat" remained.[6]

Among Italian families who had loved ones settled overseas, migration was as an option for a better life. For couples like Antonietta and Loris, the migration project had already been initiated before Antonietta's departure in September. In January 1949, the application process for Loris's migration to Canada had commenced, and their migration project appeared on course. Antonietta's and Loris's letters attest to the realization of their project with optimism and relative certainty of their reunion. Yet, despite a positive outlook on their future, a significant portion of time needed to pass before their long-awaited reunion.

Time and its slow passage inevitably gave way to layers of melancholy, an emotion defined by Julia Kristeva as "amorous passion's somber lining."[7] Melancholy or melancholia is closely associated with loss, creativity, and reflection. To Freud, it signalled signs of painful dejection, cessation of interest in the outside world, loss of the capacity to love, and a "reaction to the loss of a loved object."[8] Roland Barthes defines a lover's melancholy as akin to fading or fade-out in which "the loved being endlessly withdraws and pales."[9] The couple's physical separation at moments seemed insurmountable with the Atlantic Ocean serving as a metonym of their separation. The time difference and the overarching geopolitical and cultural differences between them, commingled with the renewed political tensions emerging on the global stage, engendered feelings of melancholy between them, even while they endeavoured to sustain a positive perspective on their fate. A dynamic, transnational love melancholy results in the letters. To write love sonnets or prose in a state of melancholy, particularly related to romantic love, emerges from a literary tradition dating at least to the Renaissance and Romantic period.[10] Here, the proliferation of the imagination was a

---

5 Judt, *Postwar*, 95.
6 Gabaccia, *Italy's Many Diasporas*, 153.
7 Kristeva, "On the Melancholic Imaginary," 5.
8 Freud, "Mourning and Melancholia," 245.
9 Barthes, *A Lover's Discourse*, 112.
10 Lawlor, "Fashionable Melancholy," 38.

key component to melancholy in much the same way, as scholars suggest, as its chronic characteristic. In addition to co-presence, melancholy and its imaginary echoes were particularly suited for the creative person who felt alone in the moment.[11] While Antonietta and Loris do not show signs of a chronic melancholy over the long term, shades of melancholy – fluctuating in intensity – are identified in their transnational writings.

Reflection, a practice that is imbricated in the process of letter-writing alongside memory, also intersected with the couple's melancholy. In the epistolary process, as Patrizia Gabrielli notes, the white paper facing the letter writers became the mirror through which they reflected and interpreted their lives and the realities around them.[12] And, as each reflected and contemplated their past, present and future lives together, melancholy kept them from falling over the edge into outright despair, and helped them to prolong the emotion of remembrance facilitated in their writing.[13]

— Venice —

New Year's Day 1949, 11:15 p.m.
Indimenticabile mia Nietta,[14]
It's cold in this new room of mine, a room that offers me nothing but a gloomy silence, yet I need the space to induce a reaction in my heart. It's a silence that inspires a voice; a silence that echoes the beatings of my heart.

> 'All is still, and yet all to the heart speaks to me ...
> This peace away from here where can I find it?
> You are lovely, season of springtime,

---

11 Ibid., 38.
12 Gabrielli, *Col Freddo nel Cuore*, 19.
13 Brady and Haapala, "Melancholy as an Aesthetic Emotion," n.p.
14 My Unforgettable Nietta.

164   January 1949 to July 1949

Renews flowers and love'[15]
Of your memory, I embrace my every thought,
Of your love, I crown my every sorrow

It is easy to speak while the heart dictates, it is easy to remember
when every single thing leads you there, there to your homeland, to
your home, to your heart. Oh yes, my little Tetina, no greater memory than the one in my heart lives on this day, no recollection more
invincible than the memory of this day two years ago has been carved
in my soul. But all of this furiously passes by in the same way that the
thought of not loving each other enough also passes, we hear these
cruel words of doubt perhaps because they stir in us, without reason,
or in the case of reason, all of this is superfluous, because I know how
deeply I love the woman who loves me. Even this is a reality, though
with reservations, that awakens those who wish to remain dormant.
For me the doubt of not loving you enough sets off alarm bells, always
fixed and likely to rust because they will never toll loudly for me. The
beating of my heart is loud enough.

All of this furiously passes by with the irony of not being able to
relive the joys of our past, all vanishes skeptically like a fragrance,
but beyond that, we see clearly, even in the darkness of a cold winter
night, like tonight, tender-hearted like this night. A light brightens
our path, a light already flickers for us in a little church, yes Nietta,
the little church that faces us, there we will respond to our hearts,
there we will envelope our matrimonial affections, there as we face
God whom we serve affectionately as messengers of His love. A
light brightens our path, this is the truth we must believe in, this
is our sincere reality of a love that has been waiting, and if we arm
ourselves with these words, once again an unknown future will bring

15 Mascagni, *L'Amico Fritz*, 688. The citation is drawn from Mascagni's opera,
L'Amico Fritz. The plot centres around a prosperous landowner (Fritz Kobus)
who leads a contented life as a confirmed bachelor until his friend, the rabbi
David, an enthusiastic matchmaker, tricks him and marries him to the daughter
of the steward of his estate, Suzel. Pietro Mascagni's opera *L'Amico Fritz*
premiere in Rome on 31 October 1891 was hailed as the most important operatic
event since that of *Otello*, and the opera immediately had many subsequent
performances. See Ross, "*Amico Fritz, L',*" 109.

Optimism and Melancholy Gazing into the Future 165

us happiness, it will be once again, a heroic poem that will unite us in body and spirit.

Oh, memories of years past, why do you torment me? Will my love for Tetina make history? These questions have no value, far too vivid are my memories and they cannot be sedated, it's useless to deny breath to our reality, a reality that cannot die, it must not succumb to a brutal fate, that would deliver a harsh reality for both of us. We must harvest stimulating ways to overcome it as every reality is part of our destiny, it barricades our path. For this reason, today's reality, which we have alluded to in our conversations, is fruit of our will, a turning point that we have traced to diminish our sufferings, a short cut, if you will, that we have decided to take in order to secure our happiness earlier. May this new year be propitious and conspicuous about this in every way. The new year is here, a new year is born, it is here and perhaps it will help us in our journey, it has emerged right at the beginning of our pilgrimage.

This is the way things are this year, we must work to crown the year's success, the year must energize us so we can be victorious. May the proverb speak the truth for us: a new year, a new life. This is the way it must be, a new year begins at the break of dawn of a new year, a new era, and we will build a new life; this new life begins today with these few paltry words, may these words preface a great novel that will recount our story for all of the 365 days, a story that will unravel forever until one of the characters leaves. It must be so, yes, my dearest Nietta, if your dream is to have me near you, this is the way it will be. A new year is born, almost urging us to proceed with the rescue, may this be the time for us to monitor our struggle, may this be the time we will reach our objective.

A recounting of our story could not deny us the reason for our drive to reach our objective this year, no one can accuse us of exuberance at this point; too many sacrifices, too many disappointments are proof of our immunity, for nearly three years we have continued along this path, and always without opposition, three years of this torment have already passed, how many events, decisions, sorrows, sacrifices, and joys have we experienced. Our writings, our thousand and more letters, signal events overcast with disappointments, their meaning cannot be confused because the meaning is the same for all, even in the case of a few meagre joys shining like a star at the centre of a sombre black sky. A thousand letters are proof of our constant struggle to start our new life, a thousand letters have documented the advent of our long-awaited day, and all year our letters have asked, when will that day come? There is no reason to doubt now that the day of joy is beckoning, it is here in this new year, the day of our renewed embrace; numerous interruptions have preoccupied our minds, a thousand reservations have justified our anxiety. But all of this has passed, they are now history, and if three of those years are now extinguished, this year will never end (I hope), it will never end because for us our life story will be one continuous year in which there is no finishing line, a marathon of generosity, affection, and love so that we may crown and grace the fruit of our love that we have so ardently desired. A child will be our joy, a child will follow at another stage, it will prove to us how far we will have travelled.

The year 1948 has ended and a single memory hypnotizes me: your departure. In one page, your goodbye would have signalled or marked a note of convention, but in my heart, it signified something very different, it bore a deep ridge in my heart, it was as though it wanted to sow a perennial feeling of defeat; however, my spirit did not surrender and it has enclosed this ridge with a joy that has not yet bloomed. This joy that imbues me, that makes me smile a little today, is the only privilege that allows me to constantly speak about you, it is the singular source of conviction that you love me and that I love you. This is the only memory of 1948, the year which was wiped out like two pieces of coal whose withering I carefully observed on the fire at midnight of the 31st of December. It was as though I assisted these pieces of coal in their last breaths, providing at times a drop's cooling until they were extinguished forever as the bells tolled, announcing the birth of a new day.

May this new day be propitious for us, the harbinger of our ardent happiness, the guardian angel of our bliss. May my wish be a prayer to you, may it bless you in your endeavours, may you understand my truthful wishes for you, may it reveal to you how much I love you, the wishes of my heart, and a safe journey toward you, may you believe in my wish that you remain always beautiful, healthy, happy and motherly. My dear ones join me in sending you dearest wishes, they too are

Optimism and Melancholy Gazing into the Future   167

a little more relieved that they are not being abandoned; I will take care of them, it will be my responsibility to take care of my elders. May it always be this way for the rest of their lives, may their days always be filled with warmth, like today when I saw them smiling again after the disastrous fate that affected my *padre*.

It is also for this reason that I am smiling today and feeling happy, but nothing has given me more joy than the hope that enlivens me always, and that is the ability to count the days of the year and believe that in one year I will be with you. It's very cold at the moment, I am freezing. I have stopped writing in a straight line, my hand is frozen, my eyes are heavy, but before I close them, I must send you the best wishes from a dear gentleman, a friend of mine who cares for me very much and who has done much for me, it is a wish that is entirely sincere from this Genoese friend who highly covets the hope and certainty of our happiness. I should have been at his home yesterday, but what could I do? You know how much . .

My thoughts are extended to all of your dear ones near and far, give them my most affectionate greetings as you did to your *nonni* and *zii* with the hope of seeing them soon, embrace them and kiss them for me. For you, I think of you devotedly, may you always be my only Tetina, my only girl whom I shower with kisses now and always so that you may be happy and cheerful. Kisses from my family and from W ... and especially, the nephews.

From me, a thousand and more kisses until I can give you one, a real one. your Loris

Keep me posted on any news you have on the paperwork, be prompt and remember to let me know. A letter that you mention in your last letter must have been lost in the mail. *Ciao*, Kisses Loris

[Note written in opposite direction of one of the sheets:]

Many greetings to the C ... Family and to your [girl] friends.

Write to me about the papers, remember to make inquiries and always remember to advise me. One of the letters that you discuss in your last letter must have been lost in the mail. *Ciao* to you. Kisses, Loris

Infinite greetings to the C ... family and your friends.

— Montreal 3-1-48 [1949] —

Mio amato Loris,[16]

Even 1948 has ended, a new year is about to begin, a year filled with grace and joy for us, we hope; the beginning of last year was far more beautiful for us, it was a time that witnessed us together and jubilant in Ampezzo's small dance hall, do you remember my darling? I realize only now that when we have joy, we appreciate it very little, that is, we are not aware of our happiness when it comes to us, this is the way it was for us, we were happy but we were not aware of it, and especially in these days, I envy couples walking with their arms wound around each other, gazing into each other's eyes and devouring each other with their glances. It's lovely to see them pass by, to watch them is a pleasure, their smiles are jovial, their lips move to the sounds of sweet words of affection, but now, all of this is denied to us, none of this is possible for us, why, why is this? We must not despair, no, we must remain strong, perhaps the most arduous stretch is behind us, and now, the easiest path awaits, this cheers me up, you know my darling, it sustains me and gives me the strength to resist all things only because I love you, because I know you are mine, and because I adore you. With what intensity have I recollected the evenings of last winter when we were alone resting on the long chair enjoying the fire's warmth, there was no entertainment, but what better delight than having you close to me?

This year, instead the evenings are very different! We were seldom at home, G ... my godfather, invited us, and I can tell you that we were not lonely, and I must be honest, on Friday and Saturday I went to bed at 4 in the morning. Believe me my beloved Loris, I did not stop thinking of you for one second and on several occasions I drew away from everyone to relive in my mind the evenings of last year, oh my Loris, nothing can make me forget you, I love you too much, my past with you next to me was too beautiful, and the present is nothing but a memory, a memory of something that once was. Here everyone finds me cheerful and carefree, they admire my personality but they don't know that I often suffer for one thing or another. Some people are not able to hide their sorrow, their worries, I can, actually

16 My beloved Loris.

Optimism and Melancholy Gazing into the Future 169

I am unable to show others who I am and how I feel; no, no one can understand me, so, why share my sorrows with others? It's not worth it, each of us has enough of our own problems, am I right, my darling? (I took a break of a few minutes as I listened to parts of the romantic aria, "One fine day we will see," in Italian and I hurried like crazy to the kitchen to listen to it, my *papà* did not want to listen to it as he had lowered the radio's volume so I could write to you. Yesterday I listened to *Cavalleria Rusticana* and *I Pagliacci*[17] both in Italian; they play them on the air every Sunday, the operas of Italian musicians are in Italian, the ones of French musicians are in French, they have announced that an Italian tenor will be coming soon, I'm not sure if it's Gigli [Beniamino Gigli] or Tagliavini [Ferruccio Tagliavini].[18] I will certainly not miss the chance to hear him, that is, if I get the tickets on time, because who knows how many people will be there.

And you, my darling, how are you? You mentioned in one of your letters that you were going to tell me about my *nonni*. How they are doing, as your *fratello* [brother] reported to you, but you did not say a word, did you forget? Tell me something, I will be so pleased. And your *papà*? I imagine that he is feeling a little depressed after being laid off of work. Remember my darling, as I mentioned to you in one of my letters, it is now up to you to be the head of the family, you must know how to be a good provider for your parents to be happy, be good and generous like them, and for this, I will always admire and respect you for it; for me it assures me that we too will live in peace and security in the future. I will be delighted to know if in this way your parents will be happy.

17 The operas *Cavalleria Rusticana* (premiered in 1890) by Pietro Mascagni (1863– 1945) and *I Pagliacci* (premiered in 1892) by Ruggero Leoncavallo (1857–1919).
18 Beniamino Gigli (1890–1957) and Ferruccio Tagliavini (1913–1995) were two famous Italian tenors of the mid-twentieth century. Gigli was regarded the legitimate heir of Caruso. A favourite of Mussolini, he reappeared after the war to sing at the Rome opera in 1945. His long career continued until his death in 1957. Shawe-Taylor and Blyth, "Gigli, Beniamino," 847–8. Tagliavini made his debut in 1939 in Florence and by the end of the war was one of the leading tenors of the Italian stage, until he retired in 1966 He excelled in the bel canto operas of Bellini and Donizetti and in Mascagni's *L'Amico Fritz*. Shawe-Taylor, "Tagliavini, Ferruccio," 925.

Today, I went back to work and I will keep working there, I feel good working there, and it is not labour intensive, I have not yet received my paycheque, but I believe they will pay me $20 per week, this amounts to more than 10,000 Italian lire, as the English say, "nais eh!" [*sic*] (good eh!) for a woman it is not bad, right? Of course, the more intensive jobs pay better, but I already gave those a try, and you saw how hard it was for me. What else can I tell you? The old year, that is, on the first day of the past year we were together, on the last day we were apart, let's hope and wish for the opposite for this year, on the first, we were apart, on the last, oh yes, we must be together and forever. (My *papà* is here now and he is asking me to go to bed since I need to wake up early tomorrow.) Many kisses and greetings from my *papà* and *mamma* who think of you, and from me, a thousand and more kisses and a warm embrace.

from your Nietta

Did you receive my Christmas card? And, did your *fratelli* [brothers and sisters]? And, your *mamma* and *papà*? Kisses to everyone. Kisses to you again.

— Montreal 6-1-48 [1949] —

Mio adorato Loris,[19]
Last night at around 6, that is when I returned from work, I found your very dear letter. I read it like all your other ones, with indescribable expediency to the point that if someone had asked me what the letter was about, I would not have been able to answer. It's always like this, the desire to know what you have written is so strong that I don't read the letter at first, I devour it, as a result, I understand everything and nothing at the same time. Upon reading it a second time, I understood everything in your letter and I was very, yes, very sorry to read your very sad and melancholic writing, I did not expect this kind of a letter. I believed that the holidays would bring you some joy, this is what I had wished for you and repeated often, I wanted you to be happy even if you missed me, that you would remember as much as possible our past Christmases so that you would not suffer, but it was not so; the woman who loves you, who wishes for you to live in peace

---

19 My adored Loris.

Optimism and Melancholy Gazing into the Future   171

has given you sorrow, Loris, I who loves you, who wants to see you happy has done nothing but double your sorrow. Forgive me, my love, forgive me. Something like this must never happen again, you must not accelerate things in this way, try to reason, try to understand the motives why you have not received correspondence, and there is no reason other than a postal delay like last time. I replied to all of your letters, you should have known that during the holidays a higher concentration of correspondence travels to and fro and the delay is entirely plausible. Where did your trust go? Did you forget the phrase you once wrote to me? "A love without trust is like a flower without fragrance." These are your words, do you remember them? Now, do you wish for our love to become an unscented flower? You must not, you must not do this, my Loris. Remember that I love you, that I adore you, and that I will come through with my promises. If you don't believe me and you don't trust what I'm telling you over and over again, it means that you don't know me well enough, that you don't know who I am and what my feelings are. It is difficult to understand one another, as much as you live with the other, you cannot know her deeply, you need to observe her, follow her actions, and maybe then you will learn about her good and bad traits and determine if you can trust her words or not. Please forgive me if I try to reason too much about this, but perhaps it is better to speak clearly, in that way we can know each other better and understand one another more deeply; There must not be a shadow of falsehood between us, everything must be said without fear, everything must be clear and transparent between us, I am telling you this now more than ever because I am learning more and more about the consequences of couples who do not understand each other.

Enough with this, I was very, very sorry to hear how grief-stricken you were and I hope that my letter has responded to your wishes, also I was disappointed that you were not able to go to Ampezzo, L ... wrote to tell me that they were waiting for you, but what could you do, you are not to blame; it will be for another time, right my darling? Did you advise them that you could not go? I urge you to do so if you have not done so already, they will be pleased to hear from you. This evening I received a letter from R ..., my sewing teacher, I would like to send you a copy. You cannot imagine how much I cried while reading it, my eyes are still red from the tears, all of my past leaped to mind, my adolescent years, my youthful years when I was my happiest, I'm sure! Last night I visited *Signor* S … the travel agent, and I immediately received information on when you will be able to travel. He replied that in one year's time everything can be completed, even before, we don't need any papers from you at the moment. I gave him your name, date of birth, etc., now my *papà*, myself, and the agent will be going to the emigration [immigration] office, do not worry, my darling, in a year you will be here, you believe me, don't you? I close this letter now, tomorrow I need to wake up early, hoping to receive your news and hear that you are a little happier now, I kiss you with much affection.

your Nietta

PS My parents and I received your greetings and your family's wishes, all of us are grateful to your family. Did you receive my Christmas card? Or was it delivered to Ampezzo as well? How careless of me, no? What can I say? I sent so many cards and mistakes happen. Good night.

Forgive my bad writing.

Greetings to everyone. Dear kisses from me and Vittorio. Your *mamma*.

— Montreal 9-1-49 —

Mio adorato Loris,[20]
I don't know how many days have passed since I wrote to you. In the past little while, it is as if I am not aware of anything, I come and go, I talk, I move, I rest without knowing exactly what I am doing, nothing troubles me recently (that is, in the past few days, fortunately!). My *mamma* is more or less well, and consequently both my *papà* and I are overjoyed to see her like this, but the days pass without anything brightening them up or diminishing their monotony, every day is the same, no sunshine, cold, grey skies, this is perhaps why I am unaware of time. As I mentioned to you before, nothing troubles me aside from one thing, yes, that is what I feel, your absence, the more time passes, the more I feel it, and I believe more than ever that until you get here, I will see nothing but cloudy grey skies even when everything seems

20 My adored Loris.

Optimism and Melancholy Gazing into the Future 173

splendid and rosy. This will make you understand how much I love you still and how much I long to see you. You might say that words are not enough, action is needed but with patience that will come too, do not doubt it.

We went to meet with the notary and we are now waiting for a telephone call from *Signor* S ... for a meeting at the emigration [immigration] office, a little late, perhaps? What can I do, my Loris, I can only do this when my *papà* is available, I can go to the office only with him, not alone that's for sure. Do not despair, my precious, everything will come in good time, do not doubt it, you will see; my *papà* already speaks of you as if you are part of the family, we talk often about many things here, things that lift my often low morale (you know my darling, my morale is not always low, if you still know me (I'm kidding) you know how easily I become enthusiastic and discouraged, from one hour to the next, it seems I change moods dozens of times, perhaps all of this depends on age, ah! to be young!!). Joking aside and continuing my discussion, yes, my Loris darling, you must have faith and constancy, love me as you say you love me, do not forget me, remember that we were separated so that we could see each other again, remember that I love you. Why am I saying this, am I not confident of your love? Oh, yes, yes, I know that you love me, but it will not hurt you to hear these words, sometimes life weaves invisible webs and we need to be ingenuous, brave, and determined to free ourselves, it is good to reflect on these words, both you and I need them for now and in the future, we need to be strong in life and we need to fight to win.

Let's move onto other things. Last night my parents and I visited a gentleman who has just arrived from Italy, he is from Forni di Sotto,[21] he brought me various letters from I ..., W ..., N ..., and D ... who writes about you, Ferrara, and L .... However, I honestly did not understand what she was saying. Did you go to Ferrara? L ... has complained to you that we don't write often? I am telling you the truth, if I had to write to everyone who has sent me news, I would have enough writing to last me a week; I will write to everyone a little at a time every night. I received news from your *fratello* C ..., thank him for

---

21 A small neighbouring town of Ampezzo Carnico, approximately nine kilometres away.

me, tell him that I will certainly write to him. Do you see Loris? You complain that I do not write to you often, but you don't consider the fact that I have many others whom I should please with my writing, including my *nonni, Zia* A ... etc. with whom I regularly correspond.

Now I must tell you how many letters I must compose, one for I ... and A ... and D ... and M ... and your *sorella* [sister], W ..., and R ... and my *nonni* now, and your *fratello*, and first of all, you. Now, don't you see that you are not alone? When I think of all the people I need to respond to, I become nervous and anxious, seriously, you know! The fact is that during the day I am always out, and in the evening, I don't feel like writing as there is always something, then there are the evening classes that absorb a lot of my time, and so, all in all, I don't get anything done. This evening too I went to class and returned home at a quarter past 9, I then combed my *mamma*'s hair, and started to write to you. It's a quarter to eleven, and I want to go to bed, tomorrow morning I need to be up at seven. I have here the newspaper article that features a traditional Friulan Epiphany, thank you for this thoughtful gift, I was so happy to read this and see the striking landscape of Gemona, I could not help but think about my little hometown and the dear Monte Tinisa and Monte Pura,[22] they are always in my heart. However, it is now useless to think about this so much, I am here now; I can hope only for one thing and that is to see you soon, in that way, Italy will be here for me, the sun will be here, happiness will be with me, only in this way can I forget a little what I have left behind. Remember me always. Many many kisses, your Nietta.

— Venice 10-1-49 —

Nietta mia indimenticabile,[23]
Yes, I did delay by a few days in writing to you, but if I must be truthful, I wanted to first receive news from you, more than ten days had passed since I had received word from you. I did it out of obstinacy, or better yet, it was a decision based on my loneliness, alone, without you, without your words, without your affection. Perhaps it was a little

---

22 Monte Tinisa and Monte Pura are located in the Carnic Alps, in the vicinity of Ampezzo.
23 My unforgettable Nietta.

Optimism and Melancholy Gazing into the Future 175

excessive of me, but I was tired of waiting needlessly. When I received your second to last letter I became calmer, even if I understood that any delay however slight was likely caused by the holidays, or better yet, from your recent excursions. It was a bitter pill to swallow in those days, and I was alone in my grief because no one could understand me, and who could I talk to? It would have only aggravated my resentment. Epiphany arrived, and while I had gifts for everyone I hoped that someone would also remember me. That day I was like a little boy, a child again, innocent and without prejudice, yet quite enterprising when it came to those famous stockings. And so the misery in my heart passed on that day, one of countless days in which others saw me happy and cheerful as though I were holding a toy in my hands. A letter on that day would have brought me immeasurable joy, the kind of joy that children of this world feel, but nothing of the sort materialized.

Despite this, and not out of arrogance, I thought of you on that day like never before, and in my bitterness, I tried to make sense of your sorrow as I imagined you alone, and I thought of something that almost justified my state of mind, a photograph of your new home struck me painfully hard, but I held on to it so I could send it to you, and that same evening, I started to write to you, but I just couldn't. A few days passed in a similar state of mind until I received a letter from you. How much joy melded with my own pessimism, and with extraordinary delight my spirit was lifted, at the same time I carefully read the lack of plausible, or at the very least, interesting justifications.

Don't look sullen if I tell you this, you know very well that I say what I think, and I don't keep secrets. With regard to the parties that kept you away from your familiar surroundings, I cannot reproach you, for the same reason that I can understand, but I did not tell you of the hellish days that harboured my soul, certainly I did not stop myself from writing to you, not because the holidays compel us to write, but I did not do it before either, actually in the past few months my correspondence with you has intensified with a few extra letters so you would always have news on the circumstances which you are familiar with. For this, don't think badly of your Loris, he worries a lot about the future for his family and he is anxious over your news and your correspondence. Your writings lack a little of their usual enthusiasm, even if they are no different from the others, the fact that I do not find solace from my nightmares, and this is easy to understand, it's similar to the time you were feeling anxious over the uncertainties I wrote to you about the exam results. It's the same for me now as I await your replies, or better yet, your news. Your news is missing from your writings, that is, you are not writing about your thoughts, your concerns, you know how much I treasure reading them. Certainly, you did not forget the declaration that I made to you on that infamous September 21, now you must know that there is no limit to my desire to hold you again in my arms, there, now I have told you explicitly the reason for my current state, the reason I have been anxiously awaiting your letters to read your words, words that make my heart sing. Be good and tell me what you are doing for me during these days, talk to me about my being there, it is all so bittersweet for me to hear now. But I want to make peace, as my conscience requires it, and it is peace that is delivering my trust to you, my constancy, my sorrow, and my love, may my desire for peace explain my grief and my passion in loving you. I read about all the gifts and affection that surrounded you over the holidays, but you missed mine, you did not receive not even a small gift from me! Oh it's so difficult now, the distance is enormous, I can only make it up to you by reaffirming my devotion to you, and my deepest affection for you, in this way, the gifts you received will appear more beautiful to you.

Begin the paperwork for my immigration, this is the most important matter that must brighten your days, I am *"stuffo e agro"*[24] (as they say in Venetian) to keep living like this, at this point my life without you has no meaning or direction, my life is all about pleasing you and being dear to you. In the meantime, these thoughts managed to calm my exacerbated state of mind, and I softened my demeanour, I am becoming less interested even in soccer and, even less, in dropping by the Bar Campanile, all for one reason, all so that I can be more conscious than ever of my responsibilities as the son of my family. Yesterday on Sunday the 9th I worked all day until late in the evening, exhausted, I concluded the day with my family, and was in bed soon

24 "I am thoroughly tired and fed up."

Optimism and Melancholy Gazing into the Future **177**

enough. Now you can see how the changes inside of me have intensified my sorrow in having you so far away. But, while your body is far away, your heart is safely enclosed in mine, and my heart beats in synchrony with yours. Just like my kisses are joined with your kisses, your Loris.

All of us at home have received your Christmas card. I believe C ... has already written to you to thank you. About your *nonni,* he returned twenty days ago or so and reported that they are in excellent health and their work continues well. He was very pleased to see that O ... is growing. L ... wrote to me a few days ago informing me of this news. I will do my best to travel to see them soon, that place reminds me so much of my Tetina and my in-laws to whom I ask you to extend my greetings and a faithful kiss. To you, I send once again peace enclosed in a thousand kisses on your unforgettable mouth. your Loris.

— 6 —

"Imagine your Nietta, sadder than ever"
Traumas of Separation and Displacement

MIGRATION IS A LIFE-CHANGING EVENT. In the words of psychiatrist Salman Akhtar, migration

> from one country to another is a complex, psychosocial process with significant and lasting effects on an individual's identity. Leaving one's country involves profound losses. Often one has to give up familiar food, native music, unquestioned social customs, and even one's language. The new country offers strange[-] tasting food, new songs, different political concerns, unfamiliar language, pale festivals, unknown heroes, psychically unearned history, and a visually unfamiliar landscape. However, alongside these losses is a renewed opportunity for psychic growth and alternation. New channels of self-expression become available. There are new identification models, different superego dictates, and fresh ideals.[1]

Similar to the present day, transitions in a migration process involved "changes in personal ties and the reconstruction of social networks, the move from one socio-economic system to another, and the shift from one cultural system to another."[2] With many of migrants' life conditions changing, the health of migrants was, and remains, affected.

1   Akhtar, *Immigration and Identity*, 5.
2   Kirmayer et al., "Common Mental Health Problems in Immigrants and Refugees," E 961.

For instance, psychiatric studies have shown that resettlement usually brings hope and optimism – as the letters of Antonietta and Loris also illustrate. Concomitantly, disillusionment, demoralization, and depression also resulted during stages of a migration process with forms of loss as one of the major factors.[3] To leave the comforts and knowledge of home and the company of loved ones in an environment in which every crevice, every glance, every whisper was familiar, made acculturation in Montreal unquestionably hard for migrants like Antonietta and her mother. While few details are revealed regarding to what extent Antonietta's mother became acclimatized in the industrial city of Montreal in the first months since her arrival in 1948, we do know from Antonietta's letters to Loris that at least in the beginning, she refused to answer the phone and step outside of the home (see letters 25-10-48 and 30-10-48).

In historian Susan Matt's book *Homesickness* (2011), illustrations of loneliness and longing among immigrants in America tell a similar story. For instance, Italian immigrant Filomena Mazzei reported in an interview in 1978–79, "America – I didn't like it … I couldn't speak the language, I had no relatives … I had the little children. I stayed home, alone. My husband worked, and I felt like a lost person."[4] Longing for the familiarity of the homeland, missing loved ones, and facing new constellations every day in North American industrial urban cities like Chicago and Montreal were exacerbated by feelings of solitude and loneliness. And, as Susan Matt suggests, mental breakdowns were not a rare occurrence among migrants.[5]

In the letter of 16 January 1949, Antonietta wrote in distress. Her mother had suddenly fallen into a severe nervous breakdown, and Antonietta recounted in a few details what had transpired and why she felt like a "crazy woman in search of something that could revive her." In describing this moral and psychological crisis, Antonietta reflected on her panic and distress, and on the importance of having loved ones nearby. In writing to Loris about the incident – part of

3 Ibid.
4 Matt, *Homesickness*, 150. Originally quoted in Filomena Mazzei, interviewed by Antoinette Lo Busco, typed transcript, 7, box 1, "Italians in Chicago" Oral History Project.
5 Matt, chapter 5, *Homesickness*.

a family's untold stories[6] – Antonietta experienced what Akhtar refers to as psychic growth and alternation alongside new forms of self-expression. Here, Antonietta's unequivocal resourcefulness and responsibility toward the well-being of her loved ones were reaffirmed in a context of crisis and displacement. They offered further proof to Loris of her commitment and dependability – two fundamental attributes he needed to hear over and over again as he prepared to make the monumental move to join Antonietta and leave his world behind.

— Montreal 15-1-49 —

Mio amore,[7]
Even this time I would deserve to be punished a little with few explanations, you know why I say this, I am a little late in replying to you, but I must say that you are starting to imitate me. Several days have passed since I received your news, but I don't worry too much about this, there are countless reasons for the delay, of course I hope neglect is not one of them. I believe you think of me as much as I think of you, that you love me as much as I love you, for the moment this is all I need for my heart to be at peace and to leave behind my worries. I don't know why I didn't write to you in the past few days, every night I would return from work with the intention of doing so, but then, in part because I was tired, in part because of the homework for my English class, I would end up in bed exhausted desperate for sleep, and I worried that I had not written to you. It is always like this, believe me when this happens to me, I think of you more than ever, and I remember you with an intensity that you cannot imagine.

    I continue to work and it's going well enough, often the Italian girl next to me tells me that I must be deeply in love, do you know

---

6 As an exception to the lack of scholarship on silence, see Baldassar, "Transnational Families and the Provision of Moral and Emotional Support," 385–409. On associated guilt feelings in a migration process, see Baldassar, "Guilty Feelings and the Guilt Trip," 81–9.
7 My love.

Traumas of Separation and Displacement 181

why? It's easy to guess, you are the only one I talk about, your name comes up all of the time, every day I remember something new, every song, every single thing, and often reality beckons while my gaze and my mind are absent, and my mouth is silent to any other call, isn't it strange? Perhaps it's not strange for someone who knows what it means to love; what can I do but recollect the past? Only I know when I can call the past back, and so, I would like to keep dreaming, fall asleep now and wake up and find you next to me, it would be too beautiful. Sadly I must wait, and open my eyes to reality, accept the circumstances that fate has reserved for us, hoping always that it will be kind to us and grant us the happiness we believe is well deserved. Yes, all I dream about is to see you soon, believe me, I miss you so very much, not for nothing but I truly believe that in you I have found a friend, a confidant, someone I can depend on to comfort me. Believe me, my Loris, not every day is rosy here, we have our worries, our tribulations, yes, my darling, each of us has a cross to bear, small ones, big ones! I will end this letter now as I am writing in bed and it's already nearly midnight, I'm a little tired, and tomorrow, Sunday, I will write a long detailed letter. I will explain many things, about this, I wanted to tell you that my *papà* went to the bank for the first set of papers, now we need to meet with the emigration [immigration] office as a family. We will go next Saturday because I had to work today. Accept this letter as a prelude of the letter I will be writing tomorrow, remember me and love me forever, may your love be as deep and sincere as before, never do anything to diminish it, know that I love you so very much. Many ardent kisses, your Nietta

Kisses to your *mamma* and the family

Greetings and best wishes to your parents whom we remember always.

— Montreal 16-1-49 —

Mio infinitamente caro,[8]
May this be one of the many testimonies of my love that I have given to you, if I write to you this evening, I am doing it to keep my word that I gave to you yesterday, and because I have no doubt that my

8 My infinitely dearest one.

182 January 1949 to July 1949

eyes will not close tonight. Imagine your Nietta, sadder than ever, her face distraught in a way you probably never witnessed before, try to imagine what she looks like, and you will know what I mean, what I have just lived through a few hours ago, I don't think I ever experienced before. My *mamma* became sick, she suffered a severe nervous breakdown and heartache, she looks like a rag, and to see her like this tonight, makes me feel dreadful. Oh! Loris there is so much sorrow in my heart! What agony! Just imagine that I rushed out of the house like a crazy woman in search of something that could revive her, without knowing it, I ended up at the home of my *papà*'s business partner with my heart on my sleeve and breathless. I don't know how it is that I am still standing, maybe it's my nerves that keep me going, and of course, I am not able to sleep, oh no! I am always worried that my *mamma* will collapse again. She is resting now with the help of an injection of morphine that the doctor gave her. My poor *mamma*! Loris, do you see what life holds in store? I feel so disheartened, I don't even have the strength to think of anything, if you only knew how desperate I have felt, sobbing a few moments ago in my room, and how much I appealed to my *nonna*, a good and caring woman, and I thought of you too, yes, even you.

You see this letter was supposed to be about something else, it was supposed to give you some of my *papà*'s helpful advice, in a few words, a short summary of what life is like here so that you can see things as they are, so that you can clearly understand how we live here – so that, in a word, we are free of responsibility and so that one day, you will not regret coming over, as other recently arrived Italians do. He will do everything he can to help you, all he needs is the reassurance that you will not one day come to regret your decision to come here, as many men have experienced when they sent for their own families. Of course, these are harsh words to receive from someone whom you believe is helping you. You see, I did not want to write these words to you for fear that you might delay things a little, but I felt compelled to do so for no other reason than for my own conscience. But all of this is meaningless for you, it must not matter, you will see, you will like it here because I am here, because we will learn to create our own happiness, and we must be together, my Loris, we must see each other soon. Oh! How much I wish for it, I believe that if we must suffer, it's much better to suffer together, whether here or at the end of the Earth, we must see each other again, we must live our days together, we must be close to each other to love one another.

Oh Loris, how horrifying it is to be alone, especially when things go wrong, it's very hard, now for the first time, I have felt it, not only today but for a few days since my *mamma* has fallen ill, more than physical, it is a moral anguish. I cannot say anything more, when you will be here, it will be easier for me to talk with you about it. Loris, please, don't go telling a word to my family about this, it must remain between you and me, they would suffer terribly from it. Let's hope that my *mamma* will feel better tomorrow and always. If I have time, I will write to you again tomorrow to tell you about everything else and to explain certain matters. Tonight, I don't feel like writing or thinking too much about things, my head is spinning and I will try to get some rest. My *papà* didn't call me, my *mamma* must be sleeping. Loris, my darling, please, love me forever, think of me, think of our reunion, which must take place because we wish for it and because we love each other. Please give my greetings to your family, and my dearest, most affectionate, sincere kisses. I love you.

Your Nietta

Forgive my messy writing, try to understand what I am saying even if the sentences are not clearly written. Kisses

— Venice 16-1-49 (Sunday 1800) —

Amatissima mia Nietta,[9]

Never will I forget, or try to forget, those phrases and anecdotes that we composed declaring our love for each other, even if we have had a few moments of opposition or doubt, which at times compromises the sincerity of a phrase or two, these are memories that are proof of our trust and our promises. Sometimes we make mistakes more out of our euphoria than out of rational causes, even if in certain situations the reasons are negligible, nothing escapes me as I do things right, nothing overtakes me with obsession, because I tend to be objective about us, and aware of every detail. May this assure you that though I am in pain and feel discouraged, I do not exaggerate my ideas and

---

9 My dearest beloved Nietta.

thoughts because I carefully explain things in the best possible order, first so that I do not regret or change my ideas.

Your analogy is wise though a little too profound, which I happily accept as it allowed me to learn about your diligence and good sense in reading me. Good girl, my Nietta, tiny but bright, as fast as a spinning top and perspicacious, even if you ask me if I have forgotten that famous phrase: A love without trust is like a flower without fragrance. No! My answer now is, no! Most firmly no, since a flower without fragrance is deprived of its beauty, while our love is inscribed with the most sincere trust that was born in our hearts, despite our desolation and the long distance between us, beyond the spiritual beauty of our bond that connects us in indissoluble ways with conviction and hope, that we may embrace this love and with your head leaning against my heart as we breathe the winds of a sensible individual who eagerly and passionately wishes to make us happy. For this reason, others view me as demanding and difficult to please; it is not right that you are the one who bears the consequences of this, but I understand your concerns and your principles, yes, I understand you and I appreciate you. You are a good woman because you love me, you are a good woman because you care for me like a mother, and I appreciate your perfections and your virtues. You must be sure of this, you must believe it and convince your state of mind when it is lost in dangerous stormy seas; I understand how much you love me, your concern for me and your love. And the different conditions we now face are humanly reasonable in our peaceful objective, and for this, my error comes to mind, rather, my exuberance, when I was feeling down. For this reason it is my duty to share the negative outcome between us, and not to let it rest only with you, because it is logical to convince oneself that delays are our fault or of our doing, many times they are not.

Let's be clear that we should always try to be thorough in our observations, in our writing, and our time as we depend on its development and continual progress. May our continuing attachment, may this path be the way for me to reach you soon, and may time this year move more expediently than any other year, so that I may receive in a flash the confirmation of my imminent departure. May fate be kind to us during this interval, may it grant us health and happiness, may it concede the most extraordinary joy of my life, that is, to join you with

Traumas of Separation and Displacement 185

all the trust and confidence, with all the happiness and willingness
that has made me a more mature man during the anguish of waiting
so that I may erase all of your regrets and embrace all of our desires.
I await from you the latest most positive news possible, from you I
await news on the latest developments regarding my application. Send
me news on everything, keep me informed about everything, and
with this, you will be making your Lorissin infinitely happy! Inquire
constantly about my application, you will see it will be for our benefit.

I am leaving some space here for my *mamma* who wants to thank
you for your greeting card and confirm that we received it. Sincere
enormous kisses for you now, with all of my affection, your Loris

Today, the Venezia team won 7–0 and they are now in 4th position.
That's good, isn't it? Or better yet, they are good, no?

– Montreal [n.d.][10] –

Mio Tesoro,[11]
Here I am writing to you after a break of several days with a soul
that is calmer and a heart that beats more ardently with love for you.
Throughout all the highs and lows of these last few days I never forgot
about the one person who thinks of me. In reality, you were present
more than ever, and I thought of you with indescribable constancy.
All has passed now, the storm that turned our family upside down
has subsided, peace has returned, let's hope it will continue in this
way, always. My *mamma* is feeling much better; during these days, I
was especially close to her, I was a real little homemaker, I took her to
see the doctor every other day, and did everything I could to comfort
her. It's Saturday and my *papà* who is home, took her to the doctor's
(we never work on Saturdays here), and I stayed home to write to you,
because today, I just could not take it anymore. I felt terrible for not
writing to you after that desperate letter I wrote to you on Sunday, but
believe me, I had not one free moment to myself, and in the evening
when I could have had a little time, there was always someone coming
over to visit my *mamma*, they would often leave late, and I could do
nothing but go to bed and close my eyes. Even today as I was starting

10 The letter was likely written a few days after 16 January 1949.
11 My precious.

186 January 1949 to July 1949

to write to you, actually, just as I was holding the writing paper in my hands, the brother of G ... arrived at the door, he arrived a month ago from Italy, and so I had to keep company with him. He stayed for supper, and is now talking to my *mamma* and *papà*.

I received your letters several days ago, though I had wanted to respond immediately, one of the letters vexed me a little, I won't deny it, we could have many discussions about this, but it's better to leave things aside, that is, even if I wanted to tell you what I thought about it, I would not be able to do so. You know that I am unable to harbour resentment, and before I express myself, I consider my words carefully because I do not want to hurt anyone. You see Loris, my adored one, you tell me that my letters lack teeth, I know what you mean by this, that is, perhaps I don't say too much about your arrival (even though I believe I have always told you everything), we must be a little more patient, you must not believe that things get done in two days. My *papà* has already paid a visit to the bank to complete the papers for the deposit of the funds, he then called the agent for him to visit at the emigration [immigration] office, but he was told that we must first meet with a notary and make a declaration. Now, do you see how much my *papà* is helping us? I urge him to do everything as soon as possible, believe me, I wish all of this would be over and done with, and that you would be already here, this is all I wish for, this is all I dream of, this is all I aspire to, but we need to be patient for the required time for the papers to be processed, and then, we will be able to embrace each other, and start a new and beautiful life together. You will see, my darling, this year for sure, you will be here with me, near me, close to your Tetina, who loves you so very much.

I hear the brother of G ... complaining about not being familiar with the language, it's really very hard for someone who comes here. This is my *papà*'s biggest concern, he is afraid that you will not be happy here, there is plenty of work here, and he will help you without a doubt; however, as long as you don't speak the language, it will be difficult for you to find work in your trade. Just the other evening we were talking about this in reference to an aviation officer who was very capable of working as an electrician here, but they told him that they will not be able to hire him unless he can speak the language, this is the way it is, my Loris, don't worry, and don't give up, the first

Traumas of Separation and Displacement   187

months will be hard for you, as they have been for everyone, but then, you will get used to it, hopefully your diplomas will help you. Don't feel discouraged, just think that every immigrant has had to experience a difficult period before finding work, everyone has a story to tell, stories that recount the most painful and least painful of stories, for you it will be different, very different. Here, you will find what most of them did not have upon arriving, a home, a little Tetina, a second family. Oh! Loris, how happy I am to think about all of this and that most beautiful of days when I will be holding you in my arms. Together with your letter, I also received a letter from W ... I was very pleased to hear from her, tell her that I will respond soon and thank her kindly for me. Please extend my greetings to your family and to you, my most dear and affectionate kisses,

Your Nietta

PS Did you have your hair cut as you said you would in Rome? You had written in one of your letters that you had some work done on your teeth, you must be even more handsome now. Make sure you are handsome just for me. (I haven't changed, I am always jealous!)

[written on the paper's sidelines:] Many kisses and greetings from my *papà* and *mamma*.

— Venice 23-1-49 —

Mia Nietta carissima,[12]

The current date tells you what day we are today, and how much I care for it. It's Sunday, a Sunday that is as grey and colourless, as stupid and languid as ever, this is what a day of rest amounts to after a stressful week. If I revealed to you that besides going to Holy Mass and basking in the sun on the Riva degli Schiavoni after lunch, both done over two hours, how absurd all of this is to me despite it being true. But I won't stop here to tell you the pros and cons, my memories quickly transport me to the past when I wrote about and confirmed a similar experience at other times. In the past, I disapproved of my reasons for feeling this way. You will certainly remember this occasion, and compare it with my present feeling, I am certain that you will not find contradictions. This way of venting through words is

12 My dearest Nietta.

188 January 1949 to July 1949

all true for me, it's an acceptable release that is permitted I hope to me, whom in dealing with uncertainty and loss, I do not create hyperboles or tragedies. Mine is a moral form of venting that finds solace in speaking with you, in writing to you my feelings. I am very conscious of the fact that this will not make you smile nor will it please you. This is the life I lead, these are the days I live.

Many things have altered my youthful spirit, they have equally altered my optimistic view on life and for this reason, I am thinking more consciously about the path that will lead to the future, I look at tomorrow with eyes wide open, with the conviction that thorny roses adorn my path perhaps all the more since I believe that a rose without thorns is worthless, even more so since the rose wraps its stem with thorns to protect itself from the violence of man who will easily sow any vile act, here is the good fortune of this simple flower, beautiful for itself and its surroundings as it seeks to injure nothing and protect itself from harm. I look at tomorrow more conscientiously, I see and foresee joys and sorrows, with my experience I seek a way out of a situation hoping to overcome any challenge. In the past few days, or months rather, life has thrown a few balls my way, some of which were inevitable; I became more understanding, more reasonable, more responsible. All of these are privileges that add to my experience, so that one day you will sing about your friend who is very aware of family consequences. He is more than a friend because he will love you even more and will find courage in sorrow and in love. Maybe I miss this, maybe this is compensated by initiatives, and if I miss it, it is because I am alone, and I have no one to turn to.

And yet, I am at peace, perhaps a better tomorrow awaits me, and it is for this reason that my day is filled with the conviction that I am doing this for the benefit of my family, that it is my responsibility to ensure moral delight, something that was missing today, and as such, it is so much more difficult to trick the slow passing of time to reach my objective, which is simply to join you as soon as possible. Your letter that I received yesterday comforts me a little more than the others because it transmits all that you are doing for me, it is the imprint of your love, it is the sign of your preparations in light of my arrival. I hope your letters are as auspicious as this one, replete with more conviction, and I hope to receive soon a consoling confirmation. I am

Traumas of Separation and Displacement   189

always anxious especially because of this, in trepidation just for this, these days offer interesting narratives for my progress.

My faith in your words knows no boundaries because I know that it is your heart that compels you to write these words. May my faith galvanize you to succeed in your endeavours for me, may my faith sustain your undertaking which will receive recognition from my heart.

All of this gives me enormous gratification and happiness, it helps me to understand how much you love me, as your last letter confirms. Let's continue on this course, oh my Tetina (not always so late, please). (I'm kidding, truthfully even my letters are never late, I can assure you of my utmost punctuality.) (Compare the dates and you will see if I am not speaking the truth.) Yesterday, Saturday, I received your letter and read carefully one of your lines, it led me to think immensely about you and your family. Just as I had hoped, you paid a visit to the emigration [immigration] office for more information about my application. This made me very happy, and it strengthened your promises to me. At this moment, however, I leave you by thanking you and sending you many kisses and greetings. And for you, a thousand special kisses, because you are the only one I want to kiss on the lips and hold close in my arms.

Loris

— Montreal 24-1-49 —

Mio adorato Loris,[13]

This evening I left at 7 to go to school, which begins at 7:30, but I had planned to stop by *Signora C ...*'s home and I left half an hour earlier. But the first half hour passed quickly, followed by the next, and I was still there, by the time I reached the school all the doors were closed shut, I would have wanted to wait but I would have caught a cold for no reason, and so, I headed home. Here I found my *mamma* and *papà* already sleeping, I had no choice but to do the same, my eyes looked around with a certain sadness, the same sadness I feel when I am alone, as always, my missing you overwhelmed me, with it came my desire to write to you. I remember the words my *mamma* said as we boarded the airplane for Montreal: "Who knows what it will be like for

13 My adored Loris.

us to live there, Antonietta," and I replied while sobbing: "Oh! For you it will be beautiful, you will be near your husband. For me, instead …!"

For me, as long as you are not here, nothing appeals to me, nothing pleases me, and if at times, I find myself there, all I do is think of you, and I am surprised at myself thinking, "Why am I alone? Is it because Loris is not here with me? How much he would love being here!" I think this would especially be the case if the activities are to your liking, it's always like this. For instance, yesterday I went to see an Italian play, performed by Italian actors from New York (who knows if you will understand that word! What a loss if you don't attend English classes, right Loris?) The play was entitled, *Cuore di mamma*.[14] A moving story that was highly appreciated, from my perspective, they were actors of second or rather, third rate — with the exception of a few who gave a fairly good performance. Of course, if Venetian critics had been here, for instance, someone like your brother or like Loris, who are used to the more famous, the more renowned plays at the Goldoni Theatre, they would have abstained from applauding, in order not to be caught by others, they would have applauded silently … with their nails! Don't laugh at my expressions, please, I enjoy talking with you like this because I feel like the same Antonietta who lived in Italy, understood and understanding, reflective, and at the same time, cheerful. Here I feel like a stranger to everyone, the truth is that I am, because no one here knows me profoundly, no one knows what is going on in my little brain. In any case, even if the play wasn't the most exhilarating, it once again stirred in my heart all the nostalgia I have for my Italian land, the play brought us all back to our Italic blue sky, it compelled us to imagine the seashores, our valleys, our cities, and, I would have wanted you to be near me to feel what I feel, so that you too could experience what "nostalgia for the distant homeland" means.

My adored Loris, only one thing I ask of you, if I thought for a moment that I would not see you here I would feel the worst punishment ever, only one hope sustains me, that is to see you, to see you here, and to never let you go. The other evening as I was walking, a lady we know, saw me and asked me to stop by her home for a few minutes,

---

14 The play was later turned into the film, *Cuore di Mamma* [*A Mother's Heart*], directed by Salvatore Samperi in 1969.

Traumas of Separation and Displacement 191

she is the sister of *Signor* S .... The agent, shortly after, he came by as well, and told me that soon he will be looking at your application, and that he will not let it go until everything is finalized, encouraging isn't it, my precious? This year, the process of emigration [immigration] has been simplified. You will see that everything will work out for us, according to our wishes, you believe me, don't you? As a matter of fact, let me give you some news, yesterday for the first time since I arrived in Montreal, I met the gentleman who had travelled with me on the Rome-Montreal flight. Do you remember the dark skinny man dressed in blue? Perhaps you do, you don't have a poor memory as ... I do! Well, I met him yesterday at the theatre, he is now married. I don't know if you know his story, ten years ago, he let his fiancée leave for America, during this time, they wrote to each other continuously, now she has called him over; what resilience, no? Or we can call it "true love." I asked him how he felt about being here, and his wife replied that he wants to return to Italy, except he won't go back. I am convinced of this, everyone says this in the beginning, and then they stay here, my *papà* is an example. We exchanged only a few words because people needed to pass in the hallway, but perhaps I will see them again, do you see that even in a city like Montreal, it's possible to run into people that you know?

Don't scold me, I still didn't have the photographs taken, I have another promise to keep, I didn't forget. Oh yes, the ring, everything will come to us a little at a time, of course, I would like you to buy it in Italy because they are more lovely and less expensive, what can I say, with the first dollars that I earned I made a gift to my *mamma* and *papà*, then I bought a little something for myself. Don't worry, I will do everything that I promised you. *Signora* C ... called me this evening to tell me that she has prepared a package for you, a nice calendar, I saw it this evening, and I will send it to you tomorrow. Kisses and best wishes from my parents. I wanted to write to your *mamma* to thank her for her words, but there is no space left here, tell her that I will write to her another time and that I think of her often with much affection together with everyone there with you.

To you, my darling love, a dear embrace and many kisses on your beautiful mouth.

Your Nietta

— Venice 24-1-49 —

Nietta mia amatissima,[15]

I cannot wait a second longer to reply to you, from the time I received your letter and now. Under these circumstances, one second is like an hour or rather, a year of silence, your letter of tonight tells me so much, it was a letter that I had been waiting for (in reference to your last letter in which you tell me that you will provide more information in your next letter) though I felt something unusual, as I anxiously hurried home hoping to have received a letter from you, and there it was. You were there waiting for me, to tell me many things, so many, I believe, as I read your letter. Of course, I could not imagine your grave sorrow, such immeasurable sadness, but I wanted to join my profound sorrow with yours, a sorrow that you are feeling so deeply now. Your *mamma*'s illness has traced a deep groove in my heart, you can see it in my eyes. Poor *mamma*! This has profoundly turned my spirit, filling me with human thoughts and doubt, contrary to my own, because I love your *mamma* like I love mine, and I would doubtlessly have saddened her further with my deaf-tone remarks. Your *mamma* whom I cannot distinguish from my own, has loved me always like my own *mamma* in joy and in sorrow, she has shown an extraor-dinary understanding of my disappointments, she has nurtured an affection that was then reciprocated to her. If her affection was her instrument for comforting me, by way of recognition I cannot offer anything but affection, it is a veritable quid pro quo, here emerges a pain similar to yours as her true daughter, I understand how terribly sad you must feel, now that such horror has struck your *mamma*.

A paragraph more steeped in sorrow could not have ended my day, of course, it's normal to be aware of everything and it's logical to also partake in the sorrow. It's a sorrow that is generated through a feeling of privilege, a feeling that is constructed through concrete proof that is not only made up of words, it's a regret, perhaps, that eclipses the joy of when I saw you together both glowing with serenity and good health. This is a sudden blow, an unknown calamity, never could I have imagined a similar incident, even if I read between the lines a little bitterness in your reflections. I read and not for nothing did I

---

15 Nietta my dearest love.

Traumas of Separation and Displacement 193

understand why you feel so sad, when a few nights ago you repeated the sentence: we all have our worries, we all feel and carry the weight of our cross, that night, I almost wanted to speak to the wind for you to hear my conviction, for you to be reassured that my road too has its share of slopes and rocks.

Let's not overestimate or underestimate this important reflection, it's a reality that everyday life is made up of crosses and agonies that surround us. It's also true that the fate of each of us is already written, whatever good or bad we will experience, we don't know about it, and when exactly will it strike? Oh Nietta, my precious, I cannot comfort you in this enormous sorrow; my sorrow is as deep as the urgency for me to stay calm. I have no one to turn to, I only have my words, my prayers, and with the exception of my poor heart, I do not possess treasures that can surround you with care and consideration. Oh, dear hearts, small and wide boundaries that circumscribe you, seal even this drop of love, may you be the high mountains that have always enclosed every episode in my Tetina's life. The heart is the fabric that most easily tears from sorrow, it is for this reason that the wound takes so long to heal. Oh, please cheer up, my little Nietta, reason is no match for these forces, and it's certainly not going to help diminish the pain, but my heart still possesses some courage and tranquility. May this tranquility serve as a model for you to overcome the pain, may this courage of mine strengthen you for the love of your *mamma*, and since no greater ill is possible, pray now, and entrust the Lord, our Father with hope. May this be the spring of trust that reveals to you the sentiment of faith in believing that we are all subject to danger. May your strength in loving me, as you confess, be the same as the wilful sacrifice of having me so far from you, as long as, and despite this, we will be reunited soon, on this I did not waste words in letting you understand. I am always the same when it comes to my principles, I am always the master of my will, this indicator of my decision and awareness is discussed in my previous letter, whose tone is similar to this one. [?] I could never go back on my decision, or my steps, especially now that a path is opening for me. Only for this reason and with extraordinary awareness I write my destiny, only for this reason and with much responsibility, I carefully consider my every decision. What a tragedy it would be if it were the opposite. If

I did not love you enough, I could have imposed myself on your will and I would have made every decision on your behalf. Since only one fact can attest to the absolute trust you have in me, any other comment is void of meaning.

Let it be clear and undeniable that one singular objective leads me to share our wish for eternal happiness, that is, the desire to love you entirely and forever, and to be close to your loved ones, to whom I gratefully remember. It is only for this reason that I see any comment as senseless because you have always been my wish, it was I who had taken initiative on every word, every thought, it is for this reason that I deny a moral return to my own decisions. I have no doubt of the kind of unpredictabilities that are in store for me in the new world, but I am more and more ready to meet them, and how horrible it would be for me to give this all up. Life is made of experiences, and I am making a collection of them – I am aware of this. Believe in these words, if only because they are spoken by the mouth of someone who has provided a memory of himself, a consent to a promised love and a faith in love. The consciousness with which you wrote all of this is not extraordinary for its loyalty and sincerity but rather it is an instrument of the strong-willed, a virtue of the pure. Do not think for a moment that you offended me with this, I can only be happy for the way that you are, all of this pleases me especially so that I may carefully consider this new world.

Reassure your *papà* of my well-being, and my realistic view regarding his concerns, of course, it is also true that I would not want to take advantage of your kindness. You, my little Nietta, my only hope, the only friend of my heart, you can understand my language better, you who has had intimate relations with my thoughts and my heart, you will know how deeply important my words of joy are. A clear and sincere yes must reassure you more than ever, and remind you of my immeasurable need to be near you again. For you, may a thousand joys serve as encouragement. For me, may sorrow be a sign of my indelible desire to love you. Kisses and greetings from your Loris.

— 7 —

"It almost feels like you are already here"

The Metonymy of Writing and Feelings of Proximity

MISSING EACH OTHER was hard work for separated couples. It required constant negotiation of the other lover's absence in the everyday commingled with the need to postpone communicating to the other until the advent of a day's quiet moment. In those moments, the letter's material existence (the paper, the pen, the ink, the calligraphy, and the envelope) represented a form of respite for the separated lovers. At the same time, letter-writing served as a physical reminder and an emotional remembrance of the other and the imaginary with the other into the present, past, and future. It is thus not coincidental that enormous importance was assigned to every letter – along with other artifacts posted in the envelope.[1]

The letter afforded distance and proximity in a person's existence. Through its recollection and reflection of ideas and events, the letter produced, in the words of Cécile Dauphin, a theatrical show that offered an invitation to dream.[2] The desire to dream was rooted in the performance of writing the self and in the reading of that performance by the recipient.[3] Letter-writing demanded also inventiveness and interpretations from its correspondents, in which lovers of epistolary relationships summoned up images of each other, without the visible presence of the other, and sometimes reacted joyfully to their own creations.[4]

---

1 Passerini, chapter 7, *Europe in Love, Love in Europe.*
2 Dauphin, "Letter-Writing Manuals in the Nineteenth Century," 141.
3 Milne, "Email and Epistolary Technologies," n.p.
4 Milne, *Letters, Postcards, Email,* 9. Cited in Perry, *Women, Letters, and the Novel,* 101.

Defined as "fragments of experience" by historian Martyn Lyons, love letters may have striven for spontaneity and in the process, affected a planned disorder in the writer's thoughts; however, if too much contrivance transpired in the message, suspicion of the contents' authenticity would likely arise.[5] While corresponding lovers tried to evaluate how their messages would be received in response to fear or to "*l'angoisse de la réception*," aptly described by Jean-Louis Cornille,[6] the spontaneity with which they were written cannot be underestimated. These letters thus underscore fractured mirrors of a life, though not without offering a close reading of micro-stories told in their own voice, and set against a broader historical context.

References in letters to the letter writer's body, writing scenes, the places in a home where a letter was opened or read, contribute to the creation of an imagined presence, whereby a sense of immediacy, intimacy, and presence are conveyed. In the letters of Antonietta and Loris, the letters were treated in significant ways with a symbolism that determined how letters were communed with, kissed, embraced, and forced to stand in for the absent lover in epistolary novels.[7] In this "intimacy of absence," shared dreams were woven, and in the realness of writing, sending, and receiving of letters, the dreams were assured.[8] Moreover, in the references of the "here and now" time and distance were collapsed, and as Milne writes, depending on the eloquence of the letter writer, the recipient could feel as if they were actually face to face.[9]

When reflecting on epistolary writing in relation to face-to-face communication, physical presence (or co-presence) tends to be understood as more authentic, less performative, and less mediated. Face-to-face communication represents the ideal paradigm of the

---

5 Lyons, "Love Letters and Writing Practices," 233–6.

6 Cited in Lyons, "Love Letters and Writing Practices," 233. Cornille, "L'Assignation, analyse d'un pacte épistolaire," 34.

7 Milne, *Letters, Postcards, Email*, 14. Cited in Perry, *Women, Letters, and the Novel*, 101. On Italian postwar migration writing, see also, Ricatti, "First Love and Italian Postwar Migration Stories."

8 Milne, *Letters, Postcards, Email*, 55. Cited in Bossis, "Methodological Journeys through Correspondences," 69.

9 Milne, *Letters, Postcards, Email*, 15.

The Metonymy of Writing and Feelings of Proximity   197

meeting of minds.[10] To borrow from philosopher Andrew Feenberg, "Communication seems most complete and successful where the person is physically present 'in' the message. This physical presence is supposed to be the guarantor of authenticity: you can look your interlocutor in the eye and search for tacit signs of truthfulness or falsehood, where context and tone permit a subtler interpretation of the spoken word."[11] Yet, epistolary communication brought a unique voice to the relationship between lovers and migrants. Through absence, "the genesis of all letter writing,"[12] letter-writing became a creative, spiritual, literary practice opening up a discursive space in which constellations of subjectivities and intimacies might not otherwise be articulated.[13]

Letter-writing entailed a physical action as well. In the words of calligrapher Francesca Biasetton, handwriting left traces of the gesture of writing: the hand holding firmly a pen or a pencil, moving in space and on paper or on other writing surfaces. The contact often created a friction while producing a pencil's rustling or a fountain pen's squeaking. Writing was also about organizing words on a sheet of paper, dimensions of which (in the margins as well) were memorized by the writer.[14] With the thoughts and words insisting to be written, the author would shuffle blank sheets to the front of the writing pad.

Taking the practice of writing love letters further afield, the role of handwritten letters in today's age of information and digital technologies is worth reflecting on. As Clare Brant argues, letter-writing is not dying but rather mutating, cross-breeding, and developing new identities in conversation with fax, phone text, online chats, and especially email. Ironically, it is through the introduction of digital technologies that the practice of letter-writing has gained newfound energies. Like other forms of ego-documents (biographies and autobiographies), Margaretta Jolly writes, letters persist as historical and biographical resources, journalistic petitions, correspondence courses, therapeutic exercises, celebrity or literary artifacts, and they also morph into faxes,

10 Milne, *Letters, Postcards, Email*, 16. Cited in Feenberg, "The Written World," 22.
11 Milne, *Letters, Postcards, Email*, 16.
12 Ibid. Cited in Lowenthal, *Lady Mary Wortley Montagu and the Eighteenth-Century Familiar Letter*, 24.
13 Milne, *Letters, Postcards, Email*, 52.
14 Biasetton, *La bellezza del segno*, 11.

emails, testimony, personal ads, and visual communications. In the digital economy of writing, letters have "returned to the foreground of the cultural imagination."[15]

— Montreal 1-2-49 —

Mio adorato Loris,[16]

I should be replying to both of your letters, one that was received on Saturday and the other one yesterday, but I will limit myself to the first one so you will not complain. I wanted to write to you last night, but honestly, I was not feeling well enough. I had returned home from work with a bad cold, and I did nothing but drink something hot and go to bed. I feel much better now, even though I am not completely out of the woods yet, but there is nothing to be done, seasonal colds! I did not take a day off work because I didn't want to miss a day, and tonight, more than anything else, I feel tired (you will notice it from the errors here). It doesn't matter. I am writing to you anyway, and don't think it's going to be a short letter, no, it's going to be the usual long letter. I could not fall asleep without writing to you, I just couldn't, tonight, we talked a lot about you, about our future, about us and my family, you cannot imagine how comforted I am in discussing these things, it almost feels like you are already here with us. This gives me courage, it gives me tremendous courage, so much so that I feel happy to the point that I forget the insignificant and boring life that I lead every day, and so my adored one, don't think that I lead an exciting life here. I need to be at work at 8 o'clock in the morning, this means I need to wake up at 7, sometimes even earlier, since it takes me over half an hour to reach the factory by tram, the streets are impossible to walk on, they are covered in ice and snow.

I leave it up to you to imagine how tired I am at night and how much I feel like going out to enjoy myself. Even last Saturday *papà* wanted to take me to the Casa d'Italia especially since *mamma* was

---

15 Jolly, "Introduction," 4.
16 My adored Loris.

Montreal 1-2-49 3

Mio adorato Loris,

dovrei rispondere a due tue, una ricevuta sabato
e una ieri sera ma mi limito a rispondere solo
a quella prima perché tu non abbia a lamentarti –
Ieri sera volevo scrivere ma ti dico la verità non ne
avevo nessuna voglia sono venuta a casa con un raffred-
dore forte alla mano e non ho fatto altro che prendere
qualche cosa di caldo e andare a letto, ne invece mi
sento molto migliorata sebbene non sia del tutto
a posto, ma cosa vuoi fare, malattie di stagione!
Non ho potuto lasciare il lavoro perché mi dispiaceva
a perdere una giornata e questa sera più che raffred-
data mi sento stanca (puoi notare dagli errori). Ma
non importa, ti scrivo ugualmente e non credere
una lettera breve, no, sarà lunga come di consueto,
non potevo andare a letto senza scriverti, non avrei
tutto, questa sera abbiamo parlato molto di te, del
nostro avvenire, di noi, della mia famiglia e non
puoi immaginare quanto mi consola il discutere
di tali cose mi sembra quasi che tu sia più qui
con me e m'incoraggia ciò, m'incoraggia tanto
che mi sento felice al punto di dimenticare la
vita insignificante e noiosa che finalmente trascorro, e sai mio adorato, non credere che sia
tanto divertente, la mattina alle 8 devo trovar
mi sul lavoro, sicché devo alzarmi alle 7 ed anche
prima perché quasi sempre mi vale ½ di tram per arriva

feeling better and was willing to go out, but I preferred to stay home and rest, I really don't feel like going out much, especially in the winter when it's so cold. I have even stopped attending my English classes; if I don't learn it in one year, I will learn in two. In any case, I get by better in French, it's much easier. You see my dear Loris, I am not able to enjoy myself, it makes sense, you are not here and without you how can anything appeal to me? I bet that if you were here, I would not be tired in the evenings! But even that day will come, won't it my darling? If you only heard the conversations we have on the sewing floor, the girls tell me that I shouldn't be so in love, that it's not worth it, that all men are the same. Instead I insist on telling them that it's not like that for me, that my man is different, that it's worth feeling this way for you because you deserve it. They joke and laugh about how I feel, but for me, all of this is of no importance, because I love you, and I am not ashamed of telling anyone, I think they say this more out of envy than anything else because a love as powerful and sincere as ours is rare.

As you know I stayed home for a few days to be with *mamma*. *Papà* didn't want me to go back to work, but the factory supervisor called me several times to tell me that she has found the right girl who is willing to work hard. I caught the fish by the hook and do you know what I did? (It was obvious that she needed me.) I asked for a raise, so now I make $6 more per week. I will let some time pass, and then I will ask for another raise. Otherwise, I will change jobs. Here, there are many opportunities. There's something for everyone. I am sure she won't fire me, she needs me too much. So, while before I was paid 45¢ per hour, now, I am paid 55¢, not bad, right? And if you come down, I can keep working, here we work, but we gain a lot of satisfaction from our work, that is, if the good weather ever gets here. It will be fun to visit new places, not now, however, let's be honest. What else can I tell you, my precious? That I love you, that I think of you, that I ardently hope for your arrival, that I live to see you again and to adore you. In the next few days I will write to you again in response to the last letter I received yesterday. My *mamma* is feeling better again as she continues to be treated by the doctor. I realize I just wrote a letter with scattered thoughts, forgive me, the next one will be better. Many many kisses, Antonietta.

[To Loris's mother:]

The Metonymy of Writing and Feelings of Proximity 201

My dearest *mamma*, I don't want to close this letter without writing a few lines to you and thank you for your very kind writing which made me very happy. I think of you, always, because you are a dear person to me, because you are the mother of Loris. I know you care for me, and why wouldn't I reciprocate your love for me? For me, you are my second *mamma*, and honestly, I'm sorry that you are so far away. This is what fate has decided for us, but we will be able to keep loving each other, hoping that God will allow us to see each other again. Many kisses to you and to papà, L ... and M ... and A ..., L ..., and the little V ... Many kisses for you, your Nietta

— Venice 4-2-49 —

Nietta mia carissima,[17]

I am the one this time who was not punctual, but please don't blame me as it is not my fault. I cannot be ambiguous, or rather, I must be precise, and I must pay attention to your writings because I know how much you love me and how much you need these lines to feel close to my heart, to love me, and to love me more. I cannot do any of this, not even remotely because I love you so dearly, and I know how awfully the long silences dishearten you; experience has shown me the torment of long and short periods of starvation, that it is always a condition for pain and worry. How many reasons have I given you in my defence now that I am in the wrong, a wrong that is justifiable nonetheless. Here it is. Since last Saturday, 29 January, I was sick in bed [?] yes, in bed with a minor infection, rather a mild form of diphtheria, which as you must know, is accompanied by high fever that knocks me out quite a bit. My throat hurt the most as my tonsils swelled and the infection induced awful pain to the point I was tossing and turning for days and nights on end. It's over now, all has passed without consequences, and I am still at home, it's been eight days, as the doctor advised me. Do not worry, I am fine now, since yesterday morning I even got out of bed and walked around the house. On Monday, I will go back to work. This is the reason I was compelled to delay writing my letter to you, however by Tuesday I still had not received a letter from you. At around 10 o'clock on Tuesday,

17 Nietta my dearest.

202   January 1949 to July 1949

while in bed, I saw my *mamma* deliver two letters to me, you can imagine that in that moment I was so excited to receive the mail that I no longer felt any pain. I don't remember if I began reading the long letter or the short one. I looked over the dates first, but one of the letters had the date written, the other did not!

The fact remains that I frantically read both, even though in my heart I was a little afraid of reading them, and was about to stop altogether to avoid reading bad news, just in case there would be any. Instead, the letters brought nothing but good news, and the joy they gave me was boundless. From the day I received the letter about your *mamma*'s illness, I had no other news, so of course, reading your good news in the last letter was a huge relief. I am happy because I can imagine your *mamma* once again in good health, I can imagine her content with her dear ones, because I can imagine you a young woman of the household busily helping her *mamma* with domestic chores. In the end, I am delighted to think of you, knowing that you are happy, and so, peace and joy have been restored, only remotely obscured during those days of tribulation. Good girl, my Tetina, I know that neither sacrifice nor hard work bother you, you will see that I will be more work than your *mamma*. You will see and you will remember this.

Joking aside, come on, let's be serious as we have always been, and let's think about other things, the more pressing and urgent matters. I understand my application papers have already been initiated. Thank you my dear Tetina, and thank your *papà* and your *mamma*. I cannot bear living so far away from you any longer, I would give my soul to be close to you. Keep at it, make sure all the papers are in order for my arrival in October this year, otherwise I'm done for ... Please think of me in total apprehension every moment of every day, I am literally counting the days, you cannot imagine how intense my desire is to see you again, to see you again is nothing, it's about having you next to me, loving you, being close to each other forever, and being forever grateful to the Lord for this blessing. I was very pleased to read the kind words that *Signora C* ... has for me, please tell her that I do not know yet how to thank her, and that I send her and her family my most heartfelt best wishes and a thousand greetings and kisses to her daughters, I will be sure to bring them a little souvenir of Venice. As for you, which of the most splendid gifts can I bring to you from

The Metonymy of Writing and Feelings of Proximity 203

Venice? I know, my heart, which is Venice along with a thousand kisses on your mouth. Your Loris

[Top of first page:] For your *papà* and *mamma* whom I think of with great affection, a huge kiss and greetings, Loris

— Venice 6-2-49 —

Nietta mia amatissima,[18]
To close this day with thoughts spun into words for you, that is, in words for you, seems to me the most beautiful, perhaps the most precious of thoughts. These thoughts came to me this morning as I woke up and glanced at your photo on my bedside. Immediately now that my mind is rested, my truest of thoughts turned to you with a prayer to the Virgin Mary, to her I pray so that she may protect you, keep you well and happy. This holiday morning, I prayed to her as usual, and I looked back nostalgically to all the holidays we celebrated together, here and in your hometown, those were real holidays because even our spirits were up, even our souls were celebrating, everything around us was radiating with joy. They were holidays and days close to you, even when there was some sorrow that spoiled our peace. The days were few, you will remember them because you were always cheerful, dark days were never part of our happiness. There was never a serious reason for them, we loved each other with the right dose in our hearts, and we love each other still, a deep and great love, nurtured by our strength and willingness to continue along this path. These words leap from my heart, much like dew draws tiny droplets in the verdant grass fields, it's like the dew of my life that opens and closes every single day in order to bring you joy, or at least, to try to make you happy. May my thoughts bring you happiness, much like my way of being, my traditions, my habits that are unchanging, only because I live with skeptical indifference for anything that is not part of my idol, that is, my love for you.

Oh, my Tetina, it is in this way that life finds me in slight disagreement and indifference, nothing in this life can give me back the glimmer of joy that I basked in when I was next to you, or rather, that I could have completely with you when you were close to me and I loved you near your home, near your places, near your heart. I find

18 Nietta my dearest love.

indifference, because, as you know well, I dislike a carefree life corrupted by today's modernity, which annihilates people's good habits, it distracts people from their good ways, compelling them to forget all that they had learned as adolescents. I honestly detest these things, only because they are not in agreement with my principles, that is to be a person of dignity, well-behaved, and a lover of beauty and goodness. It is especially because of this that I love you deeply, my darling little one, so beautiful because of your kindness and modesty, which make up who you are. Oh, when will I be able to tell you these things loud and clear? I hold onto the hope that this will happen, and soon, I hope that my papers will have reached a good point in the application process, I will discuss this in my next letter because I need to ask you for a few clarifications so that we do not make mistakes and waste time, because my most precious time is best spent speaking with you, telling you about my frustrations, telling you that I love you forever, and that I kiss you, always, forever your Loris

[At the top of the first page:] Kisses and greetings to your *mamma* and *papà*, your Loris

— Montreal 15-2-49 —

Mio indimenticabile Loris,[19]
This is the right word, the most accurate word, nothing can stop me from writing it, I cannot cite the moments that I do not think of you because you are always with me, you are always in my heart, and this is why the word *indimenticabile* [unforgettable] is not inaccurate or casually written, oh no my darling, no, believe me, even if I am occasionally not on time with my letters, I do not write late because I have forgotten about you or the promises that I made to you. No, if it were the case, I would not be worthy of your respect, of your love, which I believe is profound and sincere; every moment I have spent with you remains with me, indelibly in my mind because it was too beautiful. I know everything will work out if I wish it to, and why would I refuse my happiness? Believe in my love, have faith and trust always and you will not be mistaken, you will see that our dream will come true, I promise, believe in everything I tell you, believe in my love, a love that

19 My unforgettable Loris.

The Metonymy of Writing and Feelings of Proximity 205

fears no obstacles, I love you Loris, I love you, and I wish tomorrow would be our long-awaited day, oh, what bliss!

But everything cannot be solved in a moment's time, you know that. We are always discussing this at home; just yesterday my *papà* called S ... for more information, which I do not need to explain to you now, I will tell you later when everything will be resolved, until now all is proceeding well. We now have other matters to attend to, we are moving house, and in the first week of March we will have moved into our new home, on Sunday I visited our new place with my *papà*. It's a lovely apartment composed of 5 rooms, electric heating, and all the necessary amenities, he has rented it for one year. I think that in that time he is planning to build a little house, we will see if the plans work out, just the other evening as we were talking he said, "If Loris will come down, he will give me a hand," I don't even doubt it remotely because I know how much you enjoy working, isn't that right, Loris? Besides, it's for our little home.

Some time ago I received a letter of yours while you were still convalescing, you cannot imagine how sorry I was to hear that you were sick, even if you were not gravely ill. This is what it means to be far away, your dearest love suffers and you are not aware of anything, you cannot comfort him or relieve his pain; it's horrible! At least I now know that you are well, and this pleases me enormously, please my darling, take good care of yourself, eat well, and rest, you will make me happy like this. Will you do it? Your letter of sometime ago cheered me up, in your letter you write about your decision to join me here, congratulations my darling, I admire your decisiveness and your iron will, this too is proof of your love for me, of course, I am telling you the truth, I never doubted you, I know you too well, and I know you would not have backtracked nor foregone on the promises you made. We are made for each other, and we will be together wherever we will be, together we have made this choice, and so let it be, together we have chosen this path, and together we will pursue it without complaints or admonishments. May God illuminate the path for us, this is all I ask, for the rest, oh! Everything is possible! My dearest, I leave you now, I am tired and my head is pounding, kisses to your *mamma* and to all your dear ones, to you, my precious, a thousand kisses and affectionate caresses from your Tetina forever. Kisses from my parents.

— Venice 16-2-49 —

Amatissima mia piccola,[20]

Several days have passed since I received your news, despite it being my turn, I delayed writing to you so that I could have in my hands this last letter that I just finished reading. Last night I had all of the best intentions to write to you, but I did not follow through because I had a feeling I would receive news from you today. This is exactly the way it was, and not for nothing am I now replying to you, nothing stands in my way, I know this one should already have been in the mail, and soon with you, instead it's still here in my hands. I am now focused on one thing alone, and that is to try to please you by composing phrases that will lift you and inspire trust in you again, something that you have been missing lately. I too should bemoan and despair over everything that altogether has happened to me, things that have changed me since you left, fortunately in these moments of suffering and depression I manage to always find the positive that lifts me.

As you say, the suffering around us has been intense lately, and on this I could write a novel. I won't do it because I don't want to make you feel worse, this alone prevents me from elaborating. It is an enigma for me to explain the bitterness of today. Many things contrast starkly with my thoughts, others are part of my regrets, and for this reason, I do my best to alter the perspective on things, this is the way I spend my days clinching these ideas, hoping to erase them when I reach you. This is the crux of my thoughts, the apex of all my thoughts. Coming to Canada will be the realization of a dream, not so much for you, but for me. Let me be clear, I do not dream of America, I dream of you, and altogether I dream of a new life. You discuss this in your last letter, not in your second to last letter, but it's not important, of course, everything depends on you, that is, on all of you, and for this reason, I don't think I have explained myself adequately, or rather, I don't think I mentioned to you that I have a deadline for the time in which I can leave, that is, I have until November 1949. After that, I will be stuck with the exam ... Imagine that to reach this point I had to jump over many hurdles, as you can envision, and for this reason, I would not want to be left empty-handed. You know what

---

20 My most beloved girl.

The Metonymy of Writing and Feelings of Proximity 207

I mean, even if it were the case, I have not mentioned it before, if I am saying it now, it's because you need to know this. Therefore, you should know that everything must be completed by November (at the latest); do you think we will make it? You already replied to me about this, I know, but I have no choice but to advise you again, at this point, the Canada of my Tetina has become an obsession, yes, because everything about it reminds me of you with intensity, and I dream of you and our new life, of our family, and a new era that will be marked by love. These thoughts constantly provide comfort to my pessimism, they strengthen my trust in reaching our goal, there is a lot of talk about Canada all the time, I have never heard so much talk about it until now, and with this, oh, what melancholy! I even saw bits of it the other evening, it was a film taking place in Montreal and Ottawa last year, that is, *Il Sipario di Ferro*.[21] In my mind's eye, as I watched the projection of the magnificent streets and boulevards, I envisioned our shadows while I dreamed of my Tetina whom I sought to see through the lens. But nothing materialized before my eyes, perhaps because my eyes are dimmed, what remained was the bond of a strong and pure love between you and me.

Oh Canada, why are you so far away? I would have already joined you if things were different. Send me always news in your next letters, I eagerly await to hear more. In an earlier letter I wanted to ask you something. Here it is! So, when I come down, we will need to marry as we agreed; for such matters, do you not need documents for our marriage, including any of my documents? Should I get the papers ready or will we be doing this at a later date? Or don't we need them?

21 Loris is referring to the film *The Iron Curtain* (1948), directed by William Wellman. The film is based on the memoirs of Igor Gouzenko, a Soviet clerk who worked in the Soviet Embassy in Ottawa to encode embassy mail traffic. As he was about to be sent back to the Soviet Union, Gouzenko fled the embassy on the night of 5 September 1945. The Soviet documents he carried with him exposed a Soviet spy ring active in Canada, the United States, and the United Kingdom. Gouzenko's defection caused an international crisis that many historians consider the beginning of the Cold War. Among the numerous studies on the topic, see Rudner and Black, *The Gouzenko Affair*; Knight, *How the Cold War Began*; Granatstein & Stafford, *Spy Wars*; Whittaker, *Cold War Canada*; and more recently, Molinaro, "How the Cold War Began ... with British Help."

208 January 1949 to July 1949

I don't think so! On the other hand, if that's the way it is … Give me
precise details so we do not waste precious time. I understand that
my application has already been initiated, even if *Signor* S … has yet
to begin with the paperwork. Tell him that if he doesn't do things
right, he will have to deal with me afterwards. I understand your
work is moving along well, and that you have earned the right to a
pay increase, that's very good, congratulations! For this reason, do
not worry about the ring you wanted to give me. I don't need it my
Tetina, I have the steel one which suits me fine, do not worry. Instead,
I wonder what I can bring for you and your parents. A gift now could
not make you as happy, I hope, as a thousand of my kisses sent to you
with all my heart, your Loris.

I cannot wait to receive your photograph, in fact, I can't wait to see
you in person. I leave it up to you.

Greetings to C …

[Top of first page:] A thousand kisses and many thanks to your
mamma and *papà*. Yours

Loris

— Montreal 20-2-49 —

Mio adorato,[22]
I wanted to wait a day or two before writing to you, since I had just
written to my family at home [in Ampezzo], and now I'm feeling very
tired, but as I went about replacing the writing material in the drawer,
I reread your last letter imbued with words of sincere affection, so
much so I could not help myself from getting back to the task and
write a few sentences to you. I will be brief tonight, I cannot stay long
to write because I need to wake up very early in the morning, and
if I don't go to bed, I will be a zombie tomorrow morning. In this
letter, I will limit myself to describing to you my day and tell you
how delighted I was to read your letter which is here with me, yes,
always be like this, my darling, show me the love that you hold for
me, be expansive, sincere, affectionate as much as you can, I need it
dearly, I desperately need to feel surrounded by your love, your care, it

22 My adored one.

The Metonymy of Writing and Feelings of Proximity 209

doesn't matter if these are only written words, I know these are your thoughts, your wishes.

The life that we now lead, we must admit, is very hard, we are young and in need of love, because we love each other, we need to be close to one another, instead, distance denies us this, it denies everything that we wish for, oh! When I think about this, everything around me becomes sombre, but hope lives on, the hope of seeing you again, soon and forever, imagine, my darling, my life, forever. Oh! I love you, yes, I love you. I am more than ever sure of the words that I am saying to you, believe me, I would die if I lost you. Today, I attended the 11 o'clock mass at the Italian church,[23] there I met a friend who invited me to the movies, *La Traviata* is a beautiful film, in English it's called, *The Lost One*,[24] sung in Italian and explained in English, the singers and actors were marvellous, it was a real masterpiece. There too I could not forget you, because I know how much you love the music, how much it moves you, isn't that so?! My Loris, believe me, my life is only a memory now, I cannot wait until the memories fade so I can begin to live again, and live a life that was interrupted a long time ago. I leave you now, my darling, hoping to receive news from you soon, and any clarifications that you need from me. A dear kiss to your *mamma* and to your family. Write soon, kisses from my relatives who remember you always, and from me, the woman who adores you, the most affectionate, sincere kisses ever. Your Nietta

Excuse my bad writing. Many many kisses, *ciao*

[on separate sheet of paper:]

I forgot to mention that we will be moving on the first of May. For the moment, write to me at the address of *Signora* C ...

7016 Drolet

I will send you my new address after. Please give my dearest greetings to your sister W ... whom I remember fondly, tell her that I have a calendar for her new home, she will receive it a little late, no? Kisses to your little nephews and to *Signor* B ...

---

23 Antonietta is referring to the Church of the Madonna della Difesa, also known as l'Église Notre-Dame-de-la-Défense in Montreal. See the introduction in this book for further explanation.

24 *The Lost One* was the English title of Verdi's widely popular opera *La Traviata*.

— Venice 23-2-49 —

Mia Nietta carissima,[25]

Though quite exhausted, with eyes red from fatigue and an injury on my right eye (nothing serious), I begin this letter to you this evening, even if it is a little late, I write in response to the letter I received this evening, a letter I had a hunch I would receive today! To begin with, please excuse me for writing with my bandaged hand, this is the best I can do, and excuse me again if the letter is not composed with its usual elegance, I am at the hospital for a few days (nothing serious, I swear to you), as the expression goes, when you are your work ...

By now, I could call myself a professional in the field, or work, even if I am still young. Every event in our lives is part of our lives, including the years I completed in the field. I started working when I was a young man, oh! Not at eight years old, of course, but rather when I turned sixteen because frankly, it was the only path that interested me. I had just completed high school when I became interested in art, I became employed in the large company, part of SADE, and from there, little by little I began to understand the value of work in a spiritual sense. There, step by step, I began to build my experience and responsibilities to the point that now, I think about how much more I need to do to become as good and qualified as I wish to be, as I want to be.

How different my perspective was when as an adolescent; I neglected the importance of work, how different I foresaw my future, maybe because nothing weighed on my shoulders, maybe also because in my family I was spoiled, until, as the days passed, and the years turned into ten and over, I thought of expanding my work in an office so I could improve my work. I remember that when I completed the mandatory two years of technical school, actually I did not complete them because of the war, I thought that shortly after I would have had to move to Vicenza to be conferred the degree of Industrial Technician, but ... many things came along that pushed me back. Family contingencies, the war, too many expenses, this and more, all of which interrupted the pursuit of my ideals, and soon enough I began to think about giving back, I thought carefully about becoming useful to my family and to

---

25 My dearest Nietta.

The Metonymy of Writing and Feelings of Proximity   211

myself. And so, on February 16 of 1943 I started at SADE, and learned the trade over time, I learned what is meant by sacrifice and humility, these were useful to me to improve myself, even if the path was long and hard. All of this is a summary of my life, a model for my decision.

The dawnings of our past days have now changed, the optimistic horizons in our lives have changed, and yet, I am very happy, with all the difficulties, I would not change any one of my life goals, perhaps because fate has granted me much happiness, much joy, and I leave it up to you to imagine the ways that this twenty-second spring has come about. All I can tell you is that if I had not responded to fate, I would not be close to you, and now, I would not be loved by you, all of this is because of fate, even my suffering because you are so far away, but fate has reserved the most extraordinary surprise of seeing us again together, hopefully soon, because with you by my side, I want to work for us, for our children, for our home. By the way, regarding our home, tell your *papà* that he can count on me because I too want to be part of the birth of our new home (I am not at all able to make cement or pile bricks and stones) but we will have to see once I am there, isn't that so, my darling. Now we need to have the documents in our hands so that I can come down and a new day will begin. Give me news on this, and let me know how the process is moving along, I am always thinking about this as this dreadful situation merges with my most vivid memories of the days we spent together and the regret of not kissing you and loving you enough while you were here.

your Loris

[Top of the letter on first page:]

Kisses to your *mamma* and your *papà*, and wishing your *mamma* a swift recovery Kisses, Loris

— Venice 26-2-49 —

Amatissima mia Nietta,[26]

Nearly one year has passed since the day we were at your home, if I remember correctly, avidly listening to the soccer match played between Italy and France. This 365th day is at the threshold of our long

26 Nietta my dearest love.

winding path, we are approaching the end, nearly one year has gone by, yes, it is today that I remember precisely this day, there is no better moment than now to listen one year later to the Italian team playing against the Portuguese visiting team. Today too, our team won, today too, the hearts of fans are screaming with joy, even on this day their faces are gleaming with rays of sportsmanship.

Can I rejoice too? Can I think of myself as jubilant as I was one year ago? The response must not hesitate in denouncing a change, my soul is as always enthralled by sports, but the same is not true in the way I express myself. Perhaps it would be better if I too send my greetings and best wishes to the journalist whom with his subtle voice called to commemorate and unite all the Italians living abroad. How many have heard his voice, how many of them have called out to their *Italia*, everyone I think, for a moment feels tied to their *Patria*, everyone, regardless who they are, has travelled to unknown spaces to find once again within themselves their home again, their land again, of this I have no doubt because sports bring people together. Everyone today was thinking this, because sports, like love, keep us grounded.

For you, not only did my thoughts connect with the opening words of the journalist but a continuous recalling entered my mind even during the program, yes, because, the day could not be more perfect, and alone, I dreamed of abstract and impossible things, but like the past, which is always present, more than any other day, you were in my heart today. Sports and love tie me to you in a profound feeling of veneration; I offer it to you as a pledge of trust in my words, as a reality revered many times over, as a truthful faith and commitment to love you in all circumstances. Nietta, my girl, my love knows no words or phrases to express my substance, which you know already and value. Of course, we are being tested, and under these conditions, I can only unite my determination with yours for us to overcome all things, I can only join my thoughts – my body, my mind – to you hoping always we will find peace in our many dark days ahead. The belief in one thing alone remains with me now, it is the faith with which I let you leave, it is the faith which you placed in my eyes so that you may always be with me, but the image did not turn out as the lenses were obscured by the tears, a shadow appeared before us, the shadow of a space that divides us, the shadow of fate that steered us to its will. But

The Metonymy of Writing and Feelings of Proximity 213

our thoughts are so much more clear, more truthful in our reasoning, not overwhelmed by our emotions, in our actions we can see how everything has passed like the rushing water of a waterfall, however our love has not passed, it continues forever, there is place for our hearts to keep our feelings warm, to keep any bitterness at bay, and to steer our will to all places until it reaches the nucleus of your heart, a heart that may be small in size, but possess immeasurable goodness. My dear Tetina, here I am with you on this day that bids farewell to this day, this Sunday, bereft of everything and everyone, only in this immense solemn silence around me can I join my voice to these words dictated by my heart. Will this day come soon? Yes, Nietta? Will that day of seeing you again appear? I pray that it will for the faith that I have in you, for the will that moves me to change my life, I hope so for the need of more beautiful days with greater luck than these is enormous. In your heart I place my faith, even if I am a pessimist, but if this is your wish, so it shall be, this is how you are, whereas I am a little different, and perhaps more difficult, I will draw from this to help me in the days of our family, you will see the benefits. It is 1830, and so, even this day has passed, between home and the little time I had for Mass this morning. I hope this letter finds you in good health, as is the same for me, my hand has healed and so has my eye, I wish the same for your *mamma* and *papà*, after those days of illness. Hoping to receive your good news, I close this letter sending you many kisses and lasting embraces, your Loris

[Loris's mother adds a note to Antonietta:]

My dear Nietta, I send you a kiss and my dear memory of you and your loved ones, even though there is not much space for me to write, my affection for you is clear. I would like to have more time to tell you many things which will certainly please you. Please extend my affection to your *papà* and your *mamma*, and to you, my dear Nietta, I send you dearest kisses from me, M ... and E ... affectionately yours, *mamma* who thinks of you always.

— 8 —

"Did you think I was sleeping here?"
Women's Agency in Migration

ANTONIETTA'S RHETORICAL QUESTION extracted from a letter to Loris on 3 March 1949 merits reflection. It signals a woman's agency in a transcultural space, an "emancipatory effect of migration for women,"[1] as noted by Loretta Baldassar and Donna Gabaccia. This emancipatory effort is evidenced, for instance, in Antonietta's contact with official bureaucracies in a foreign country to ensure her fiancé's immigration. It echoes her desire for recognition from her fiancé for whom the complexities involved in his sponsorship to Canada remain necessarily obfuscated. Moreover, the question alludes to her role in assisting her father to sponsor Loris and ensuring his migration to Canada. More broadly, it underscores the central role that women occupied historically in a migration process, a gendered process that reflects the different positions of women and men in society,[2] beginning with the initial considerations of departure in the homeland to the settlement and adjustment stages in the receiving society.

In the decades immediately following the Second World War, a large percentage of economic immigrants admitted to Canada arrived through the sponsorship program. Of the 2.5 million immigrants who reached Canadian soil between 1946 and 1966, 900,000 came as a result of family ties and networks mostly from Italy, Greece, and

---

1 Baldassar and Gabaccia, "Home, Family, and the Italian Nation in a Mobile World," 15.
2 Harzig, "Women Migrants as Global and Local Agents," 15.

Portugal.[3] The family unification program not only favoured the migration of already established ethnic nationals – and thus perpetuated the country's "cultural texture" – it also contained, as historian Christiane Harzig argues, an element of explosive growth since most sponsored immigrants could again sponsor others and provide initial help and support in finding shelter and work, as the letters of Italian immigrants evince.[4] In this postwar era, Canada also witnessed the arrival of the largest number of women from Italy, accounting for over 40 per cent of adults immigrating to Canada between 1952 and 1961.[5] Until at least the 1950s, it was widely believed in most countries that a woman should follow her husband's citizenship in the case of binational marriages.[6]

While many Italian women arrived after their husbands or their fiancés, others like Antonietta arrived before. In reaching Montreal before Loris and supported by her father and mother, Antonietta set out to prepare for Loris's arrival. This included the need to take on different roles and functions – factory worker, student, friend, daughter, caregiver, and long-distance fiancée – and to participate in the building and maintenance of social relations in Montreal's transnational community, which she was becoming acquainted with, engage in contact with the nation's administration (travel agents and government offices) to ensure a swift processing of Loris's application, and reflect on her decisions in her letters to Loris. Her agency is also mirrored in the content and style of the letters, that is, in her decision to describe one situation over another and the writing style in which she disclosed it, as we witness in the first letter in the chapter.

The letters elucidate historical evidence of soon-to-be married men following women in international migration processes, a pattern seldom illustrated in early migration movements, yet increasingly evident in contemporary labour migration processes. This exciting new direction for research in earlier migration movements contrasts with the normative approach in traditional migration studies that

---

3 Harzig, "Immigration Policies," 44.
4 Harzig, "Immigration Policies," 44. See for instance, Cancian, *Families, Lovers, and their Letters.*
5 Iacovetta, "Scrivere le donne nella storia dell'immigrazione," 27.
6 Harzig, "Immigration Policies," 24.

viewed women as moving on the coattails of husbands and fathers rather than as active agents in the migration process. Engaging with women's and men's epistolaries of this nature casts additional light on agency and gender roles in migration patterns that were perhaps less common, yet no less significant.

— Montreal 3-3-49 —

Mio adorato Loris,[7]

Just this minute my *papà* said to me, "You are exhausted and you are starting to write a letter now?" to which I replied, "It's been some time since I wrote to him, and I have decided to do it now, but he too, he hardly sends news." It's true, I have not heard from you in several days, and I don't know why, but I'm a little worried, what happened? I thought I would certainly have received news in these past few days, but nothing. I can't complain though it will all come to roost, that is, I cannot do very much except wait and sit tight. I too am a little late in writing to you, and I am here to tell you that I'm sorry, I don't know how it is that I delayed in writing to you, especially since I had so much to tell you. Of course, you are always on my mind and in my heart, even if I have not kept my end of the bargain, even today, this morning we moved the furniture into the other house, imagine the chaos, everything upside down, pandemonium everywhere, all day, feeling edgy, in part because I wasn't feeling well, monthly discomforts. Tonight, I am so worn out, my eyes are a disaster. My poor *mamma* is still cleaning at this hour, I just can't wait until everything is over and that we can finally settle down once and for all.

Loris, you should see what a beautiful home, lots of light and sunshine, oh! How I wish you were already here with us, instead, you are still so far away – let's hope it won't be much longer. I went to the emigration [immigration] office for the application, they told me that we should receive a response from Ottawa in a minimum of five weeks, then we will send you the papers, and you will do what you need to

---

7 My adored Loris.

Women's Agency in Migration 217

do. You will see that you will be here for the month of November, do you believe me now, you incredible cynic? Do you think I don't understand all of this? Did you think I was sleeping here? My desire to see you is just as intense as yours, but we cannot do everything in one day; of course, if it was up to me, oh, what I would do! Now we have taken care of one thing at least, all we need to do is wait for an answer from the Capital; I think it will be definitely a positive response, right, dear? Oh! How horrible it would be if it were the opposite!

With regard to the marriage documents, I asked *Signor* S ..., he advised me to speak with the priest of the Italian parish, I still have not done it because I don't think it's urgent, but I will do it as soon as I can, and I will let you know. I am here with the pen in my hand, my love, and I don't know what else to write to you, if you were here, then of course, I would know what beautiful words to tell you, I would know how to hold you tight in my heart, I would know how to kiss you with so much ardour. Instead I have to settle for thinking of you with intense longing, my goodness, that long-agonized day must come!

Shall I tell you about my days? The days pass as usual, between work, home, and school, constantly, and some leisure time is spent only with my parents. The truth is, I sometimes avoid going out. On Tuesday, for instance, my *papà* wanted to take me dancing at the Casa d'Italia and I preferred to stay home, I don't want to be distracted, I want to stay focused, I want to think only of you and I don't want to face opportunities that might tear me away from my thoughts. It's better this way, I am sure you will agree, it's already devastating to be so far apart. You see, my darling, I'm making too many errors in writing to you at this hour. It's best that I close here, my warmest greetings and kisses to your *mamma* and your family, and for you, the most ardent kisses, the dearest, the most affectionate kisses and a gentle touch!

Your Nietta

Kisses from my parents who always remember you.

The new address is:

7601 De la Roche

218   January 1949 to July 1949

— Montreal 5-3-49 —

Mio adorato Loris,[8]

I did not receive one, but two of your letters today, I am so very grateful. I had a feeling I would receive news from you today, and, in fact, I was right. My dearest, my infinite dearest, what can I tell you in this hour overwhelmed by memories and quiet reminiscing? It's 10:30 in the evening, I am alone in my new home, it's a little isolated, this one, just outside the city, a powerful silence reigns as the radio plays a soft sentimental piece that makes it even harder to bear your absence and all that surrounds you. "Stardust"[9] is the song, perhaps you have heard it before, they play it a lot in Italy as well. Listen to it when you can and remember me with intensity, knowing that your Nietta enjoys listening to it. Will you do it? How many, how many thoughts imbue my mind, how many things I would love to share with you, and yet, as I begin to pen these thoughts on paper, the ideas become confused and all remains locked in my heart, perhaps my heart wishes to keep everything to itself until the day it will be able to beat alongside your heart?

Loris, how dearly I think of you always. Yesterday for example, as we were having lunch, I noticed an empty place at the table, and I thought of you and imagined you among us; as I watch the crowds walk on the streets, I think "Couldn't he be here too, among the many others who are here? One additional person will make no difference to this big city." Today as I was returning home from work I thought about how much more wonderful it would be if I saw your smile, your gaze, upon arriving home, as I would have delighted in your touch, I don't think I am asking for very much, every young woman my age, I think, has a right to a little affection, what is life about otherwise? In this moment, a line you wrote to me some time ago comes to mind, "Man does not live on bread alone." No explanations are necessary, everything is clear

---

8 My adored Loris.

9 The song "Stardust" (lyrics by M. Parish) was originally composed in 1927 (with lyrics added in 1929) by American songwriter, pianist, bandleader, and singer Hoagy Carmichael (1899–1981). The song was intensely popular. It was recorded more than 1,100 times and translated into thirty languages. Hasse, "Carmichael, Hoagy," 157. The Italian version of the song, "Polvere di Stelle," has been interpreted by numerous popular Italian artists, including Natalino Otto, Bobby Solo, and Mina Mazzini.

Women's Agency in Migration

for you, because this is how you think, this is your life. You need to be strong, still and always, the worst is over, all we need to do now is reach the finishing line, and soon we will have news about your arrival here, as I already mentioned. Your papers need to go to Ottawa, actually, they left some time ago because I was at the emigration [immigration] office 15 days ago, now we wait for the response, more than this we cannot do, do you believe me? And ... please, don't be a pessimist, I don't want to hear you speak like this, you must believe in me, just as I have always believed in you, be strong and don't be discouraged, this is fundamental. I came here so that you could join me, because I want to live with you, if you did not want to come here, I would have stayed behind, because I want to live where you live, where you are, do you understand, my love?

Tell me, how is your hand? and your eye? My poor darling, all these things are happening to you this year? Please take care of yourself, don't wear yourself out, and tell me if you're all right. The truth, please! I was telling my friend at work today about the international game that you had described to me, the journalist's appeal to all Italians abroad and the game's results; both of us couldn't stop ourselves from crying, not to mention the shivers that were running down our spines. We didn't hear the broadcast, and frankly, we were so sorry. Here, there's talk about the Juventus team coming down this summer, is that true? That's what Italians who have just arrived are telling us. Now, my beloved Loris, I want to go to sleep, I have to go to work early tomorrow morning. Honestly, I must admit I almost never got up so early in Italy. But, this is something I want and I won't complain about it, oh no! I kiss you with so much affection, even in the name of my parents, from me, however, the biggest special kiss ever. Your Nietta

In another letter I asked you if you went to Ferrara, I never received an answer; on numerous occasions I ask you things, but you don't answer, try to remember to answer me. Kisses.

To your *mamma*, whom I remember with affection, many dear thanks for her writing to me, which I very much appreciated. Kisses to *papà* Gigio, to M ... and A ..., L ..., *Signor* C ..., V ..., W ..., husband and children. To your *mamma*, especially, affectionate kisses from me, *papà* and *mamma*. Your Antonietta

220 January 1949 to July 1949

— Venice 9-3-1949 —

Nietta mia amatissima,[10]
It is a duty for me to begin this letter several days after the last one I
wrote to you on February 27. It is a duty for me as well to apologize
to you for having been mistaken, that is, I did not err, but I wanted
to, even if I was not fully committed to it. Of course, ten days add
up, especially when we are waiting for something. For me those days
moved with such apparent speed that it seems hundreds of days have
passed, but it's also true that nothing had stood in my way, nothing
had imposed a forced silence, rather, I was a little lazy, that's about it
(a veritable curse for me) because I don't usually allow myself to be
defeated by laziness, but it's not easy to tell you about my fatigue and
the need to rest after long days of work. If I told you everything and all
the details, it would never end, especially since my fatigue is perpetual.
You say you know something about this, especially now that you have
work, school, home, etc., imagine then what it must be like for me.

After supper last night, I decided to begin writing a letter to you,
but upon starting to write the address, I fell asleep on the paper, it
was so obvious that everyone urged me to go to bed; it was only 8:45
and already the fatigue had taken over. The same followed in the next
few days, except Sunday when I was in Ceggia[11] at the home of my *zio*
[uncle] G … for some business. I spent the whole day with my cousins
at their home, I returned home by train around midnight. Because
of these circumstances, I sat here at this table unable to do anything,
and I had to postpone my duty and give my mind some rest. Tonight,
I was able to make up for it a little, I wanted to overcome my own uncertainties and put myself to the task to write to you. It's very early in
the evening, and because of this, my mind is fresh and ready to write
to you – everything is the same, nothing has changed in any way, my
desire to write to you, to speak with you, to tell you words that restore
your faith, all of this is always immense, it's always the same, that
is, because only one thing has never changed (Love). The words that
will delight you are several, the sentences that will bring you joy are
infinite, even if they may not be convenient [?], and it's for this reason

10 Nietta my dearest love.
11 Ceggia is a town located approximately fifty kilometres from Venice.

that I want to leave an imprint of my true feelings in my words to you, even if you recognize my style, even if I write with little elegance. By now, it's obvious that you are familiar with my style, you know what I think, and you can recognize my love, this is why you should not have any doubt as you wait bitterly.

But, I understand, I understand very well, it's a human weakness to doubt and to distrust, isn't it also true that I have never nor have we ever previously doubted our mutual behaviour toward each other. Evidence of this nature is in your letter in which you bring to light my own mistake, that is, my lack of conviction (not trust), in which you write: are you convinced now, my darling incredible cynic? You cannot imagine to what extent this phrase injected a renewed energy into a dead body, it infused a breath of vigour into an open wound, an avalanche of love in addition to the love you already possess for me. The phrase in itself has a double meaning and I had no trouble reading it. I read two meanings in the word "cynic," that is, first the decisive meaning of the adjective, and second, the challenge that it spoke about, but in both cases, this phrase gave me much confidence, as much as I expected from you. The nobility of your words was like water poured onto arid land, yes, my heart was pried open that night, I was moved by the purity of your confidence that cannot betray me any longer.

I never imagined receiving the news I received in your letter yesterday, at the very least, I had limited myself to waiting. This is the most wonderful news I have ever received from you until now, this news has reactivated the confidence I was lacking during these days, the news is a masterpiece of a profound love. Just imagine our joy when we will be in each other's arms again, there will be no other practical or logical considerations on that day, our hearts must never slow down; therefore, at this moment they are on their way to preserving their energy for that day, no, they must be in constant motion to pave the way for our hearts later, that long day of constant suffering will end in a truthful, faithful sacrifice, in which a new day will begin more luminous, more joyous than ever. The news of my application reaching the Capital makes me live my days waiting patiently, it's true, these are days of anxiety and anticipation, but the day of harvest will come, and what celebrations will follow. For the marriage papers, find out what the deadline is, so that I can have them prepared, if necessary, better yet, don't wait, also because, as soon as I will have received your papers, I won't wait a day to prepare mine.

I received the calendar you and *Signora C* ... sent me. Please find the appropriate words to thank her, you know her better than I do, please tell her on my behalf that such a sweet gift could only be a demonstration of her kind heart. On that calendar I will count the days that still separate us. I will gaze at the calendar, and I will think of you more, and I will mark the dates and memories that witnessed me happy. I thank you warmly. In Ampezzo, the F ... brothers won 11 million [lire] from the SISAL lottery.[12] Do you know them? Even if you don't, you now know that in your town there are a few more wealthy gentlemen, but I am the one who is a noble gentleman, I have no money but my heart lives for your happiness. Many kisses, your Loris forever.

For my dear in-laws, a most beautiful thought of our memories, with affection and kisses always, and many thanks in return, your Loris

— Montreal 15-3-49 (time 8:20 p.m.) —

Mio infinitamente caro,[13]
As you sleep sweetly in your bed your Tetina watches over and wonders, she silently watches over your sleep so that you may sleep peacefully, for you to rest; you see my Loris I am with you always and everywhere; not only in this moment while I write to you, but always, in every moment. It is now 1 minute to 8, but in Italy we are six hours ahead, in that case, I am very certain that you are sleeping sweetly in your bed. I don't know why, but recently everyone is talking about you more than usual, in every conversation your name is mentioned, and even my *papà* now has asked me about your previous letter. If you were here, we would not be mentioning your name more, we are already thinking about your arrival here and imagining your enthu-

12   The Italian lottery company, SISAL (Sport Italia Società e Responsabilità Limitata), was founded in 1945 in Milan by three Italian journalists (Massimo della Pergola, Fabio Jegher, and Geo Molo) for the purpose of reactivating Italian sports after the war. Their initial capital led to the reconstruction of sports facilities especially for soccer/football in Italy. See http://www.unastorianatapergioco.sisal.com.
13   My infinitely dear one.

siasm for travelling here, naturally, it is the same for us. Many times, when my *mamma* and I are alone, we surprise ourselves by saying, "at least if Loris were here, we would have some company," our new home has lots of room, and there's only three of us, three lonely souls. Fortunately, we have my cheerful *papà* who does everything to keep our spirits up, even now, he is here making me laugh with his latest finds. (I took a 20-minute break, the couple is remembering their adventures of when they were young, and I cried laughing.) When will we be all together and happy? Can you imagine what those days will be like? It's useless to try and describe them, like me, you can imagine what those days will like be for us, I cannot wait, my precious, to hold you in my arms, and to kiss you with all my strength.

I won't continue in this vein, you know that everything reminds me of you, everything I do I dedicate to you, I do everything for you, you alone, are you happy about this? Do you know what compels me to do this? Your ways, your way of doing things, your demeanour, your feelings, so sensible and wise, this makes me love you always more. I am constantly waiting for the reply from Ottawa, which I hope to receive soon, you will see that everything will work out for us. I am working as usual, they increased my pay by 5¢ per hour, without me asking for it; this means I deserved it, right? And you, my darling, always the same life, isn't that right? Are you in good health now? And your family? Your *mamma* and *Signor* Gigio? I send them my best wishes for good health as I hope the same for us. My *mamma* has gained some weight since we are here, she is looking very well. My *papà* tells me that he would like to write two lines in my letter to you, he is asking me to hurry with my letter because he cannot wait much longer. He has recently bought a car, but during the winter season, we won't be enjoying it much because the roads are inaccessible. Once the warmer season is here, we will be able to take some nice drives, let's hope that you too will be among us then. I now close this letter, I want to tell you again that we are having some terrible weather, snow, storms, so much for spring! You on the other hand must be basking in that warm Italian sun as you enjoy the first smells of spring and the flowers in bloom. We are immersed in full winter here, we must be brave, the warm season is on its way, God willing. Many, many kisses to your whole family, and to you, a million kisses and an enormous embrace.

224   January 1949 to July 1949

Forever yours, your Nietta
Kisses from my *mamma* who remembers you always with affection

— Venice 15-3-1949 —

Nietta amatissima,[14]
Tuesday is according to my logic, or more accurately, my eagerness,
the propitious day in which I receive your news, and this Tuesday did
not betray me; actually, it confirmed to me that the frequency with
which you are writing to me is slowing down. I don't remember specifically how many weeks it's been since I received mail from you on
Tuesdays, it must be a few months, this means progress on your part.
With this, let's call it certainty, I spend better days, not always peaceful or easygoing. No disasters, thank God, but many kinds of worries,
especially related to the family, or of a general sort, about the home,
work, and the rest. I now know first-hand what it means to sacrifice,
and what a family does to you. Essentially, it's everyone's fate, that is,
it belongs to almost all men. But you won't believe what I am resigned
to, my trust in a better world. Acceptance and trust stand in opposition to each other, they are a contradiction in terms, even though they
are not generally recognized as such, because in acceptance (at least
for me) I find ways to seek solace and think about a reality that has
not yet been attained nonetheless, all of this is a confirmation of our
project. While we do not seek out anything that can cause us trouble,
these things still come along, we don't try to abandon or forget, yet
all is lost and forgotten, this is the logic of life, it has in store many
mysteries for everyone, mysteries that help us to resolve the good and
bad things of life. May these always help you with your experiences,
I mean as you take steps forward or back persevering in reaching for
your objectives, by experiences we also mean other things, something
that reshapes our feelings or ideas, something that changes one's life
or one's thinking [?]. It's a joy for me to think with greater responsibility, it's a joy for me to know that there is someone who hopes and
trusts (in me, even if I believe that youth only comes along once, even
if I believe that it is duty that awaits me first and foremost, and that
without duty I could not achieve anything).

14 Nietta my dearest love.

Women's Agency in Migration

Unfortunately, these are hard days, unfortunately, everything has changed, and consequently, I am indispensable for my family, whom frankly, without bragging, I sustain with a good dose of wisdom. I believe I have always had a bit of this in me, but now, more than ever I acquired it and adopted it, yes! I have done this so that I can lighten the weight, to make my time with my family more agreeable. But I don't always find gratitude in the faces of others, that is, in the other persons who weigh on my shoulders. Oh, I would not want to accuse anyone, because I feel I would offend my own family name, but it's equally true that A ... accuses me of doing everything without prejudice, even if I can confess to you now because I am not ashamed to speak the truth, she would do well to be more autonomous, or at the very least, understanding about the situation, and be a little different in my regard. In truth, she is the only tyrant here despite her good qualities (I would be wrong to deny this), she should not be this way toward me, even though I am not easy to live with, I am no slavedriver. These things don't exactly tear down my ideas, my words, my days, but frankly, they do not excite me either, first because I give them relative importance, secondly, because I don't want to be bitter over this, even if my heart suffers more than my body, words hurt, they hurt my spirit, my morale, while I am far away, a thought or word from you helps me a lot.

In you, I find so much comfort, your words nurture my soul and my faith in you is strengthened. I long for this deeply. I am sure, as sure as the hours that separate us, that you are not as grateful as I am. Oh no, it is absolutely certain that I have always allowed myself to love you deeply to make you happy. Returning to the point I was remarking on before, if I now try to relieve a little bit of my moral pain more than my material pain, I should not be treated in this way by a woman who in the end needs everything and everyone. You are well aware of the differences between me and her, you know how she is, but it's better to pretend than to blow it out of proportion. I will add this, that my parents give me so much happiness and courage when I see them gratified. [?]

Enough about this, I am sure that you feel a part of my sorrow, but be sure that I am a man who is willing to respect others and be respected, this gives my sister hope. You asked me if I travelled to Ferrara, first, I don't believe I answered you, but the truth is, I was not able to. I did not have the time nor did I have a reason, I would have preferred in that case to go to Ampezzo and enjoy the affection of your dear *nonni*, the beauty of your town, so dear and unforgettable to me. I will be there at Easter, this time, at all costs, even because, I plan to have more free time. During the week, I will write to your family, who probably think that I am dead. I received the calendar, if I'm not mistaken I have already mentioned that. It's 10:30 and in this remaining space, I can only write these words, I love you, I think of you, I talk to you, I remember you, I kiss you

Your Loris Kisses

Greetings and kisses are returned to your *mamma* and *papà*. I am always waiting for good news from you, including a photo of you.

— Venice 24-3-1949 —

Nietta mia amatissima,[15]
Though it's late and I am very tired, I have had to decide right now whether or not to write to you. Time has passed not so much in terms of hours, it is now 10 o'clock, but more in terms of the usual time in which I go to sleep, this is unusual for me. Next, work has taken up all of my time these days. So much work this week to the point that I am wiped out from not sleeping enough, it has taken all of my time, including the little time I had to write to you, which I know, or at least I can imagine you aching for news as you wait for that person who belatedly runs and rushes to write to you so that you may receive news soon. This is the wish that enlivens me as I think of you cheerful, it is the wish that animates my thoughts, which a thousand times brushes against the white shores of fate as it rides over the mountains and the seas to return punctually on that day that closes joyfully with the certainty of being in your thoughts, of being loved, remembered and comforted. How many of these days follow one another like a chain, and how many of these days adorn our lives, enclosed in one single objective, the desire to live and to live for you and with you is enclosed in each of our [?], the image of a young kind girl, the image of a pure woman, the image of an only child gripped by the desire to love and to be loved. This is the only ring in our lives that ties us, this is the only purpose that makes us

---

15 Nietta my dearest love.

love each other always, this is why I feel my heart accelerating its beats a thousand times over, this is why I feel my body shaken by the human need to feel your deep warmth which contains the life of my determination, the life of my thoughts, the life of my flesh.

Despite the many difficulties and oppositions, and the numerous uncertainties, these drops of life are not lost in wells of weakness or confusion, but rather, they fall upon the warm soul of my love, so that she may feel strengthened, more confident, everything that you need to feel reassured that love is the essence of this trust, the essence of this generous devotion we have for each other. I spent much of the last few days at work. What I have just written is the essence of my will's relentlessness to do otherwise, but you must know that on Saturday and Sunday, two days of holiday on the occasion of Saint Joseph's Day on the 19th, and Sunday, the usual holiday, I have had to lock myself in my second home, the Central Office, and there, I spent all of Saturday, Saturday night, and all of Sunday until late at night, and so, my umpteenth days at work ended without distractions, without boredom, anger, or envy. They ended with the joy of finding myself away from the troubles of the soul and the body, away from situations that could sever the chain-link of beautiful days of purity and unfettered happiness. Infinite affectionate kisses, your Loris

— Montreal 27-3-49 —

Mio amato Loris,[16]
It was my turn to write to you a few days ago, but as usual, daily obligations, and my laziness delayed me in composing these thoughts for you until today. I have in my hands two of your letters to which I have not yet replied, one was written a little late, and I waited eagerly for this one, and the other one I received a few days ago; there was nothing in the first letter that made me angry, it was a letter like usual with you longing to see me, (our souls are constantly talking about this ever since that day in which we were separated), lines of affection, (and you know how happy I am to read these), so the letter that I long awaited gave me great joy and delight in knowing that you are well and that you are always yearning for my love. The second letter, on the

16 My beloved Loris.

other hand, was very different, there was disgust, annoyance, discouragement, you cannot imagine how terribly sad I felt after reading these words of crude, malicious behaviour, directed especially to a heart as sensitive and kind as yours. Please, my dear Loris, try to understand and forgive, try not to take all of this to heart, it's not worth troubling yourself over it, don't you think so? There is one thing that I hope for and wish for, that you may be here with me soon, I wish for this so much, then, even if there will be some sorrow or disappointment, both of us will be suffering, and I think it will be easier on us, isn't that so, my darling? It is certainly a continuous tribulation to be so far apart, it's hard not to be able to express yourself, and allow yourself to be comforted when there is pain, let's hope it won't be long now. I am still waiting for the sponsorship application, of course, an hour hasn't even past, but you know what it is like to wait for something!

With regard to the papers for our marriage, can you inquire as well with your parish church? I am confident that they will give you the most accurate information, do you mind my dear? I am living a little far from the Italian church, and it's more difficult for me to find the time to visit them. I too should write to the parish priest for my documents, but since you are thinking of going to Ampezzo, it would be better if you could talk with him personally, do you mind? In that way, when you come here you will bring my papers as well, it will be faster and less complicated in this way.

Did you write to my family? They must be so excited to see you. Or perhaps they are afraid that the same thing that happened to you at Christmas will happen again now. How many days are you planning on staying? You can imagine how I will be spending the Easter holidays, thinking about you in my home in the company of my *nonni*, my *zii*, my cousin O ...! Oh, Loris, there are already tears in my eyes, you see? Nostalgia is still with me, oh! I have lived too long in that home that I have loved. I urge you to be the bearer of happiness on that day, fill the void that we have left. I will be thinking of you intensely in those days together with my loved ones, my friends, give them my greetings, and wish them a Happy Easter. One last thing, be good, stay away from bad company, do you understand? If you tell me that you don't, I will tell you more in another letter, which I hope will

Women's Agency in Migration 229

find you still in Venice. Do you remember what we talked about in Ampezzo, you, me and M … before I left?

My *papà* left for Toronto last week, it's just me and my *mamma* now. Today we did not leave the home, and if I must tell you the truth, it is 9:30 at night and I am still here in my pyjama and housecoat, we woke up very late, it's a rainy day, and so, where could we go? I ironed and put some order to my things, I did a few chores that I had not done yesterday because I worked for half a day and I spent the rest of the day with *Signora* C … I had lunch there at noon, and then I was so tired that I had to take a nap at 5. She herself walked me home, in the evening, *Signora* P … and her husband visited us …

[Top left corner]

Kisses to your *mamma* whom I remember always and to your family from my *mamma* as well

— Venice 1-4-49 —

Nietta mia piccola,[17]

In part because of everything, and particularly, because of your delay, I too abstained from the task of writing to you, remember that it's a delay of two days, so keep the scolding at a moderate level, in part because of work, on this I am sure you have no doubts, the third factor is that I absolutely wanted to wait for this date, a date that will not surprise you especially since I can already imagine you the target of a number of April Fool's jokes. Knowing that this day is popular in Canada too, I did not send you a thoughtful gift coupled with a little trick, more or less traditional as far as you are concerned or vice-versa, it would be better if you are ready for it. Fundamentally and truthfully, however, I awaited this day not so much for the holiday, but more for its significance of one year ago today, exactly today when our love was renewed, a love that knows no boundaries, no restraint, a love that rejects any reason for separating us, a love that must never end in rancour or disagreement, but rather in hope and sacrifice for this love to be clear and transparent, a love that we will never bring to a close. We will work to build a skyscraper of peace and harmony, of smiles, joy, affection and fidelity. This is the summary of a year that

17 Nietta my girl.

has fleetingly passed us by, on the outside it was attached to an arrow that pierced my heart, today the pain is not a result of the arrow's tip but rather from an arrow that for many days now has worn me out. A year has now passed, it has passed so skeptically that only the memories that we experienced can reawaken our thoughts. It is for this reason that I wanted now to imagine ourselves together again in the sweet serenity of that lush brush, to the cool gurgling of a delightful poetic stream, whose sweet rush is likened to a phrase about us, one that I sought to reveal to you on that day, I was overjoyed and thrilled. I loved you then as deeply as I love you now.

With this photographic scenery, perhaps you will wonder how and where the events unfolded, but I give you a hand, I who remembers all the details of all that has brought me joy. My explanation will bring you back to the places where you met once again your Loris. That day was the first of April, and with your *papà* and A ... we had gone trout fishing and wishing to take advantage of the occasion, we wet our feet as we jumped wildly from one bank to another, climbing over the large rocks of the tributary, you will recall our conversations were frequently interrupted by the crashing sound of the water fall. From all of this I reserve one pure thought, a thought that is brought back to life in that place on this Earth. At this point, one year has passed, one year is over as we lay to rest those memories, one year has passed, yet it feels like yesterday that our hearts stopped beating, but our days of bliss will return, splendid days glowing with happiness will be with us again.

I cannot stop thinking about what I just wrote to you and the real April Fool's Day trick that your *papà* gave you as your curiosity was heightened by the parcel that was so carefully wrapped with paper of multiple colours.[18] Perhaps even this year you would have fallen for such a trick, especially if I had been there, don't you think so? In that case, which would be the best April Fool's joke that I could send to you? I have many to tell you, and many will come back to mind today along with that blind bad luck, many things in the past few days have brought

18 Antonietta's father had played an April Fool's trick on her. He had left a parcel at the post office for her to pick up. When she opened it, she was surprised to find a mound of colourful rags inside. Personal conversation with Antonietta Petris.

Women's Agency in Migration

me to the point of exasperation. Things of great importance, things that would undoubtedly almost kill you, but let's hope that things will follow favourably, actually, let's hope they just stay the course. I cannot give you details about this because it's too dangerous, but should I have the good fortune of finally seeing you, you will understand everything then, and everything will have been done to strengthen our love.

Rather, and this is the question you will need to answer, this applies to both of us, perhaps it's not a question but rather an explanation. Tell me, given that here in Italy they are talking about Communists being denied entry to America, does the same regulation apply to Canada? As you know, the reasons I had registered are negligible, and for over a year I have not participated in the group because I don't agree with their ideas. Try to obtain as many details as possible about this, but I believe that Canada is part of the English Commonwealth, yet nonetheless this regulation has been in place for over six months in South America, the Italian police headquarters are now applying these rules introduced by the consulates in Italy and the police head-quarters. Try to find out all the details, and ask your *papà* about this, and let me know as soon as possible what fate awaits me. Just this evening C ... [Loris's brother] returned from Ampezzo and brought me greetings from your *nonni* and your *zii*. They are all doing very well, he mentioned that O ... is blossoming into a beautiful little girl, they say she is as beautiful as her aunt Antonietta, there is no doubt about that! Try not to be jealous!!! You told me I still need to wait for the photo, how long the wait is taking ... '*un po' per celia, e un po' per non morire.*'[19] Perhaps I will have time to send you one that I have just taken for you. April Fool's Day is almost over, it's exactly 4 minutes to midnight. The kisses that I send for you are not a joke, but they are an infinity of kisses for you.

Your Loris

[Top of first sheet: note to her family]

Give my kisses and greetings to your *mamma* and *papà* with many thanks for their constant care toward me. Many kisses from my *mamma*, and greetings from the others [?].

---

19 "A bit to tease, and a bit so as not to die." Puccini, *Madama Butterfly*, 334.

— 9 —

"You are lovely, season of springtime"

The Poetics of Nature and Writings of Distant Love

NATURE AND ITS SEASONS are observed in the letters of Antonietta and Loris through myriad lenses. As in the case of other collections of letters, the letters of Antonietta and Loris point to themes and subjects we find in novels, poems, and essays that were studied in school or learned as the correspondents came of age. This literary interweaving shows – as Luisa Passerini notes in her analysis of the correspondence of another couple, beginning in 1938 – "the deep links between the literary imagination and the imaginary present in daily life."[1] In this chapter, the description of the Carnic mountains as the queens of the valley, the verdant fields and a serene sky are written in connection to nostalgia and longing infused with a striking awareness of the forces of change that will define their lives together. These forces are motivated by Antonietta's migration and Loris's anticipated migration to Montreal.

There is a long history of turning to nature as a source of inspiration for poetry and prose from at least the fifteenth century. The description of nature in the letters seems to me an acknowledgment of this long history in literature and other writings, and is particularly reminiscent of a literary tradition situated in the Romantic period, when "poets subjected nature to an unconditional interior meditation."[2] Loris was very likely familiar with the work of Italian nineteenth century poet and philosopher Giacomo

---

1 Passerini, *Europe in Love, Love in Europe*, 281.
2 "I poeti assoggettano la natura ad un'incondizionata meditazione interiore ..." Camerino, "'E il piacer ... farsi paura' Leopardi e la percezione dei fenomeni naturali," 338.

Leopardi. As one of Italy's greatest writers, he likely learned poetry and prose through his studies, and would model himself on romantic ideas of nature. Leopardi's work points to nature's constellations of behaviour as similar to the laws of individual feelings, with nature thus guiding the imagination in both spontaneous and pure fashions instead of in arbitrary and abnormal ways.[3] In addition to the poetic transparency with which nature appears in the letters, there are other ties to nature in the letters.

The description of nature no doubt also created an imprint of the homeland that Loris wished to remember and share with Antonietta in his letters and possibly re-evoke in the future once he had joined her in Canada. These bountiful, verdant fields and white-tipped mountains represented the locus where the couple first declared their love for each other several years ago, a period that to Loris likely felt very distant. In his descriptions, it is as though Loris has already crossed the Atlantic Ocean as he endeavoured to pre-empt and imagine in the present the "mental pain" of separation that his migration would cause to him and his family and friends. While he had not yet embarked on the oceanliner, the imminent departure began to weigh on him, as he reflected on what he would need to renounce in his promise to migrate to Canada.[4]

Nature, in connection to literature, music, and art, inspired Loris and Antonietta. They consequently reflected on nature in relation to distance and time, nostalgia and longing as they experienced separation and migration. Nature and its landscapes represent a significant lens through which emotions and metaphors of experiences related to mobility can be paralleled with future directions of research.

— Venice 10-4-49 —

Nietta mia piccola amata,[5]
A blue ribbon with myriad shades of the thousand and more colours of the iris stand out in this moment, they illuminate the evening

---

3 Ibid., 339.
4 Similarly, see Akhtar, "The Immigrant, the Exile, and the Experience of Nostalgia."
5 Nietta, my darling girl.

against a dark, ashen sky as dense and dark as the colour of lead. All
of this appears on the horizon as we look south of the resplendent
Carnic mountains glowing fiercely red from a spray of colours, these
mountains emerge majestic and regal as the queens of our valley,
the custodians of our land. With their own unique authority, they
circumscribe a serene sky and a vast extension of verdant fields at this
time of spring embraced by the sun and its warmth. How beautiful
they are! The white tips adorn here and there their classic greyness,
pointing to the enamel green of a tiny forest in bloom; how much they
bring back the truth of a day absorbed by love's euphoria garnering
nothing but happiness and joy. When will the days I see before me
match those quiet peaceful days? When will we savour happiness
together once again? Everything around me in this hour speaks of
a memory that profoundly whispers to my heart, my feelings. We
were happy and together with the splendour of the sun before us, one
year ago I was close to you as spring was blooming, we had by now
already received and seized the peace that Easter blossoms, and we
were delighted by a generous, kind man, your *papà*, Vittorio. Those
days were an extraordinary, sincere joy, one that already then was
anticipating a bitter separation of things and people, a separation of
intentions and objects. Of that bitter decision, I am the one to remain
on course. That day will come, there is no doubt, especially because I
believe wholeheartedly that the day of redemption will come for me,
something that has not manifested itself in these days, it will come,
I am sure about it in my heart, but let's hope …

As we hope, many things will happen, many sorrows will pass,
many moments of happiness will ripen, and many minds will change,
this is not a game of fate but a willingness on the part of our destiny,
which has granted me so much! I cannot explain myself fully because
I don't want to at this point though all is definitive, may this be good
news for you, many things have changed for me in these days, I will
not provide more details because I want to surprise you if I will travel
to Montreal, and this will perhaps give you joy and happiness in the
same way it has worried and preoccupied me in these past few days.
This is why I started this letter describing the calm that brings splendour once again to the dark sky, this is why I could not write to you

The Poetics of Nature and Writings of Distant Love 235

until today. In a few words, I was away from Venice for three days,
I arrived last night and today, here I am with you.

On your part, I thought I would find news from you upon my
return, instead I found a void of hope and certainty. It was some time
since you had not delayed in writing to me, now, you fell for it again,
get better quickly my dear Tetina, do not make me wait a long time,
always assure me that you are mine, only mine, I believe I am the
only one who has stolen your heart. Together with your news, I hope
to also receive the certainty that I am eagerly awaiting, I leave to you
then every decision, to you my certainty. In my last letter I wrote
to you that I would have travelled to Ampezzo for Easter, I am now
confirming this to you that I will most certainly be going and with
the greatest of pleasures, I will be visiting them with infinite nostalgia
and immeasurable sadness. You will receive this letter in time for
Easter or later perhaps, of course think of me, I will be there in those
days, those moments, and from there I will be thinking of you, the
smells of your lands imbibed, sealed by the sacrifice of your Loris.
This is the way it will be forever, until I will remember every single
thing about you, it will always be like this until I join you, until our
dream is realized. May this year's Easter bring us the serenity and joy,
that happiness and peace that was granted to us last year, may this
Easter be the last Easter we spend apart, may this day be the summit
of our waiting.

On this occasion, I cannot prevent myself from sending you my
wishes and greetings for a Holy Easter on that land which witnesses
you together on this day. May my most affectionate kisses serve as
a reawakening from a long sleep on this day of Peace and glory and
happiness for you. Your Loris

To your *mamma* and *papà*, please extend my sincerest and kindest
wishes, on this day in which I cannot be with you I return to your
loved ones in the land of Ampezzo now only for me, as I think of you
and kiss you. Affectionately your Loris

— Ampezzo 19-4-49 —

Nietta mia amatissima,[6]
To return to this place is like turning back the clock, and since time designs its own history, these places preserve a life lived here in its entirety, and they compose a long diary, a long history, a story about joy and happiness discovered here, like a gem in a field of flowers among hundreds of roses, between two hearts. To return here is akin to fuelling a fire that has already been kindled, certainly, it does not burn beautiful thoughts, but rather rekindles memories, purifies thoughts, chains of details are woven into our spirit, keeping constant our love, our affection, our will. This is the summary of my stay here, a bitter stay given your absence, filled nonetheless with sincere affection that brought peace to my face and softened my gaze. This is exactly how things were these past days, it is precisely how I felt in your house, which preserves the best part of our intimacy of our affection, of our thoughts about one another. To relive days on this native land of yours is like starting a new life again, this time under the auspices of a memory that embodies us fully, because we left a part of us in every minute thing, in the truthful fragrance of harmony and understanding we left our love, we left on this Earth a first nest in which still today the stories of your family, our *nonni* and all of our loved ones are reminisced. It was as though I was resurrected as I stood at the entrance of this home, it was as though my heart was resurrected as I listened once again to the voices of your loved ones, it was an absolute, irrefutable joy that was added to the list of memories, on the special day of Easter of 1949 in which I found myself once again in your home with your dear ones among all those who remember you and who see you, your person, your spirit, your affection in me.

Easter 1949

With a new season of spring, at this point blossoming with intense natural beauty, Easter has returned with peace in every heart, just as the fields are green and the trees bloom once again on this dear land of ours. Spring has returned, peace is restored, Easter has returned framed this time by nostalgia and regret, everything is replicated with

---

6 Nietta my greatest love.

The Poetics of Nature and Writings of Distant Love   237

the same simplicity and naturalness that we have always recognized. Everything is the same with similar gratification, making these days delightful for all of us, with this however, the days of bliss that we lived were not reproduced, they are amiss from the exhibit of springtime, "All is still, and yet all to the heart speaks to me … this peace away from here where can I find it? You are lovely, season of springtime, renews flowers and love, the sweet April,"[7] sweet April. What enchantment awakens in me and in every flower? This awakening grew more intense with your absence, now that every memory renews the existence of a joyous past, now that on this Easter day your tender and sweet voice is missing, the voice of my Tetina, away in another land over the ocean, especially these days that are rife with memories and without a word from you. Your letter will arrive I am certain, before I leave, everyone here is waiting for it, even I am eagerly awaiting word from you, especially since I had not received any for Easter. On Good Friday, fifteen days of your silence had passed, now it's more than that. I will discuss this later, for now, I want to continue on my first point.

So, on this Easter Sunday, your silence in this home deepened the furrow of sorrow in my heart, to return here in Ampezzo marked even more gravely my spiritual thirst, to reappear here among your loved ones was a vivid repetition of the bitter memory of seeing you leave. Oh yes, my Tetina, you need to live it to believe it, and understand how profound my sorrow is, how despondent my sacrifice is. What is missing in this euphoric springtime, this scaffolding of beauty is something that would have enriched these days. A series of things and details tied to a chain of memories cannot evade my gaze, a gaze which looks back with intense melancholy at everything that we witnessed together, everything that is buried in my heart, much like a constant concatenation between a past and present life, between the present and the future. You know what I mean, and you will immediately understand the state of mind with which I write to you, now that it is only through memories that I speak, now that I connect my memories to an active reality, now that alone, I must do all that I can to relive the past with innumerable details, evocative,

7 Mascagni, *L'Amico Fritz*, Act 2, 688.

238 January 1949 to July 1949

and powerful memories. Everything here speaks to me, every person reminds me of a day, every day reminds me of an event, every event revives a love. Your mountains from Monte Tinisa to Monte Pura, from Monte Pura to Monte V... [?], all of them have your imprint, all of them embody your spirit, they have not changed, just as you too have not changed, your spirit is akin to theirs, their spirit which restores new life today and tomorrow, almost by tradition when they give courage to all those who are crestfallen.

News

Saturday was then a rehearsal of last year. I arrived in Ampezzo, the joy of your family, especially your *nonna*, was immense, almost moving. Like before, I was surrounded by everyone's care and consideration. With this letter, you can be assured that everyone is in good health and satisfactorily resigned. Frankly, I thought I would find them in a different state, instead I was delighted to be mistaken. You can be sure in absolute ways that everyone continues to be very, very well. You should see how beautiful O ... has grown, a truly beautiful girl, a big girl just like her Aunt Tetina whom I heard has gained some weight. Is that really true Nietta? While I was here, I met everyone in the town, from L ... to A ... from S ... to R ... your sewing teacher and all of your friends. I won't even mention D ... and T ... with whom I spent the evenings chatting at their home. All of these people have asked me to send you their greetings, especially D ... who told me that she will write to you this week but she, like all of us, is waiting for your news, that's been a long time coming.

On Easter Sunday I spent the afternoon in the company of I ..., D ..., O ..., her fiancé, and we managed to while away the time, then on Monday afternoon together with them again and A ... we went to Mediis, and there we were admitted to the public dancehall. Like usual the writer here limited himself to dancing a tango with D ... and together we went around the rosy in the middle of the hall. What a shame, don't you think? What can I do! I spent yesterday, Tuesday, and today, Wednesday, at home and on the main square in the company of many of our friends.

Tomorrow I leave for Venice, the festivities are over, there, a new series of tasks will begin, that is, the final set of documents need to

The Poetics of Nature and Writings of Distant Love   239

be prepared, the documents that I was authorized to begin on the Saturday before leaving for Ampezzo, that is precisely the day that I received the documents from the Canadian Consulate in Rome. It is perhaps for this reason that I was more energetic during these festive days, now I have no reason to doubt the outcome or the possibility. Now we will see what we need to do, I will talk with you about this more calmly as soon as I return home. Everyone here asks me to send their greetings to you, especially your *nonni*, your *zii*, D ..., who asked me to tell you that you need to be more accurate and punctual with your letters. I, who am familiar with the fox, let it be until the right moment when I will be able to have you, and then I will take advantage of the moment to please you, to kiss you and hold you tight against my heart

    your Loris

— Ampezzo 21-4-49 —

Please extend special greetings from all of us and myself to your *papà* and *mamma* and tell them that everyone here remembers them with great affection. Tell your *papà* that I met *Zia* A ... in Mediis, his sister, tell him she is well and that she awaits news from all of you. She sends greetings and kisses.

Soon I will leave for Venice and I will be travelling once again in sorrow because of my departure [?], what saves me is the thought that I need to complete the preparations for joining you. In this moment, your dear loved ones are sending their warmest wishes to you, your *nonno* is smiling next to me. I leave soon perhaps so that I can begin to join you. Kisses Loris

— Montreal 26-4-49 —

Mio carissimo ed amato Loris,[8]
I will be brief tonight, not because I have not received any news from you (honestly, I have been waiting for news for a few days now), this is not the reason, but rather because I am tired, after the usual day of work, I have been mending a dress, I have no idea what time it is, and with the clock in my *mamma's* room, I can't even check, though I

---

8 My dearest and loving Loris.

think it's midnight, for this reason I am telling you that I will be brief. My ideas are not so lucid, it is for this reason that my letter will be incoherent, nonetheless I think you will accept it, at least I hope so! As I was saying earlier, several days have passed since I received news from you, I won't deny it, this brings me intense anguish! What happened? Is it bitterness? Revenge? Given the punctuality with which you have always responded, one of the attributes I admire in you, I cannot find an explanation for your silence, that is, the only two reasons I see possible for your silence are those I mentioned above. I don't know if you spent Holy Easter in Ampezzo, I don't know anything, write to me, and tell me something.

I would like to share many things with you, many little things that happen to me every day, and that I experience daily, how much I think of you, conversations I have from day-to-day, but to what use? At the end of it all, they are all the same. I think of you, I think of you always and I love you, these are the words that must always be in your heart, do not forget them, Loris, my adored one, don't ever forget them, you can forget everything else, but this, you must not, you cannot forget. I await your news, now it's my turn to beg you to return to me, without bitterness, if I hurt you, forgive me, it won't happen again my precious, do you believe me? I enclose here a photo taken at Easter, keep it with you until the day in which I will be with you, physically, and forever, kiss it, and keep it safe, I embrace you affectionately and kiss you.

Your Nietta

Kisses to your *mamma* and your loved ones

— Venice 2-5-49 —

Amatissima mia Nietta,[9]

The greyness of many dark, obfuscated days seemed to take over my spirit and my will to the point of nearly thwarting my being into the worst possible state ever, its metallic ugliness, the seed of a bitter echo, the sprout of pain and sorrow. I voluntarily succumbed to an atrocious, sour silence, I yielded to a delay that has no memory, a victim of a saintly and pure fear. This is perhaps why my silence seemed

9 Nietta my greatest love.

The Poetics of Nature and Writings of Distant Love 241

forced and voluntary despite myself, for this reason I was a character of a hurtful parenthesis of distrust, and because of this, without a precedent, I was a slave of a real and particular fear. The parenthesis of sorrow that is remembered from April 1st to today, the 2nd of May, as a sad experiment in preparation of marriage, that nonetheless preserves the photographic negative of a bitter period. To me, it must serve as a confirmation, an assurance that I love you deeply as much as I have always loved you, an assurance that my heart has but one objective, that is, to know how to love and to nurture that love.

I who have always spoken to you with an open heart, I who have always had a heart that offered humble protection, I suffered enormously and bitterly and I found not even a morsel of solace. No one was able to comfort me, I alone was compelled to consume the atrocious, infernal sorrow, I alone burned little by little for 31 bitter days of trial. Thirty-one days bear the seal of your silence from the 1st of April to the 2nd of May with no word from you.

I don't know, I just don't know how to convince myself, I cannot find a reason, Why all of this? What happened at the end? "But" may this "but" offer you the sincere acceptance of a heart that for over one month could not, did not speak. What was the reason for this silence? A thousand thoughts, a thousand hypotheses, a thousand sufferings, a thousand ideas and more as I thought about a reason, but none emerged. I suffered tremendously, I held hope but it was all in vain as my head remained shrouded in darkness. To provide no word for one month is like robbing me of my sight, in my gaze there was confusion, with a stubborn look, I cried to myself asking, why are things going so against me? Now that we are halfway in our life path and everything should be brilliant with trust, happiness, and confidence. How many, how many times did I look back and wonder that perhaps I had done something wrong to deserve this, but my heart would reply: you did nothing wrong other than love someone deeply, yes, as I always have, perhaps even more than before now that you are far away. Yes, more than before, I am sure, if I did not truly suffer, I would not have been so downtrodden, so consumed; it is only for this reason that I offered to the wind a part of my life, yes, to the wind so that it could be the messenger of my wail, I thought. I know how to love you, I know how to bring happiness to you, only God knows this, only God knows how much I pray for you. All of this is nothing new, my ways, my words, I pray for this wish every day, this wish for more, to keep me faithful to my love, to cherish myself, to keep me faithful to you, you who extends her hand to keep me trustworthy and provide you with that joy I have always fought for and to make you the Queen of my thoughts, the keeper of my spirit, the abundance of my heart. I did everything always with one objective, always and everything did I do this with one goal in mind, always and everything did I do this to lift your heart and your love toward that spiritual greatness that lifts the ground to an angelic state, that unites the heart to the mind and writes the story of an everlasting happiness resting on the sincere peace of a family's serenity. These things underscore my wish to see you blissfully happy, I believe my words are clear, though mundane, but for you, I am certain you will translate these poor heartfelt words not just into words, but the breadth of expression of my sentiments for you that will never end on this Earth, they will inhabit the heavens where true peace will be filled with wonder where victors will be resistant to material tribulations, the victors of true peace, reminiscent of the Divine gift.

Oh, my Nietta, perhaps I am speaking in complicated ways, but it is all that I have for you alone, this is all that remains for me to punish you for the indescribable bitterness I felt, perhaps I should not demonstrate my utter fragility, but I cannot be mean, even if my limit was surpassed, there is no doubt that for me the best punishment is forgiveness. And since misunderstandings and confusion are never amiss in letters, I will limit myself in thinking that perhaps your letters were altogether lost; of course, it is possible that it happened to one of the letters, but two or three, no! Especially since I was receiving four letters per month from you, then came Easter, and even on this occasion, I received nothing, it is for this reason that my days in Ampezzo were not the most cheerful overall while I relived days of reminiscence and nostalgia alongside your family and your elders. I explained this to you in detail in my last letter written while I was inspired there, already in that letter I mentioned your delayed letters, as I hoped to find myself with one or two of your letters in my hands upon returning home, or at the very least, a greeting card for Easter, but nothing came in response to my wishes of peace. It was in that letter that I described to you my discoveries in your little town, a portrait of youthful charm,

The Poetics of Nature and Writings of Distant Love   243

nothing had changed, you can be sure, during this period of absence, I found everything the way we had left it on that day in September, it is for this reason that I was able to bring some joy to my despondence. Everything spoke to me about you in that sanctuary of peace and meditation, my rest there was auspicious for my soul, for my body. A place that embodied peace, warmth, affection from your loved ones, all that was missing was the echo of a certain voice, that is of two voices that I remember deeply, the echo of your speech was missing, the echo of your footsteps, of your words of comfort when I felt down, and so, your *nonna* would hold me tight, she understood and talked to me, she talked about you with the regrets of a long time past, I held tight to her affection, almost to the point that I could feel your body close, I would speak to her and hear the timbre of your echo, you are so alike, and at the very least, you are the same, in this way the days passed fleetingly by until I left with equally heavy regret.

As I left you, I meditated throughout my travels home as chatting fellow travellers witnessed me overcome with grief. And so, a new chapter of our story ended once again in Italy, yes, because though I remained, I won't need to change any part of it, rather the story will need to refine itself in its bitterest and youthful moments. I did not hesitate to start a new chapter, however, perhaps the most challenging, yet the most right of all, and so I tried with all my will to understand and capture something interesting until the gleeful day finally arrived, that is, the day in which I was no longer sulking, everything had passed by then, all was over, even though my sorrow remained with me throughout. I hope your intentions are positive, and there will be no reason to make you anxiously wait any longer. Your letter speaks to me about your remorse in having forgotten me for so long, alongside this feeling, I read your solemn need for my words and my presence. It will always be so, you can be assured, I will not and cannot forget you with indifference, my ties with you run too deep toward a pure and generous love, I would not be able to love anyone else as I have loved you; it is not the material that is important, my heart is speaking, a disinterested and altruistic heart, a heart engraved with modesty, overflowing with feelings of affection. Only for this reason has my heart suffered with abundant resignation, as it waited for a propitious, comforting godsend, and like Solomon, I never appealed for an injurious fate.

244 January 1949 to July 1949

I continue tonight, 4 May, from where I left off and as an Italian enthusiast, I give you this horrific news. Today is the 4th of May and Italy is immersed in national mourning for the tragic loss of over 30 of its beloved sons. Tonight, at exactly 1600 hours on the Superga hill near Turin a plane crashed to the ground, it was carrying the entire Turin team. Everyone died, they all left their lives there after having celebrated the patriotic colours of our nation. All 30 of them perished, including the Great Valentino Mazzola, Ezio Loik, and the Ballarin brothers, former bearers of the black-green shirt, young and old warriors of the Italian flag. Everyone in Italy, from avid sports fans to fervid Italians, is grieving the dead today. My deepest heartfelt thoughts go to them, and especially to the Venezia team. Aldo Ballarin and Dino Ballarin, two brothers who zealously heightened the lustre of the Italic sun. Sports, journalism, and aviation have today sacrificed once again its brave men, and as a sports enthusiast of a great era who is profoundly moved, I extend my first thoughts to them for their everlasting peace.

I continue from where I left off in my letter in sections, turning to you now with the same constant verve as always, as I think about your letter of 26 April. It was a short letter, but equally dear and anticipated, including your first photo. You cannot imagine my delight and emotion in seeing you after so many months of waiting. In that moment, I felt I was dreaming as my eyes observed you and I cried, it was never a dream, you can be sure, but absolute reality. It was a reality to see you still beautiful and sweet, as beautiful as the Madonna, oh my dear Tetina, as delicate as the fragrance of spring. How deeply I gazed at you, how tightly I held you spiritually in my heart. Your beauty in this photo clouded me, perhaps because you never looked like this, and my eyes witnessed wisdom in your gaze, a wisdom that circumscribes their life. You are more beautiful than you have ever been to me after so much sorrow, but all was different in a few seconds, and the more I looked at you, the more I observed you, the more you shined, you are beautiful, your gaze is glowing, the dress you wear resembles the sweetness of a delicate flower, you are resplendent as my heart has always seen you and loved you. You look like a young bride imbued with the sweet gaze of someone who is just married (but, next time, remember to send me a photo that shows the other leg because I was a little distressed at seeing you like so). Am I

The Poetics of Nature and Writings of Distant Love   245

mistaken? You are beautiful in that dress, always elegant in your style, so much so you made me think of a young bride. How I adore you in that veiled hat, perfectly combined, good girl my darling, you have such lovely taste, similar to mine. You are truly, truly beautiful.

I received the first papers from the Canadian Consulate in Rome concerning my departure, you can imagine my enthusiasm, now I am rushing to proceed with the papers in order to go to Rome, of course, the Consulate's regulations are no longer the same as last year's, rather, they are more precise. Imagine that a parent who is leaving must now bring to Rome his whole family after having had the X-rays done in the capital of his province, I will need to do the same and have the X-rays done in Venice at the office of the medical doctor designated by the Consulate, then go to Rome, but before I travel to Rome for the visa, the instructions indicate that I must have in my hands either my ticket for travelling or a letter from a travel agency confirming the availability of seats on-board. For this reason I am in a bit of a bind. You know very well (and I will be brave in explaining this to you) that in this moment my situation does not allow me to make any other move, maybe for this reason I have this concern, I don't know what you think of me now, that is, I have never before had to turn to you for this kind of situation. Things have changed for me as well now, and you must understand this without prejudice, on the other hand I know that all of this depends on your *papà*, it will be up to you to speak to your *papà* on my behalf. Please do this favour for me with no other ideas in mind and explain to me the outcome in your next letter. I have no further news concerning your letters that were lost, or the papers, that is, the application in process, at least they arrived from Rome and everything is now clear.

Consequently, I have no other news on the application of emigration of P ... What was the response? Write to me clearly, I hope nothing serious has happened. As you can see after so much silence, I wrote a long letter to you, packed, at least I hope, of truthful and sincere words, may this be the conclusion of an ugly episode, and a new beginning of a bright horizon. All is quickly forgotten by us, may the pure kisses from my heart be the seal of stone forever, your Loris

Kiss me, and give my greetings to your *papà* and *mamma* as I remember them with much affection. From my family, and particularly my *mamma*, kisses and greetings.

246 January 1949 to July 1949

— Montreal 8-5-49 —

Mio amato Loris,[10]

If I am responding a little late with news, it is only because I was waiting for your reply to the two letters I had sent to you some time ago. I awaited all this week with an anxiety that I leave for you to imagine, every day I would call my *mamma* at break-time to find out if I had any news from you, but the answer was always negative. Yes I received the letter you sent me from Ampezzo (noted) with a 15-day delay from the other letter, and then, nothing, what happened? You tell me what I should be thinking. Or, do you want me to go crazy? Oh Loris, you shouldn't do this to me, if you bear a grudge against me for the letter that I wrote to you in a moment of disgust and disappointment, you are wrong, very wrong! You know yourself that sometimes it is not reason that governs us, but rather our nerves, even people who are sweeter and less impulsive than me fall into the trap at times, we need to understand, we need to empathize.

As I was saying, I wanted to write to you this week because I had many little things to tell you, but I was so disappointed in your silence that I could not even find the words to voice what I wanted to tell you. Tonight however, I just couldn't resist, for better or for worse, I wanted to craft these words for you, in this way you would also find the document attached here, I don't know if you have begun the application process, I hope to know for certain about this tomorrow (honestly, if it were not the case, I can't tell you how disappointed I would be). In any case, together with the documents that you will be taking to Rome, you will include this one as well; however, before travelling there for the interviews and exams, you will need to have with you your boarding ticket. I will mail this to you as soon as I know where you are with the application. I would like to write to you about many little things about your arrival here, but since they are not too important, I will keep them for another letter when my heart will be more cheerful (and you know when that will be!!). I ask you, please, my darling write to me, I need to hear from you, especially now. Now, let's talk about your trip to Ampezzo. Thank you my darling, I am so delighted to hear of the warmth with which my family welcomed

10 Loris my beloved.

The Poetics of Nature and Writings of Distant Love   247

you, oh! I knew it would be so, they are so fond of you! I couldn't stop myself from crying when I read your description as I listened to you speak about my dear, dear loved ones and my dear little country, forever in my heart!

But perhaps we should not talk about this, all it will do is rekindle my sorrow that is beginning to heal, one thing alone remains for me, the hope to see you again, to talk with you about everything I have seen and experienced, and about everything *that we have lived*! ... But, why, why are you not writing? How ironic that you said, "You will be a [?]" Oh yes, if I keep this up, you will find me in a worse state than when I left! My *mamma* wanted to write to you in these days to inquire why you have been so silent, but then between one thing and another she did not have the time. I am going to sleep now, hoping that tomorrow is a new day, a day that will bring me news. Kisses to your *mamma* whom I remember with infinite affection, to *Signor* Gigio and the rest of the family, to you my life, my love, I send you my dearest and most ardent kisses.

your Nietta
Kisses from my *papà* and *mamma*

— Venice 15-5-49 —

Nietta mia amatissima,[11]

I wasted no time in replying to you and your letter that I received only yesterday, the 14th, I received the registered letter that included the document.[12] I wasted no time because I too find myself undecided at times, but I had already determined I would write to you today, and this is what I wish to do having just returned from the game. This letter will help to clarify those doubts or uncertainties, or better yet, things we had not anticipated and that followed one after another lately, replete with anxiety for the preparation of the documents. In your last letter (registered) about this you mention that you had delayed in writing to me for the sole reason that you had not received news from me, and you ask with immense apprehension and disheartening alarm, what did I ever plan to do to you? What am I doing to

11 Nietta my greatest love.
12 Cf. letter of Antonietta Petris, 8 May 1949.

make you suffer, what indeed had happened to me that I disappeared with no word in sight. It is only for this reason (perhaps justified) but nonetheless a little too impatient and with little foundation, I am telling you that you were mistaken in judging me. I am truly shocked that you, my dear Tetina, you who knows how attentive I am with you, how much I devote myself to you with my writing, how could you have thought badly of your Loris, in this case (not so much in terms of rights, but more from logic) it was I who had to think so of you, thinking of you in a new land with so many new things to discover, but I did not get to this point (from lack of ignorance) …

At this moment, everything is fine, please don't worry, just be aware that (should it not have been obvious enough in my previous letter) I was the one who waited for one month and one day for your letter, the letters must have been lost in the mail, and so, how could I respond to you as I usually do if I had no news from you while I was in Ampezzo, or when I had returned home? I understood that you also would not be pleased about my silence, but I believe it was justified by your own silence. My last letter must have provided ample clarifications of this little game, yes, it was a game, because while I waited, you waited too, you thought I was the cause, and instead, it was you, when I thought you were the cause, instead, it was me. I hope that this letter clears the air but I want to remind you: Never again think wrongly of me, I am always your Loris who loves you and thinks of you thoroughly, and that never has my head given a start to your heart. May this serve to convince you and assure you further of our future, a future that is brimming with happiness and joy. With faith and hope in God, I spend these days in feverish anxiety. Let's hope everything turns out for us now that I need to travel to Rome for the examination.

On this, here is some news. After I received the first set of papers from Rome, that is, upon my return home from Ampezzo, I began the paperwork. These are already read, and in a few days, I should have my passport in my hands, given that it was requested even through V … at the Bar Campanile, who is in touch with the officer in charge. At the police headquarters I received the authorization from the Canadian Consulate, and this prevents us from wasting time. Once I have the passport in my hands, I will have the X-rays done at W …

The Poetics of Nature and Writings of Distant Love 249

with the doctor who is designated by the Consulate for every city. They did this in order for things to flow more efficiently in Rome. Once the X-rays and blood tests will be done, I will travel to Rome for a third visit and for the visa, however, as you know, I will first need my boarding ticket. I will not add anything else about this. If all proceeds as it should, the meeting will take place soon. I pray to our good and all-powerful Lord. We are in His hands. Amen.

I will stop here because there is no point in continuing further; I will keep you posted day by day when the moment is right. Thank you for sending me the document, I will need it for my meeting in Rome. A heartfelt thank you to everyone, the rest will follow. The Venezia team won 5–0 today, and is now in 2nd position, I hope to see them move to Group A before I leave. With my soul overflowing with joy for everything that surrounds me, and with the hope to see you soon, I kiss you passionately, your Loris

Many kisses to your *papà* and *mamma*

— Montreal 18-5-49 —

Mio adorato Loris,[13]
After a break of more than eight days, here I am with you, I can honestly tell you that after receiving your very long letter [2-5-49], I lost the will to write, not for anything, I mean, not because something has changed in the way I feel about you, but rather because I found it very strange that you had not received any news from me in such a long time. I am really sorry that the letters I wrote to you ended up in this way, because Loris, I swear to you that I did not wait such a long time before writing to you, a silence of a week and more is understandable, but a month is absolutely unforgiveable. I wrote a letter to you on the Sunday before Easter, then on the Monday, that is after I received your letter in which you tell me how worried you are about what happened to your friend P ..., and in this letter I was a little angry (I don't need to explain why, I will discuss it with you when you will be here, for now, it's water under the bridge), then days later, still without news, I wrote to you again thinking that you were angry about this, and in this letter I apologized for the way I had expressed myself, the

13 My adored Loris.

last letter I sent you included the photograph you received; therefore, you see now that it's not my fault, I don't understand how it is possible that you did not receive my letters, it's so strange!

Some time ago I sent you a letter that included a card, I hope that you received at least that one especially since I sent it via Registered Mail, I worry about this, and I am waiting for your confirmation. I already have in my hands your boarding ticket but I am waiting to speak with *Signor* S ... this evening for information on how to proceed from here, and then I will send it to you. My *papà* had already taken care of everything before you advised me of this. Here everyone is talking about your arrival, my *papà* would be happy if you travelled through France, in that way you could meet and become acquainted with his brothers; would you like that? He also asks me if you could buy him a good chronometer watch; the ticket includes the trip from Venice to Le Havre, find out how much you need for the trip, and you can spend the rest on the watch. I think you have more than enough for both, I leave it up to you as I am certain that you know how to proceed best.

Signora C ... asks me to tell you not to arrive late at night because she doesn't want to lose sleep (she's kidding!), R ... (the daughter of *Signora* C ...) dreamt that you had arrived, and that you were ugly, so ugly, old and with white hair, wearing old rags. She is a bit ... off, isn't she? As you can see, everyone thinks of you, and waits for you, I, more than anyone else, as you can imagine. I believe, actually I am certain that B ... O ... the driver at SADE will be travelling here, and that he will be travelling the same route as you, his brother prepared the papers alongside my *papà*. We would be thrilled if you travelled together, write to him and plan to travel together so that we will all come to meet you in Quebec, O ...'s brother and the whole family. Here is his address: O ... B ... Ampezzo Carnico, Udine. I include here for you the two photos that were taken on the day of G ...'s Holy Confirmation, do you like them? Here you can see the other leg, the one I kept hidden in the first photo I sent you, one at a time, isn't that enough? I leave you now so that I can continue the letter that I will post tonight with the last of the papers. I wait for your arrival, which is fast approaching, I wish for it and dream of it, I love you, many kisses.

your Nietta forever

The Poetics of Nature and Writings of Distant Love 251

Kisses to your *mamma* and the family From my *mamma* and *papà*, many greetings and best wishes to you and your loved ones.

— Montreal 27-5-49 —

Mio adorato Loris,[14]

It's been some time since I sat down calmly and peacefully to compose a letter for you, both of us have gone through a period that we can call tumultuous, and if we think about it carefully, it was all for nothing. Our letters, especially mine, were mostly about admonishments, of phrases that had nothing to do with those of a long time ago, you pointed to it and understood that your last letter is clear about this; however, I don't think that it's worth discussing the topic further, like many things, at this point this too has passed, much like the eight months that have separated us, I think this is what we should be talking about more, don't you think so, my darling? Eight long months have slipped by, I still remember, as though it were yesterday, the last events before our departure. Just last night, in fact I experienced something that I have lived before, it was during a visit to the airfield of Dorval,[15] I can't explain how I felt in seeing again the majestic four-engine airplanes, the crowds busily waving goodbye while others greeted their loved ones who had just arrived, my eyes watched and my mind reflected, sadness at departure, elation at arrival. You and I can relate to this because we have lived through it, for the past three years we have been experiencing what it's like to die and to be reborn, to relive and then to die again!

The last departure was the worst, the most painful of all, yes, the last one, let's call it the last, and now, your arrival which will be the most joyous moment ever, and from then on, nothing will separate us again, because you will be here forever, and you will never leave me again, and I will never leave you, I will follow you wherever you go, even to the end of the Earth. We have been separated for long enough, and I don't want to be away from you anymore, oh! No. If you only knew how envious I am of couples walking carefree, arm-in-arm and smiling, and I envy them, yes, I do, because they are my age, and they

14 My adored Loris.
15 Today's Montréal–Trudeau International Airport.

252 January 1949 to July 1949

have the same wishes and desires to live as I do, and why shouldn't
I be as happy as they are? Oh! We don't live on bread alone, and you
had correctly noted it one day in one of your letters, we need a little
understanding, a little affection that is different from the love of our
mamma and *papà*, of course, it makes sense that we cannot have
everything that we wish for in life. I am aware of this, I know that we
will have our share of sorrows as well, but we will be able to overcome
them, we will be together, the two of us, we won't be alone. (I stopped
writing here as the *Signori* C … paid us a visit.)

I can't tell you how many sweet kisses N … has now left on your
photograph, she has learned to call you, and say "hello Loris?" She is
so cute, you have no idea, the other day, as my *mamma* mentioned
your name on the telephone, she immediately sent you many kisses. I
was thrilled to receive your photograph, after a long time I too could
finally see your face again, always the same beautiful face, a little less
lean, but always the same, it was strange to see you wearing different
clothes and a new expression, I was so used to gazing at you in the
last photograph you had sent me that it seemed you could be only like
this, a face in waxed tones wearing a sad smile, a half image, really,
many a time I asked myself why this image did not open and close
his eyes, does this sound strange to you? Yet, when you spend hours
alone, everything around you speaks to you, a flower, a brook, and
you are the one who makes them speak for the simple reason that
you don't want to be alone, you want to have someone near you, and
so, how many times I find myself talking to your photo, having long
conversations and crying when I am sad, smiling when I am cheerful.
What do you think of your Nietta? Now, I have another Loris to
admire, a more recent, more composed Loris. Your *mamma* tells me
that you are looking less tense, that you don't think about the train
that used to take you to Ampezzo, as you ran yourself dry in order to
visit me, is this why you are feeling better, isn't this true my darling?
If I am not mistaken, you are wearing a new suit, it's very much to my
liking, very nice and very stylish here, why didn't you discuss it with
me? You know that every little thing that you do matters to me. I am
also very eager to know about how the paperwork is moving along. I
asked my *mamma* to send you the boarding ticket that surely, you will
have received by now. When will I see you, my precious? That day will

The Poetics of Nature and Writings of Distant Love 253

be the most beautiful day of my life. My *mamma* asks me to tell you if you can bring a thermometer for her, the ones they sell here are not what she is used to, she also asks for a cookbook, will you be so kind, Loris? Did you write to O …? Did you receive a reply? Try to travel together, it will be very good for both of you and for us, we will all be waiting for you in Quebec. Here is the address of my *papà*'s brother, that is, my uncle.

Petris O … 8 Rue de Vico. S. Quentin

Aisne, France

If you wish to meet him, write to him and send him a photograph of yourself so he can recognize you. I will stop here as I look forward to receiving your good news, I kiss you ardently on your beautiful face, an affectionate and warm embrace, your Nietta

Please give your *mamma* my deepest thanks for her letter and many many kisses. To your family kisses and warm greetings. Kisses to you from my *papà* and *mamma*.

— Venice 31-5-49 —

Nietta mia amatissima,[16]
You will imagine, without a doubt, the reason that I have delayed in writing to you, and because of this, you must consider me deeply immersed in work these days. In fact, it could not be the opposite since you too have been hard at work on the papers, and you will certainly remember the comings and goings that work has involved. It is nothing less for me, perhaps (I'm not bragging here) it is actually more than you might think when you consider that in less than a month I managed to put in order the situation about my position … in school, and gather the necessary papers for the release of my passport, what it took to get it, travelling to and from, seeking answers from the designated offices regarding the boarding, the remittance of funds, etc., etc. During all of this, surely this is not new to you, I stayed home after returning from work, almost as a form of entertainment, and if you know me well enough, you will imagine my exuberance and my industriousness as I inquired for answers from all the saints everywhere. On Saturday, this marks a new chapter in itself, I went for the

16 Nietta my dearest love.

254   January 1949 to July 1949

X-rays and to W ... here in Venice, and today, the 31–5, I went to pick up my X-rays and the required medical referrals. Here too, everything is moving smoothly, both truly and assuredly. I will now explain to you why the medical exams were completed in Venice.

Of course, you will remember that you went through this in Rome, and because of this, you had to stay in Rome longer than you had anticipated for the authorization. Now it is no longer the case, the Consulate has delegated a trusted medical doctor in the capital city of every province, making it easier to process the applications. The migrant is to take the sealed X-rays to the Canadian medical doctor in Rome, he then approves them after having conducted a general examination of the departing individual. I will do the same, now that everything is ready, all I need to do is leave for Rome on the evening (God willing) of Sunday, 5 June, around 9 o'clock. Perhaps when you will be reading this letter, I will already be in Rome from where I will be sending you a telegram with the results. This is why my heart is overflowing with supreme happiness, and today more than ever since the nightmare of the examinations and meetings is over with a positive outcome.

Last Saturday, incidentally, after the X-rays, I paid a visit to the steamship company for information. Just that morning I received at home the invitation to meet with them at their offices. I clarified a few questions and they told me that since I will not be able to leave on 11 June, I will need to wait for the following departure, that is, on 2 July from Le Havre in France, that is. Hoping that all will go well for me to leave for France where I will be meeting your *zii*, I will leave Venice a few days before, hoping you will have sent me their addresses as soon as possible. Frankly, I did not expect things to move so quickly, so much so it all feels impossible for my family. My *mamma*, of course, is the one who feels the threat of my departure, I try in every way possible to persuade her, she understands, but she thinks about it with regret, of course she loves you and empathizes with your happiness, she participates in our excitement together with your parents, who my family speaks of with enormous enthusiasm and delight. On their behalf, I am grateful to you and thank you with all my heart. Hoping my next letter will give you more pleasant news, I eagerly kiss you again as I wait for 2 July (hopefully).

Your Loris

— 10 —

"Come on, my darling, it's your turn now"
Leaving for Love

AS LORIS PREPARED to travel to another continent, the act of leaving afforded a profoundly ambivalent experience. Leaving also required bidding farewell to his family home and to his parents and his siblings with whom he shared the uncertainty of ever being reunited with them. His family supported his decision to immigrate to Canada. Loris was emigrating to join Antonietta, the woman they had known and loved for years as Loris's fiancée. Yet, his departure marked an unrelenting void in their lives. While letters between them would help to maintain their affective ties and withstand the weight of time, the impact of his migration on his family was extraordinary.

Studies in transnational migration have demonstrated the extent in which the migration of a family member marks the lives of those who leave and those who remain behind.[1] The few letter series that offer both sides of a transnational correspondence have been particularly illustrative of the emotional and psychological implications of separation and migration on family members whether they were leaving or

---

1 The literature on transnational history in migration has soared in recent years. Some excellent examples include Baldassar, "Transnational Families and the Provision of Moral and Emotional Support"; Baldassar, "Transnational Families and aged care"; Baldassar, Baldock, Wilding, *Families Caring Across Borders*; Gabaccia, *Italy's Many Diasporas*; Glick Schiller, Basch, and Szanton Blanc, "From Immigrant to Transmigrant"; Harney, "Men Without Women"; and Reeder, *Widows in White*. On the letters of Italian families who remained behind, see Cancian, *"Una raccolta di lettere italiane inviate agli emigrati* in Canada, 1954–1955."

staying. In my earlier work on six letter collections written between Italy and Canada in the postwar years, I concluded that the differences in emotional forces that permeated the letters of those who left and in those who remained behind were acutely nuanced. In both perspectives, loneliness, pleas not to be forgotten, and nostalgia and hope for a time when they would be united resonated.[2]

As we turn to the final set of letters written between Antonietta and Loris before their reunion, the question of farewells and goodbyes is appropriate in unearthing indices on the emotional impacts of migration experienced by the migrant himself, who was the singular and youngest member of his family to immigrate to a land so distant from their cherished Venice, and his family who remained behind.

For many on either side of the Atlantic, the departure of a loved one immigrating to distant lands was experienced like a death in the family, as the first transatlantic letters of Antonietta and Loris also evince. This form of social death was linked to the feelings of loss and abandonment experienced by everyone, both the migrant and their individual families who remained behind, fearing they would be cut out "from the family networks of care and information" of their loved ones.[3] An unclear loss of the past coupled with an uncertain reunion in the future exacerbated this feeling of death.[4] Perhaps, the Second World War's ending just a few years before also had something to do with this. The suffering and devastation the war generated were still at the forefront of their memories, and its "effects were still very real."[5] In this context, the impact of separation was heightened.

---

2 Cancian, *Families, Lovers, and their Letters*, 142.
3 Baldassar, "Guilty Feelings and the Guilt Trip," 86. See also, Grinberg and Grinberg, *Psychoanalytic Perspectives on Migration and Exile*, and Marchetti-Mercer, "Those Easily Forgotten."
4 Grossenbacher Boss, "The Experience of Immigration for the Mother Left Behind," 368,
5 Sciorra, "Don't Forget You Have Relatives Here," 43. War-related traumatic events have had a significant impact on the lives of migrants and refugees well after they have settled in a new country. Memory plays a critical role in the reconstruction of these events during a migration process. As historian Luisa Passerini poignantly argues in *Autobiography of a Generation*, memory not only records the repercussions of suffering, frustrations, and violence, but also speaks from today (23). New research focuses on developing an

The fear of separation from war had given way to the fear of separation from migration.

While a "forced passivity"[6] may have led them to suffer more than their migrant family members, we can't be sure that migrants, however busy in adapting to new surroundings, did not suffer equally in the separation from their loved ones. An illustration can be gleaned from Antonietta's first letters to Loris in which she describes her agonizing sadness and her lacerating yearning for Loris, for her extended family, and her homeland. Evidence can also be drawn from Loris's recollection of leaving his family for a second time in 1964. In an audio-recorded interview, we hear his voice nearly choking-up as he discussed the reason and impact of returning to Montreal: "it was my duty to continue to live with my wife, my daughters, and for a second time, I abandoned my *mamma, papà*, everyone in the family, they were all still alive, and this was truly the second traumatic moment [*dramma*] in my life."[7]

Leaving his family in July 1949 signalled a new beginning for Loris. However, the depth of feelings associated with abandoning his family were no match for the exhilaration he felt anticipating his reunion with his long-time love. With zeal and determination, Loris, like other migrants who left their loved ones at the docks of Genoa and Naples or the airfields of Rome and Milan, embarked on a journey toward another life, with new expectations, new responsibilities, and commingling familiar and new emotions, in this faraway land that Loris and Antonietta would eventually call home.

understanding of the mental and emotional worlds of migrants and refugees, their experiences, memories, feelings and perceptions, and mentalities following traumatic experiences of war, conflict, and migration. See, for example, Cancian, "Love at the Threshold of War and Migration"; Damousi, "Legacies of War and Migration"; Damousi, *Memories of Migration*; Epp, "The Memory of Violence"; Kushner, *Journeys from the Abyss*; Leese and Crouthamel, *Traumatic Memories*; and De Haene and Rousseau, *Working with Refugee Families*.

6 Falicov, *Latino Families in Therapy*, 59.

7 "Era mio dovere di continuare a vivere con mia moglie, le mie figlie e ho abbandonato una seconda volta la mamma, il papà, la famiglia completa, erano tutti vivi e questo è stato veramente il secondo drama della mia vita." Taped interview with Loris Palma by Canadian film-maker Nicola Zavaglia, estimated date 1997–1998.

— Montreal 6-6-49 —

Mio carissimo Loris,[8]
I am replying a little late to your letter in which you advise me of your most recent news. I am very pleased to see that the process is moving along very well and that a positive outcome is in sight, it seems to me. I am very happy about all of this. It convinces me further that soon you will be here, close to the one who waits for you and loves you. I don't know if you travelled to Rome already, of course, I thought of you there these past few days, a city glowing with beauty and history, cherish inside of you all these wonderful things that our *Patria* [homeland] offers you — its sky, its seas, and once your eyes are satisfied, admire your gorgeous city, its natural and artistic wonders, because you will never see a city that is more radiant. Believe me, you will always miss the home you leave behind; however, amid all that nostalgia, remember that you will live happily knowing that you have seen and lived in a country that is admired by the entire world. My darling, because of this, do not think that we are living in hell, don't be afraid, certainly it is not easy for us to get used to living here, but what will we care when we will finally be together forever? It's a small world. Come on, my darling, it's your turn now, it was mine some time ago!

Last night I went to Holy Mass at 11. I was alone among the crowds of people kneeling at God's feet, I thought of you constantly, and about our tomorrow, I thought of how much more delightful it will be when I will walk into church with you. How many churches did we visit together, do you remember? The churches in Venice, Ferrara, Rome, Ampezzo, and soon, the churches of Montreal will witness us together, are you happy? And, we will thank God for the blessings He has granted us. I now eagerly await a definitive response from you, I am certain that it will be the best piece of news I will have ever received. I wanted to ask you if you received further information about the marriage papers. Should I be looking into this? I think it's time we

---

8 My dearest Loris.

Leaving for Love

inquired. Write to me and advise me so there is no confusion. Believe me, these last items were completed so quickly that it almost does not seem possible that you will be here soon – things are unfolding very fast. Try to reach an agreement with O ... so that you can board the ship on the same day as him. This way, on the day of your arrival, you will find a large group of people waiting for you, and then we will have a lovely ... party to celebrate the arrival of both of you! Speaking of which, I noticed from your latest photo that you had a new suit made for you. How about getting a blue or black suit done as well? ...

– Rome 6-6-49 –

Nietta mia cara,[9]
From these sites, this city, from this home I write to you, this home which has witnessed us probably for the last time together, close and happy, today I saw myself accompanied by your shadow, once again, next to me. How wonderful it is to remember the things and the moments that witnessed us like so. How beautiful it is to see everything that connected us until the final seconds. Tears divided us, the tears that I hope to see in your eyes and mine, not as a portrait of bitterness, but rather of the jubilation that emanates from an exalting joy and utter bliss. You will understand, I am sure, my desire to offer to you the purest and most justified of joys, the kind of joy that inebriates you from my highest bliss and gratitude. I am in Rome and I am certain that you understand where I am writing to you from; however, it will be a short stay, short in the most absolute form.

For the record, I want you to know that I left Venice yesterday Sunday, 5-6, and I arrived in Rome today, Monday, 6-6, on the same morning I very quickly settled the papers at the Consulate, and when I was done at 1430 I sent you the telegram that you received, and at the same time I reserved my return ticket home. In other words, I arrived and return on the same day, imagine such news, I have not slept in a bed in over 48 hours, and it's not over because I will be travelling tonight too. I plan to stop in Ferrara where I will visit L ... and her family so that I don't need to head back that way in light of my imminent trip for Canada. I will be in Venice tomorrow night and there

---

9 Nietta my dear.

260   January 1949 to July 1949

I will take care of the marriage papers for me and you. Once I finish writing this letter, I will write to D ... so that she can get started on the papers in time for when I will be visiting them at mid-month.

I regret to leave you, my darling, but my head is full and confused from the million and one things that remain to be done, for this reason I ask you to forgive me, I kiss you infinitely and with much affection, your Loris

I received the visa for the passport and on Sunday, while in Venice, I will book my departure for 2 July from Le Havre, as we agreed. Thank you and *ciao.*

Signora E ... and *Signor* G ... ask me to extend their greetings, they remember you fondly and hope you do too. Kisses Loris

Infinite kisses for your *mamma* and *papà.* Thank you.

— Montreal 9-6-49 —

Mio adorato Loris,[10]

I don't know how I managed to stop writing to you these past few days, because I tell you honestly that not one day goes by that I don't think of you, you can imagine this, surely you understand how present you are to me, and to receive that telegram on the 6th around 1:30, I can't tell you how immensely gratified I felt in that moment, I will never be able to forget it. I received a phone call from the telegraph office: "There is a message for you miss, it's from Rome, and it says, 'Very well, kisses, Loris.'" Can you imagine how I felt? And my utter happiness for this extraordinary news. My heart leaped with joy and turned to God with gratitude as it seems clear that He too wishes to finally see us together. By now, everything is done, all we need to do is wait for your departure date, and then, for your arrival here, I can assure you that together with my utter happiness, there is one thing that worries and saddens me, that is, as I think about the sorrow your family will face when you leave, especially your *mamma,* who will be in immeasurable sorrow. I know what it means to leave and to watch others leave, and I can only imagine how much more intensely a *mamma* suffers in watching her baby leave, one thing alone must console her, and that is, you will be living with a family who loves

10 My adored Loris.

Leaving for Love   261

you and eagerly awaits your arrival. Poor *mamma*! Please Loris, try
to comfort her and help her so that she suffers less in light of your
departure.

I am surprised that you managed to get everything done so quickly
in Rome, you certainly deserve congratulations. I guess you visited la
Signora E ... and G ..., how are they? I can imagine you taking care
of the last items, if you will be able to make a last trip to Ampezzo,
I ask you to please bring us back (of course, if my family is fine with
this) the coffee cup set, that is, the one that still has all the pieces, the
wooden tray, the floral vase that is in the other house, and the two
frames in our room, the one with the photo of my *mamma* and *papà*,
and the other one with the photo of my beloved *nonna*; if these last
two items are too burdensome for you, don't worry about bringing
them, in any case, do what you think is best, if there is something my
family would like to keep, leave it with them. In a letter you mentioned that you will have a surprise for me upon your arrival, this
news makes me utterly happy, I am always ready for good news, do
you believe it? I wish I knew what this is about, in any case, it won't be
long, I will wait, I can do this!

I will stop here, otherwise I won't have much to tell you when you
arrive. I wait for you, my love. As you can imagine, I can't wait to give
you all of my love, all my kisses. For now, an enormous kiss and good
wishes, your Nietta

Kisses to your *mamma* and to the rest of your family.

Kisses from my parents, distinguished greetings to your whole
family

More kisses for you.

— Ferrara 16-6-49 —

Nietta mia cara,[11]
I purposely waited for this day, not so much in terms of this specific
day, but I waited intentionally for this day to write to you from one
of the numerous places that witnessed us radiating with joy, and less
starving for each other. Now you understand that I am in Ferrara, and
specifically at the home of *Signor* A ..., as I was returning from Rome

---

11 Nietta, my dear.

he invited me to visit him and spend a couple of hours with them. It is only for this reason, that is for two reasons that I awaited this day, the first day, we are aware of already, the second, is because I was waiting for the confirmation of my boarding ticket, and so I was late in writing to you. This last news, in effect, made me forget a little my duty toward you, that is, I have been waiting for an answer for several days already, but until now, no positive news has arrived. The date of departure depends on this news, for which I await confirmation from Rome, the company's headquarters, and for this reason, I have been waiting for it, as I was advised to do by the travel agency in Venice. However, I have not lost all hope in a departure for the 2nd of July, which the agency has assured me of.

The explanations I provide here are just a summary and for this reason I am telling you that upon my return from Rome, I submitted my passport to the maritime agency, which has received from Rome the boarding ticket, these documents will then be sent to Genoa for the in-transit visa from France. For this constant movement of papers, I need a few days, and because of this, until I will have all the papers in my hands, I cannot resign from work, I have no choice, because should the departure date be postponed, and I will have already resigned, I would then lose both time and money. Therefore, I am first waiting for the confirmation from Rome that should arrive in the next few days, and then, I will be able to take my leave from SADE without any worries.

I will try my best to please you concerning the things you wish me to bring from Ampezzo, I will do it without a doubt, especially since I need to pick up the marriage papers that I asked D … to prepare, as well as say goodbye to your *nonni* and your *zii*.

You must have noticed that I did not send you my greetings for your namesake day, of course I did not do so out of negligence, but only because work and the constant preoccupation of the preparation of the papers for my departure keeps me away from our correspondence. Of course, I was with you on that day in my thoughts and in my heart, I was near you as I too wanted to make you happy and see you smiling, hoping that soon I will be sitting next to you, kissing you and embracing you, your Loris

Leaving for Love 263

Many greetings and kisses to your *papà* and *mamma*, as I hope to embrace them soon. Greetings to the *Signori* C ... and their girls.

Many dear greetings from all of us, the M ... Family

— Montreal 17-6-49 —

Mio adorato Loris,[12]

I am taking advantage of today to write to you since I am home because there was little work for me to do at the factory, it is 4 o'clock in the afternoon, we are suffocating from the heat, making it difficult even to breathe, it's been 3 or 4 days now that this insufferable heat persists, and it looks like it will never rain, my *mamma* is sewing on the machine on the balcony, and I am here dying from the heat (I'm exaggerating), it's not so bad because I am wearing a light dress with a low neckline, the dress can be considered a bathing suit since it helps me withstand the heat. By now, you must be in Ampezzo with my family, watching them in their daily lives, in their goings-on, you must be delighting in the cool air of our town, walking through the streets that are ever so dear to me, seeing people I know and love. You can imagine how much I would like to be there too, but I am happy knowing that you are there, because you are part of me, because in you, they will see me, because from you, I will learn about everything and everyone you will have seen and heard from. The days pass with astonishing speed, the hour of your arrival is fast approaching; it still feels incredible that fate wishes us to be together so soon, it feels like a dream, a beautiful dream. Just today as I was speaking to my *mamma*, I was telling her that it does not feel real, and the time I have been here feels so short (that is, now, however, day by day, time moves very slowly!) I constantly wait for your news to hear about the latest decision, to know also what O ... has decided since not even his family has heard from him. Tomorrow is Saturday, and we will be driving to the countryside, at least we will be able to enjoy some cool air for these two days, you don't know how much I long for this. Soon, you too will be here to bring us joy as an additional member of our group, if you only knew how much I think of this when my parents

12 My adored Loris.

and I visit various sites. I will stop here, the heat robs me of any strength to do what I want to do, in any case I don't think I can tell you anything more other than we are waiting for you and we are constantly discussing your arrival. Dear greetings from *Signora* C … and her family. Dear kisses to your *mamma* whom I remember fondly, especially now, the same for your *papà* Gigio and the family. For you, the dearest kisses, and the most affectionate, sincerest wishes. Kisses from my *papà* and my *mamma*, your Nietta

— Venice 22-6-49 —

Nietta mia amatissima,[13]
Just today I was waiting for a letter from you, frankly, though it has only been a few days since I received news from you, and really, I cannot complain. But today, as I lay in bed for some much-needed rest, I was waiting for your news. The reason for this rest is rather silly, nothing serious, really, just some minor gastro issues. My *mamma* wanted me to rest all day so that I can recover fully, but this is no reason for me to neglect my duty, which I know you ardently wait for. The last time I wrote to you was seven days ago when I was in Ferrara, at which point I sent you my last letter, in that letter I gave news about my departure date, which is still unclear for reasons I mentioned, this is the way things are looking at the moment. To begin with, I don't know if I already mentioned to you that the steamship company has processed [?] my ticket, and as a result, they confirmed my departure last night for 21 June, at this point I am the one who decided against the date of embarkation because I need more time to prepare all my things, to travel to Ampezzo and Udine, then to Ceggia and San Donà di Piave for the documents and to say goodbye to friends, acquaintances, and *zii.*[14]

Many things still await me in Venice, do you see that it is impossible for me to do everything in six days? And so, I postponed my departure to the 16th of July from France always, only in this way will I be able to prepare and settle everything perfectly. I would like to tell you something about the money. The company in Venice has not

13 Nietta my greatest love.
14 Uncles and aunts.

Leaving for Love 265

yet refunded me as they require the mandate or request for payment. Can you tell me if the money you sent me is available at the same bank where you deposited the funds and where they remain, or will the company refund me at Quebech [*sic*] as the travel agency here in Venice has advised me? It would be wonderful if you could find out and let me know, because if it were that the money is still there, I would request the payment or rather, its collection in Venice, as the letter included with the payment receipt and copy of the ticket clearly indicates. I will therefore wait for an answer on this question before 14 July. I want you to know that I will be working until 4 July in order to complete the entire month. I will do my best to do everything else that awaits me at the same time. Regarding O ..., I don't have any news, all I know is what D ... wrote to me about him, that he was going today 22 June for his first appointment in Udine, and then to Rome. I don't want to waste time on this, please understand, I cannot wait to join you so that we can relive those sublime moments together and I can kiss you many times over like I did on that 15 August on Monte Pura.

Your Loris

[Top of first page:] Could you let me know what kind of gifts the little girls of *Signora* C ... might like to receive. A souvenir of Venice? Or something else? How many girls are there? Kisses to your *papà* and *mamma* in anticipation of a real embrace with all my heart, Loris

— Montreal 28-6-49 —

Mio carissimo Loris,[15]
Here I am once again focused on composing a letter for you, once again bent over this paper so that I can speak with you, and tell you everything that my heart dictates. I wanted to write to you several days ago, but between one thing and another, I have had to postpone writing to you until now when I can respond to your second letter as well; in this letter, you explain many things, including the fact that it is impossible for you to leave on the second of next month, I already knew this, actually, to be honest, I had a feeling this would happen, I had an inkling that you would not be travelling, and I tried to think

15 My dearest Loris.

about the next date you could leave, but I couldn't, strange, isn't it? It will have to be for later, for the end of July, we need to wait a little longer, just a little, what difference does it make? We have waited this long for three full years, isn't that so, my darling? Here, everyone is talking often about you, you can imagine how much I think of you, wherever I turn, I see you, and I make plans, lots of plans, so many plans that I can barely sleep at night. Today has not been a day of tranquility, I feel tense, uptight, restless, as you know not all days are the same. I don't know if it's the weather, hot and muggy, I must be completely unbearable to others, please forgive my messy writing, and think of the effort I am making in writing to you, it's not because I don't feel like it (if this were the case, I would not even have started) but rather because I cannot piece the right words together, my mind is so confused.

With regard to the refund, I will speak to my *papà* tonight and will do whatever I need to, I will write to you immediately after. I understand that you are resigning from work on the 4th next month, and you will then travel to Ampezzo? These are the final goodbyes, isn't that so, my darling? Tell me the truth, are you not sorry to leave behind everything that you have loved until now? Oh, do not deny it! It is hard! Very hard! The daughters of C … will be happy with anything that you bring for them especially from Italy. They are three girls, R … is 12 years old, G… is 8 and N …, the mischievous one, is 2½, I believe. I will stop here, greetings to your *mamma* whom I remember very fondly especially now, greetings to *"Sior"* Gigio and everyone in the family. From my *mamma* and *papà*, many kisses and dear greetings to your family, from me, in anticipation of a real one, I kiss you with my warmest affection and I send you my dearest greetings.

your Nietta

—Ampezzo 7-7-49 —

Nietta mia amatissima,[16]

As you had assumed, I returned to visit your old home, a place that always fills me with heartfelt affection and kindness. I came back to write what I believe is my last letter to you, perhaps the letter that will

---

16 Nietta my greatest love.

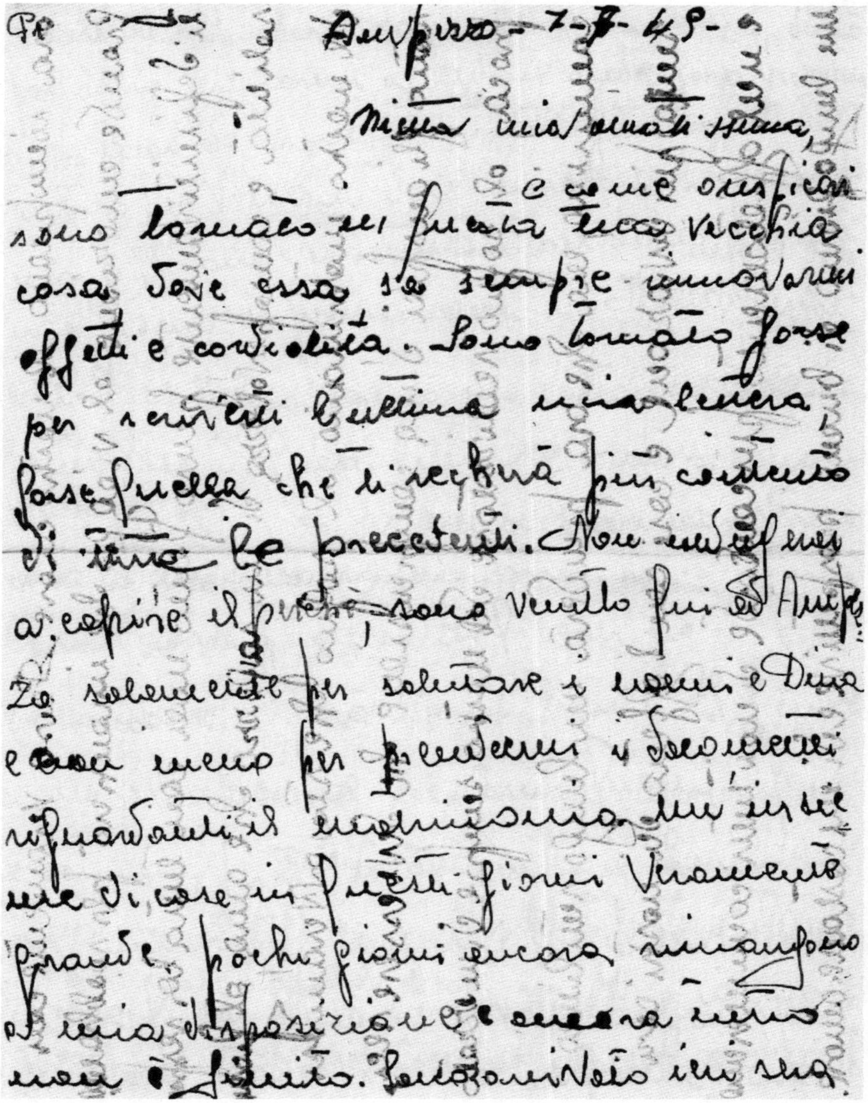

Letter from Loris Palma, 7 July 1949.

make you happier than ever. You will understand why, I travelled to Ampezzo to say goodbye to your *nonni* and to D ..., and to pick up the documents for our marriage. A number of things that are of vital importance were concluded; just a few days remain for me, with so much that still needs to be completed. I arrived last night at 6 and will leave tomorrow morning at 8, at which point I will be making a short stop in Udine where I will validate your documents at the police station. Immediately after, I will leave for Venice, where a few things remain to be taken care of. Sunday is my last day here in Italy as I leave on Monday, 11 July for Paris.

In these final days, many things have been finalized one after the other, things which I am determined to conclude with my usual modest punctuality. I wonder what you will be thinking about in these days, certainly the excitement will make your heart beat louder and stronger, of course, all of this is human, so many worries have fogged our views in the past. Everything now is moving smoothly, just as we had hoped, who knows how much joy is filling our hearts at this moment. I am excited beyond belief about the journey that I will make in order to finally be in your arms again, this time, forever. I think about it with the responsibility and consciousness of a young man who is profoundly in love, I think about our wedding day, the dream that is being realized from our constantly cloven path, which will now continue along a straight line with no longer any deviations, and so, with the affection and love of our dear ones, and in the most harmonious of unity of everyone, we will begin a new day of blessings and constant love.

You can imagine that I have had much to take care of here, between saying goodbye to everyone who knows me, not the least of course, your friends, all of my colleagues and friends at SADE, therefore a good job, a job I cared about, though it paled in comparison to my memories of you, our constant love, and this beginning to our new life together. At this point, however, we can honestly say that these are just memories, and that soon, maybe even earlier than we thought, we will seal our fateful dream with the reality of our marriage. As we agreed, I leave Italy on the 11th in order to arrive in France on the 18th. All my best to you, and infinite kisses and caresses, your Loris.

Leaving for Love 269

Before boarding for Canada, I will send you a telegram so that you will know the exact date of my arrival. I am so excited, but I will know how to remain focused and strong in case anything happens. I send you many greetings and kisses from *la nonna, il nonno, gli zii*, and the cousins, and especially from D ... and T ..., who are often disappointed in the few letters they receive from you. Everyone is thinking of you, my darling, they are thinking of how happy you and your parents are as the wedding day approaches, and you will be married, to whom? I don't know? (laugh) Try not to laugh too hard now, great news and surprises are about to reach you. Infinite kisses your Loris. Best wishes to your dear ones.

Afterword

Emotionalism and the Italian Nation

Donna R. Gabaccia,
Professor Emerita, University of Toronto

SPEAKING WITH diverse public audiences about Italy's migrants over the past forty years, I have repeatedly encountered a common perception of Italians as a nation characterized by great emotionalism. After my earliest public lectures – which focused on families and domestic life in Sicily and the United States – the first question posed from the audience always asked about criminal violence. Beginning over a century ago, Italian positivists first framed southern Italians, and later American journalists framed all Italians as people of unguarded passions, ready to reach for weapons. Film and television have reinforced those associations with mafia and organized crime. Even stereotypes that positively assess Italian males as Latin lovers, Italian females as self-sacrificing mothers or sexy babes, and Italian families as loving and warm but noisy rest on assumptions about Italians' excessive emotionalism.

In 2008–09, as Sonia Cancian and I launched the Digitizing Immigrant Letters (DIL) Project at the University of Minnesota (http://ihrca.dash.umn.edu/dil/), we began to hear different questions about emotionalism. Was it not the case, people asked, that Italian writers such as Antonietta Petris and Loris Palma were more likely to express their emotions in love letters or to express them in more colourful or more dramatic ways than others? In this afterword, I reflect briefly on the powerful popular association of emotionalism with the Italian nation. I begin with the assumption that emotionalism has long been an expectation of all who write or read love letters,[1] but I focus on what might be considered specifically national about the emotionalism of a young couple who were separated by migration after meeting in northeast Italy in the 1940s.

It is easy for readers to recognize that Antonietta Petris and Loris Palma wrote with great emotion about their romantic love. They knew they were writing love letters, the genre to which scholar and editor Sonia Cancian also attributes their correspondence. Love letters are, by definition, an exercise in emotionalism, understood to be an "indulgence in or display of emotion."[2] In 1948 and 1949, Antonietta and Loris wrote letters that were profoundly personal, very private, and also very individual expressions of their intimate feelings. The only people who mattered to them in writing, beyond each other, were their closest kin. They did not expect others to read what they wrote. I very much doubt that either Loris or Antonietta was curious about how their Italian citizenship might have shaped their letter-writing or how their *italianità* (Italianness) made their love letters different from the letters of other lovers.

This curiosity is more characteristic of scholars interested in how emotions entwine with modern nation-building.[3] In this brief afterword, I point toward two methodologies that open differing perspectives on the relationship of emotionalism and *italianità*. Analysis of the Petris-Palma collection as a corpus or body of text points not only to commonalities in expressions of emotion by the writers represented in the collection but also to variations among them. Although scholars probably do not yet have access to a rich enough array of love letter collections to allow rigorous analysis, comparisons of love letters written by Italians and non-Italians should eventually allow future scholars to add considerable complexity to scholars' understanding of written expressions of romantic emotionalism across cultures.

Analyzing the content and language of the Petris-Palma collection easily reveals both Antonietta and Loris as quite aware of their Italian, national identities. In their letters, both young lovers referenced Italy far more often than Canada, even as they anticipated building a life together in North America. Both Loris and Antonietta often and comfortably discussed the people among whom they lived as Italians, and both felt a sense of connection to other Italians. By contrast, on the

Afterword 273

rare occasion when Antonietta mentioned encounters with Canadians, she admitted to feeling uneasy around them. Still, in their letters, neither Antonietta nor Loris explicitly linked Italian citizenship or the Italian state to their love. On the contrary, discussions of citizenship and nation states carried emotional burdens of fear and anxiety.

Antonietta came closest to linking her love for Loris to *italianità* when she wrote about Italy as a place or a "geographical expression," not a nation. Antonietta's Italy was defined by its blue skies, "Italic" sea, the Alps, her hometown of Ampezzo, and a few urban sites that represented to her high Italian culture. When Antonietta wrote of *la Patria* – the term most commonly used for Italy as a national homeland, with its own state and national territory – she wrote mainly about culture, history, and the beauty of cities (Venice, Rome) that predated the modern, united, and independent Italy by millennia. Thus, Antonietta commented to Loris, "I don't know if you travelled to Rome already, of course, I thought of you there these past few days, a city glowing with beauty and history, cherish inside of you all these wonderful things that our *Patria* offers you – its sky, its seas, and once your eyes are satisfied, admire your gorgeous city, its natural and artistic wonders, because you will never see a city that is more radiant" (page 258). Antonietta also warned Loris he would miss Italy's beauty and artistry once he arrived in Canada. As a newcomer to Canada and while living in Montreal, Antonietta also clearly remained loyal to and immersed in the language, religion, music, and films of Italy. So obvious was her continued immersion that Loris once responded by extending his predictable Christmas greetings beyond Antonietta and her family to include "all Italians there" (page 137). Antonietta's sense of belonging to an Italian nation had little to do with citizenship or the Italian state but instead reflected her love of specific places in Italy, her language, and her embrace of a distinctive and shared Italian culture of music, urbanity, and beauty.

For Loris, thoughts of the Italian nation and expressions of national pride instead entered his letters to Antonietta when he discussed Italian triumphs or tragedies in the sports arena. It was on the sports field and not in exercising his rights or responsibilities as a male citizen – for example as a voter or through military service – that the Italian nation mattered to Loris. He imagined fellow sports enthusiasts sharing his strong sense of belonging together as they supported Italian soccer (football) teams.[4] He insisted that at such competitions "everyone I think, for a moment feels tied to their *Patria* ...," and he reported about a match he had recently viewed, and where he thought that "everyone today was thinking this, because sports, like love, keep us grounded." And, improbably (since Antonietta herself exhibited little personal enthusiasm for football), Loris even insisted that "sports and love tie me to you in a profound feeling of veneration" (page 212). In a later letter, Loris reported to Antonietta of his grief when learning of the recent plane crash tragedy outside Turin that had killed the city's entire soccer team. In the letter, he referred to the athletes as "young and old warriors of the Italian flag" (page 244), thus pulling together in the context of sports and fandom the nationalist trio of military, war, and flag.

Living between Italy and Canada, Loris and Antonietta were neither ignorant nor unaware of their status as Italian citizens. Nevertheless, when they wrote about national or international politics and about Italy as a nation state, they reported mainly feelings of anxiety. Multiple letters written by both Antonietta in Canada and Loris in Italy focused on the bureaucratic demands that Canada and Italy made on them as migrants; they viewed Canada and Italy as creating obstacles to be overcome as they sought to reunite. Like most migrants, Loris focused obsessively on the necessity of documents; in the top left corner of one of his letters Loris signalled loudly, "I am waiting for your prompt response concerning the documents" (page 144). Both also worried about how much military service Loris would be required to complete before he could be released to emigrate – a theme that continued across several exchanged letters.

In a rare moment focused on Italian postwar politics, Loris wrote anxiously to inquire with Antonietta about the possibility that Canada might follow the example of United States and deny entry to Communists. Loris had earlier revealed his political affiliation to her but now claimed that "the reasons I had registered [with the Party] are negligible, and for over a year I have not participated in the group because I don't agree with their ideas" (page 231). (Loris's flirtation with the Communist Party was somewhat unusual for the predominantly "white" area around Venice, where strong Catholic commitments encourage most voters to support instead Italy's Christian Democratic Party.[5])

Wishing to emigrate, Loris feared that a decision he now viewed as trivial (or perhaps instrumental?) might have profound consequences. In her introduction, Sonia Cancian also reminds readers that Loris and Antonietta, as citizens of a country with a strong Communist Party, might have had good reasons to worry about the impact of the emerging Cold War on their personal lives and ability to migrate.

Finally, although both lovers had cause for anxiety about how states could frustrate their plans, the gendered citizenship characteristic of Italy and many other nation states also encouraged Loris on most occasions to project positive courage. He thus sought to reassure his presumably less politically savvy fiancée that "with regard to your question, unfortunately the international situation is not one of the calmest, but before a war occurs … Stay calm, my Tetina, and you will see that everything will pass. Do not be alarmed, there is no reason" (page 94). In writing these words, Loris was not so much seeking to educate Antonietta for citizenship or voting but rather to calm her fears (that international politics might keep them on separate continents). Was he also perhaps suggesting her fears were feminine and somewhat irrational?

As this example suggests, Loris and Antonietta occupied differing positions as man and woman within a romantic relationship. Their intention to marry also positioned them centrally within a wider circle of kin, all of them interested in the future reproduction and new generations promised by the young couple's love and marriage. Given their differing positions within family circles, the two young lovers and their kin (who occasionally added notes to the love letters) all understandably thought and wrote about love in different ways. All the writers represented in the Petris-Palma collection were Italians, yet the emotionalism they exhibited varied considerably and found very different written forms in the letters.

A complex stew of gender expectations, place of residence, and differing socio-economic status and levels of education combined to make Loris and Antonietta rather different as writers who struggled to find the words to communicate their intense feelings. According to Cancian, Loris was from an urban family that had long lived in one of Italy's most important cities; Loris's father's work as a steward on ships not only required him to travel a great deal but also allowed him to support his son for a year at a seminary offering a classical education. Artisanal work in Venice's cultural sector done by Loris's maternal grandfather introduced first his mother and subsequently Loris himself to theatre, music, and art. Loris further cultivated these cultural tastes even after his education shifted from a classical seminary education toward the technical education that prepared him for work as a highly skilled worker in Italy's electrical industry. As a writer of love letters, Loris experimented with many metaphors for his love; he worked hard to develop an abstract metaphysics that might capture the dynamics of his emotions as he dealt with his separation from Antonietta.

By contrast, Antonietta had been born and lived in a small, rural town in the mountains; today Ampezzo has fewer than 1,000 residents (although it was probably twice that size when Antonietta was growing up). In this more provincial setting, Antonietta as a young girl had access only to the five years of schooling required of all Italian children. She subsequently learned to sew from a local lady tailor. Family finances may have limited the education of this obviously bright and capable woman. The fact that first her grandfather and then her father travelled abroad in search of work as migratory labourers suggests a family living in some precarity, and dependent on remittances sent from abroad over three or more decades. For most of the 1930s and 1940s, her father worked in construction in Montreal; he called for Antonietta and her mother only after he and a friend started a small construction contracting business. In her letters, Antonietta wrote very well for a woman of limited education, but she wrote mainly of the details of everyday life and used fewer complex figures of speech to express her emotion.

Loris began his very first letter to Antonietta, after her departure, with a dramatic metaphor: "it was as though I had died and come back to life" (page 68). In subsequent letters he repeatedly sought new metaphors for his love and his too frequent moments of despair. In one letter, he described his love as a majestic ship that "has charted a course to cross the oceans and reach you, it knows how to ride across the waves" (page 91). Antonietta also knew how to use metaphorical language (see introduction where Cancian quotes an early letter to Loris in Venice describing each snowflake in Ampezzo as "an image of a butterfly in the sky"), but one of the best metaphors introduced

Afterword   277

in her letters written from Canada was one Antonietta admitted to borrowing from her father. He had summed up Montreal's mixed population and languages as "a real minestrone."

Briefly introduced to philosophy and history as a student in seminary, Loris strove in his letters to write of his love for Antonietta philosophically or metaphysically. Having received a simple card from his lover, Loris reminded her, "The lovely and fine image on the greeting card compelled me to search for a meaning" (page 99). Later he wrote to Antonietta that "courage lifts the spirit to the point of exaltation, just as its absence leads to exasperation; I did not reach that point because our souls were not stolen" (page 111). At another low point, as he especially suffered from melancholy approaching despair, Loris even acknowledged that many who knew him did not appreciate his character, finding him "demanding and difficult to please" (page 184).

Reporting mainly on her everyday life as a young family-, church- and work-oriented woman and consistently writing in much simpler words about her love, Antonietta surely appreciated what Loris meant when he described himself as demanding and difficult to please. A reader can easily gain the overall impression that Antonietta and her family devoted considerable writerly energies to lifting Loris's frequently faltering temperament. Their efforts hint at the possibility they may have on occasion humoured Loris like a child. Loris acknowledged the possibility and responded at one point to Antonietta's persistent encouragement of him that "you care for me like a mother" (page 184).

Whatever her emotional power as "mother," Antonietta remained ever aware of her lesser education and of Loris's greater level of learning and occupational skill. She apologized for the messiness of her writing, and she worried that her writing was becoming worse because of her fatigue while working as a sewing machine operator in a garment factory. In another letter she feared, "I am sure that you have come across badly written and awkward sentences" (page 144). At the same time, perhaps inspired by Loris, Antonietta also searched in Italian literature, for example in novels loaned her by friends, and occasionally looked there for the meaning of separation and frustrated love. In one letter she reported finding in the work of an unnamed novelist an initially encouraging statement (that love and not proximity forged the truest bond) only to be disappointed when the same writer concluded that for those in love "out of sight" meant "out of mind" (page 137). The down-to-earth Antonietta responded sensibly to this contradiction by focusing on her own experience, reminding herself and Loris, "These words are fiction and we are proof that though we are apart, we can protect our hearts" (page 138).

With his more advanced education and from his masculine position in the relationship, Loris felt comfortable commenting on the format and content of Antonietta's letters, seeking to improve them (e.g., "Can you use a pencil when you write, the ink makes it difficult to read the letter," page 82) and sending her instructions about the kind of letters he hoped to receive. At one point he insisted, "Your writings lack a little of their usual enthusiasm," even as he admitted "they are no different from the others," and went on further to acknowledge it was his inability to "find solace from my nightmares" that coloured his reading of the letters (page 176).

To be fair, Loris on a few occasions offered his own apologies for poor writing, but his most memorable self-critique was offered to Antonietta only after she had already forgiven him for drinking too much wine and failing to write promptly enough. Loris lamented, "I wrote a jumble of words in which everything from rocks and earth to herbs is mixed in together. I ended up leaving it for the next day, regretting that I had not been up to the task of finishing it. Heavens, I thought, I will explain my reasons to her. Now that I should be doing this, I don't remember them … yes, I was a little merry from the wine, I was writing poorly, making many mistakes, my thoughts were not right, and I was ashamed to send you the letter" (page 109). Here, of course, Loris revealed himself as approaching the writing of a love letter as a kind of school assignment, with Antonietta in the ultimate position to judge him as a teacher would. In fact, Antonietta occasionally felt comfortable in chiding Loris, but she did so in ways that forced him to think about the impact of his words on her rather than focusing on how he might improve. For example, she reported that he had saddened her and diminished her Christmastime joy, writing "I was very, yes, very sorry to read your very sad and melancholic writing, I did not expect this kind of a letter" (page 170). Another time she asked simply, "Do I deserve this kind of punishment?" (page 108).

In comparing Loris and Antonietta as quite different writers about love, it is interesting to recall that Antonietta's mother had endured a much longer separation from her husband. How amazing it would be if an interested scholar could compare Loris and Antonietta's letter exchange to the epistolary exchange of the previous generation! Unfortunately, the rich Petris-Palma collection allows readers only to see how the close kin of the two lovers expressed in writing in the late 1940s their own feelings of familial love. Both young lovers regularly sent formulaic greetings to and from their kin and friends. It was most often Antonietta's mother who appended a short line or two to Antonietta's missives; often she signed herself to Loris merely as "*Mamma.*" On at least one occasion, unable to coax her parents to add a line to Loris, Antonietta assured him of the best wishes of her *mamma* and *papà* who were "lazy writers" (page 98). How and to what degree conventions for the expression of family love fed culturally shaped expressions of romantic love is surely a topic that deserves greater scholarly attention.

Perhaps because Loris and Antonietta wrote about love in such different fashion, several commonalities of their emotionalism are quite easy to identify. When writing of their love, both drew upon specific elements within Italian culture, notably operatic music and Catholicism. In her introduction, Sonia Cancian identifies how both Loris and Antonietta drew on the melodramatic language of Italian opera, which both had learned to love in early life. When Antonietta recounted her memory of an early visit to Loris's family in Venice, she described "one magical night" when the two attended together a performance of *Madama Butterfly*; the opera became a touchstone for their later written communication, perhaps because it is a story of a long separation (albeit one that ends tragically) for two star-crossed lovers. Whatever their considerable differences as writers of love letters, their references to Butterfly and to other opera plots and characters provided a firm, private connection. Based on the centrality of opera in their expressions of emotionalism, any scholarly researcher would want to ask further whether other Italian writers of love letters also drew upon popular appreciation for opera and music in constructing private languages of love.

To the importance of opera as a shared language of Italian love I would add a wealth of references to love as a form of spirituality rooted in Catholicism. The love letters in the Petris-Palma collection refer at least as often to God and to the "spirits" of the two writers as to opera. The use of variations on the word *adoration* and on the word *sacrifice* also suggest how key religious metaphors of Catholicism were adapted to expressing the peaks and valleys of romantic love. Both Loris and Antonietta reported attendance at church. And Loris particularly insisted that love was leading them toward a higher form of spirituality. Loris's discussions of love as spiritual connection often fed the type of metaphorical and abstract writing I have described above. In one memorable case, he reported on an Easter visit to Antonietta's home, and concluded, "It was as though I was resurrected as I stood at the entrance of this home, it was as though my heart was resurrected as I listened once again to the voices of your loved ones, it was an absolute, irrefutable joy that was added to the list of memories, on the special day of Easter of 1949 in which I found myself once again in your home with your dear ones among all those who remember you and who see you, your person, your spirit, your affection in me" (page 236).

Scholars will face at least two challenges in moving beyond the internal comparisons I have offered in this afterword: first a deconstruction of the Italian national group through attention to differences among the letter writers linked into a single letter exchange and then identification of similarities across the Italian letters. The first challenge emerges from the possibility that understandings of what constitutes a love letter or defines emotionalism may well differ across cultures. Implicitly, most scholars writing about love letters focus on romantic and not familial love, most often in heterosexual courtships, procreative marriages, or, more occasionally, illicit adulterous relationships.[6] Familial love deserves attention as it may be a font of emotions expressed in romantic relationships, too. A second and still greater challenge is introduced by the role of translation in facilitating comparisons across writers of differing national linguistic cultures. Who is the ideal translator? How can one know how translations of love letters from multiple languages create a parallel language of love that applies across cultures? There are no protocols for this kind of work, although Cancian provides a good discussion in her introduction.

Several digital collections of migrant and love letters do exist and provide a good starting place for further comparative work. The DIL at the University of Minnesota Immigration History Research

Center Archives (IHRCA) – which has been continued and expanded under the leadership of Daniel Necas at IHRCA – offers translations of the emotional language of migrant letters written in over a dozen languages. Familial and romantic love appear throughout. Necas has reported that his preliminary comparison of the DIL letters across cultures reveals the word *heart* as one of the most common ways for expressing emotions in all.[7] Letters by migrant Italians are not the only ones referring to opera, although they are few in number. By contrast references to God and to "souls" are ubiquitous in letters written in almost all languages, and might point toward variations in the expression of emotionalism in religions other than Catholicism.

My own hasty exploration of one online digital collection of love letters written by famous personages from many cultural backgrounds and digitized for readership by "romantics" (https://theromantic.com/LoveLetters/main.htm) revealed no references to opera in letters written by non-Italians. Again, however, many lovers made references to God and to their souls when writing about romantic love. I also discovered multiple male writers of love letters who addressed their female lovers as "Angel." While scarcely conclusive, such comparisons can advance scholarly understanding of the general relationship of emotionalism and nationalism well beyond the Italian case while also refining the meaning of *italianità* in the epistolary exchanges characteristic of migrants' romantic love.

Notes

1 Although heavily associated with modern romantic love in the nineteenth and twentieth centuries, the writing of love letters has a much longer history as the famous case of Abelard and Heloise reminds us. See Radice, "Introduction," *The Letters of Abelard and Heloise.*

2 *Merriam-Webster Dictionary*, online edition, https://www.merriam-webster.com/dictionary/emotionalism.

3 While framed around the love of country, early scholarship – see for example, Viroli, *For Love of Country*; and Nussbaum, *For Love of Country?* – had little to say about romantic love in relationship to the emotions of patriotism, nationalism, and cosmopolitanism: instead nations are viewed as drawing largely on metaphors of family and family love.

On romantic love, readers can usefully consult Gori, "Cultural, Social, and Personal Ways of Experiencing Love"; and Passerini, *Europe in Love, Love in Europe.*

4 And perhaps he was correct in doing so; see Martin, *Sport Italia.*

5 Diamani LaPolis and Ceccarini LaPolis, "Catholics and Politics after the Christian Democrats."

6 Holloway, "'You know I am all on fire.'"

7 Personal oral communication, Daniel Necas to the author, 24 February 2020, Vienna, Austria.

Bibliography

Akhtar, Salman. "The Immigrant, the Exile, and the Experience of Nostalgia." *Journal of Applied Psychoanalytic Studies* 1, no. 2 (1999): 123–30.

– *Immigration and Identity: Turmoil, Treatment, and Transformation*. Lanham, MD: Jason Aronson, 1999.

Altman, Janet Gurkin. *Epistolarity: Approaches to a Form*. Columbus: Ohio University Press, 1982.

Ashbrook, William. "*Elisir d'amore, L'*." In *The New Grove Dictionary of Opera*. Vol. 1, edited by Stanley Sadie, 40. Oxford: Oxford University Press, 1992.

Baily, Samuel and Franco Ramella, eds. *One Family, Two Worlds. An Italian Family's Correspondence across the Atlantic, 1901–1922*. New Brunswick, NJ: Rutgers University Press, 1988.

Baldassar, Loretta. "Guilty Feelings and the Guilt Trip: Emotions and Motivation in Migration and Transnational Caregiving." *Emotion, Space, and Society* 16 (2015): 81–9.

– "Missing Kin and Longing to be Together: Emotions and the Construction of Co-presence in Transnational Relationships." *Journal of Intercultural Studies* 29, no. 3 (2008): 247–66.

– "Transnational Families and Aged Care: The Mobility of Care and the Migrancy of Ageing." *Journal of Ethnic and Migration Studies* 33, 2 (2007): 275–97.

– "Transnational Families and the Provision of Moral and Emotional Support: The Relationship between Truth and Distance." *Identities: Global Studies in Culture and Power* 14, no. 4 (2007): 385–409.

Baldassar, Loretta, Cora Baldock, and Raelene Wilding. *Families Caring Across Borders: Migration, Ageing and Transnational Caregiving*. Basingstoke, UK: Palgrave Macmillan, 2007.

Baldassar, Loretta and Donna R. Gabaccia. "Home, Family, and the Italian Nation in a Mobile World: The Domestic and the National among Italy's Migrants." In *Intimacy and Italian Migration: Gender and Domestic Lives in a Mobile World*, edited by Loretta Baldassar and Donna R. Gabaccia, 1–22. New York: Fordham University Press, 2011.

Baldassar, Loretta and Donna R. Gabaccia, eds. *Intimacy and Italian Migration: Gender and Domestic Lives in a Mobile World*. New York: Fordham University Press, 2011.

Barthes, Roland. *A Lover's Discourse: Fragments*. Translated by Richard Howard. New York: Hill and Wang, 1978.

Barton, Arnold. *Letters from the Promised Land: Swedes in America, 1840–1914*. Minneapolis: University of Minnesota Press, 1975.

Bassnett, Susan. *Translation Studies*. 3rd ed. London: Routledge, 2002.

Bauman, Rebecca H. "Essay Reviews: Melodrama and Italian Culture." *Italian Studies* 70, no. 3 (August 2015): 416–20.

Beard, Martha Rose. "Re-thinking Oral History – A Study of Narrative Performance." *Rethinking History* 21, no. 4 (2017): 529–48.

Beck, Ulrich and Elisabeth Beck-Gernsheim. *Distant Love*. Translated by Rodney Livingstone. Cambridge, UK: Polity Press, 2014.

Belk, Russell W. "A Child's Christmas in America: Santa Claus as Deity, Consumption as Religion." *The Journal of American Culture* 10, no. 1 (Spring 1987): 87–100.

Benjamin, Walter. "The Task of the Translator: An Introduction to the Translation of Baudelaire's Tableaux Parisiens." In *Illuminations: Essays and Reflections*. Edited and with an Introduction by Hannah Arendt. New York: Schoken Books, 1968.

Biasetton, Francesca. *La bellezza del segno: Elogio della scrittura a mano*. Bari-Roma: Editori Laterza, 2018.

Blegen, Theodore C. "Early 'America Letters.'" In *Norwegian Migration to America, 1825–1860*, edited by Theodore C. Blegen, 196–213. Northfield, MN: Norwegian-American Historical Association, 1931.

– *Land of their Choice: The Immigrants Write Home*. St Paul: University of Minnesota Press, 1955.

Boccagni, Paolo and Loretta Baldassar. "Emotions on the Move: Mapping the Emergent Field of Emotion and Migration." *Emotion, Space and Society* 16 (2015): 73–80.

Boddice, Rob. *The History of Emotions*. Manchester: Manchester University Press, 2018.

– "The History of Emotions: Past, Present, Future." *Revista de Estudios Sociales* 62 (2017): 10–15.

Bibliography

Boissevain, Jeremy. *The Italians of Montreal: Social Adjustment in a Plural Society*. Ottawa: The Royal Commission on Bilingualism and Biculturalism, 1970.

Borges, Marcelo J. and Sonia Cancian, eds. *Migrant Letters: Emotional Language, Mobile Identities, and Writing Practices in Historical Perspective*. Oxon, UK: Routledge, 2018.

Borges, Marcelo J., Sonia Cancian, and Linda Reeder, eds. *Emotional Landscapes: Love, Gender, and Migration*. Champaign: University of Illinois Press, 2021.

Bornat, Joanna. "Remembering in Later Life: Generating Individual and Social Change." In *The Oxford Handbook of Oral History*, edited by Donald A. Ritchie. Oxford: Oxford University Press, 2011.

Boss, Pauline Grossenbacher. "The Experience of Immigration for the Mother Left Behind: The Use of Qualitative Feminist Strategies to Analyze Letters from My Swiss Grandmother to My Father." *Marriage & Family Review* 19, no. 3–4 (1993): 365–78.

Bossis, Mireille. "Methodological Journeys through Correspondences." *Yale French Studies* 71 (1986): 63–75.

– "Table ronde: la lettre d'amour." In *L'Épistolarité à travers les siècles. Geste de communication et/ou d'écriture*, edited by Mireille Bossis and Charles A. Porter. Stuttgart: Franz Steiner Verlag, 1990.

Bourke, Joanna. *The Story of Pain: from Prayer to Painkillers*. Oxford: Oxford University Press, 2014.

Brady, Emily and Arto Haapala. "Melancholy as an Aesthetic Emotion." *Contemporary Aesthetics* 1 (2003). Accessed 7 May 2019. https://quod.lib.umich.edu/c/ca/7523862.0001.006/--melancholy-as-an-aesthetic-emotion?rgn=main;view=fulltext.

Braidotti, Rosi. *Nomadic Subjects: Embodiment and Sexual Difference in Contemporary Feminist Theory*. New York: Columbia University Press, 1994.

Brooks, Peter. *The Melodramatic Imagination: Balzac, Henry James, Melodrama and the Mode of Excess*. New Haven: Yale University Press, 1976.

Budden, Julian. "Madam Butterfly." In *The New Grove Dictionary of Opera*. Vol. 3, edited by Stanley Sadie, 139. Oxford: Oxford University Press, 1992.

Burelli, Ottorino. "1940–1950 E in dieci anni la storia travolse un Friuli millenario." In *Buine fortune: L'emigrazione friulana nel secondo dopoguerra*, edited by Ottorino Burelli, Ido Cibischino, and Javier P. Grossutti, 18–37. Udine: Associazione Culturale Oltremare, 2011.

Caffarena, Fabio. *Lettere dalla Grande Guerra: Scritture del quotidiano, monumenti della memoria, fonti per la storia. Il caso italiano*. Milano: Edizioni Unicopli, 2005.

Camerino, Giuseppe Antonio. "'E il piacer ... farsi paura' Leopardi e la percezione dei fenomeni naturali." *Italianistica: Rivista di letteratura italiana* 16, no. 3 (September/December, 1987): 337–46.

Cameron, Deborah. *The Feminist Critique of Language: A Reader.* London: Routledge, 1990.

Cameron, Wendy, Sheila Haines, and Mary M. Maude, eds. *English Immigrant Voices: Labourers' Letters from Upper Canada in the 1830s.* Montreal and Kingston: McGill-Queen's University Press, 2000.

Cancian, Sonia. *Families, Lovers, and their Letters: Italian Postwar Migration to Canada.* Winnipeg: University of Manitoba Press, 2010.

– "From Montreal and Venice with Love: Migrant Letters and Romantic Intimacy in Italian Migration to Postwar Canada." In *Sisters or Strangers? Immigrant, Ethnic or Racialized Women in Canadian History.* Revised Edition, edited by Franca Iacovetta and Marlene Epp, 191–200. Toronto: University of Toronto Press, 2016.

– "The Language of Gender in Lovers' Correspondence, 1946–1949." Special Issue: "Gender History across Epistemologies." *Gender & History Journal* 24, no. 3 (November 2012): 755–65. (Also published in *Gender History across Epistemologies*, edited by Donna R. Gabaccia and Mary J. Maynes, 235–45. West Sussex, UK: Wiley-Blackwell, 2013.)

– "Love at the Threshold of War and Migration: A War Orphan's Story." In *Emotional Landscapes: Love, Gender, and Migration*, edited by Marcelo J. Borges, Sonia Cancian and Linda Reeder, 163–83. Champaign, IL: University of Illinois Press, 2021.

– "Love in the Time of Migration: Lovers Correspond Between Italy and Canada, 1948–1957." *Érudit: Diversité Urbaine* 10, no. 2 (Spring 2011): 91–109.

– "'My Dearest Love ...' Love, Longing and Desire in International Migration." In *Migrations: Interdisciplinary Perspectives*, edited by Michi Messer, Renee Schröder, and Ruth Wodak, 175–86. Vienna: Springer-Verlag, 2012.

– "'My Love, How Different Life is Here ...': A Young Italian Woman's Impressions of Postwar Montreal." In *Engaging with Diversity. Multidisciplinary Reflections on Plurality in Quebec*, edited by Stéphan Gervais, Raffaele Iacovino, and Mary Anne Poutanen, 439–55. Bern: Peter Lang, 2018.

– "Transatlantic Correspondents: Kinship, Gender and Emotions in Postwar Migration Experiences Between Italy and Canada, 1946–1971." PhD diss., Humanities Doctoral Program. Concordia University, 2007.

– *Una raccolta di lettere italiane inviate agli emigrati* in Canada, 1954–1955." Master's thesis, Department of Modern Languages, Literatures, and Cultures. McGill University, 1999.

Caplow, Theodore. "Christmas Gifts and Kin Networks." *American Sociological Review* 47, 3 (June 1982): 383–92.

Bibliography

Caselli, Roberto. *Storia della canzone italiana*. Milano: Editore Ulrico Hoepli, 2018.

Castel, Nico. *The Complete Puccini Libretti*. Volume 1. 2nd ed., edited by Marcie Stapp. Mt Morris, NY: Leyerle Publications, 2002.

– *Italian Belcanto Opera Libretti in Three Volumes*, edited by Scott Jackson Wiley. Mt Morris, NY: Leyerle Publications, 2000.

– *Italian Verismo Opera Libretti*. Vol. 1, edited by Scott Jackson Wiley. Mt Morris, NY: Leyerle Publications, 2000.

Catalano, Roberto and Enzo Fina. "Simple Does Not Mean Easy: Oral Traditional Values, Music, and the Musicàntica Experience." In *Oral History, Oral Culture, and Italian Americans*, edited by Luisa Del Giudice, 119–35. New York: Palgrave Macmillan US, 2009.

Catalano, Valeria. "4 Maggio, l'anniversario di Superga. Così scomparve il Grande Torino." *Il Corriere della Sera*. Accessed 5 April 2019. https://torino .corriere.it/sport/cards/4-maggio-l-anniversario-superga-cosi-scomparve-grande-torino/fiat-g212_principale.shtmlhttps://torino.corriere.it/sport/cards/4-maggio-l-anniversario-superga-cosi-scomparve-grande-torino/fiat-g212_principale.shtmlhttps://torino.corriere.it/sport/cards/4-maggio-l-anniversario-superga-cosi-scomparve-grande-torino/fiat-g212_principale .shtml.

Champagne, John. *Italian Masculinity as Queer Melodrama: Caravaggio, Puccini, Contemporary Cinema*. New York: Palgrave Macmillan, 2015.

Chávez-García, Miroslava. *Migrant Longing: Letter Writing across the U.S.-Mexico Borderlands*. Chapel Hill: University of North Carolina Press, 2018.

Chiswick, Barry R. and Paul W. Miller. "International Migration and the Economics of Language." The Institute for the Study of Labor (IZA) Discussion Paper No. 7880. Bonn: IZA, January 2014:1–95.

Coates, Jennifer, ed. *Language and Gender: A Reader*. Oxford: Blackwell, 1998.

Conway, Alan, ed. *The Welsh in America. Letters from the Immigrants*. St Paul: University of Minnesota Press, 1961.

Coontz, Stephanie. *Marriage, a History: How Love Conquered Marriage*. London: Penguin 2006.

Cornille, Jean-Louis. "L'Assignation, analyse d'un pacte épistolaire." In *Les Correspondances: Problématique et économie d'un 'genre littéraire,'* edited by Jean-Louis Bonnat and Mireille Bossis. Nantes, France: Actes du colloque de Nantes, 1982.

Cullen, Niamh. *Love, Honour, and Jealousy: An Intimate History of the Italian Economic Miracle*. Oxford: Oxford University Press, 2019.

D'Agostin, Adriano and Javier Grossutti, *Ti ho spedito lire cento*. Pordenone: Biblioteca dell'Immagine, 1997.

Damousi, Joy. "Legacies of War and Migration: Memories of War Trauma, Dislocation, and Second-Generation Greek-Australians." In *Migration and Insecurity: Citizenship and Social Inclusion in a Transnational Era*, edited by Niklaus Steiner, Robert Mason, and Anna Hayes. London and New York: Routledge, 2013.

– *Memories and Migration in the Shadow of War: Australia's Greek Immigrants after World War II and the Greek Civil War*. Cambridge, UK: Cambridge University Press, 2015.

Dauphin, Cécile. "Letter-Writing Manuals in the Nineteenth Century." In *Correspondence: Models of Letter-Writing from the Middle Ages to the Nineteenth Century*, edited by Roger Chartier, Alain Boureau, and Cécile Dauphin. Translated by Christopher Woodall. New York: Polity Press, 1997.

De Clementi, Andreina. *Il Prezzo della ricostruzione: L'emigrazione italiana nel secondo dopoguerra*. Bari: Laterza, 2010.

De Haan, Kathleen Anne. "'He looks like a Yankee in his new suit.' Immigrant Rhetoric: Dutch Immigrant Letters as Forums for Shifting Immigrant Identities." PhD diss., Northwestern University, 1998.

De Haene, Lucia, and Cécile Rousseau, eds. *Working with Refugee Families: Trauma and Exile in Family Relationships*. Cambridge: Cambridge University Press, 2020.

Del Giudice, Luisa, ed. *On Second Thought: Scholarly Women Reflect on Profession, Community, and Purpose*. Salt Lake City: University of Utah Press, 2017.

DeSalvo, Louise. *Writing as a Way of Healing: How Telling Our Stories Transforms Our Lives*. Boston: Beacon Press, 1999.

Digitizing Immigrant Letters Project, Immigration History Research Center Archives, University of Minnesota Libraries. University of Minnesota. https://www.lib.umn.edu/ihrca/antonietta-petris-letters.

Di Leonardo, Micaela. "The Female World of Cards and Holidays: Women, Families, and the Work of Kinship." *Signs: Journal of Women and Culture in Society* 12, no. 3 (1987): 440–53.

Diamani LaPolis, Ilvo and Luigi Ceccarini LaPolis. "Catholics and Politics after the Christian Democrats: The Influential Minority." *Journal of Modern Italian Studies* 12, no. 1 (2007): 37–59, n. 1.

Dixon, Thomas. *From Passions to Emotions: The Creation of a Psychological Category*. Cambridge: Cambridge University Press, 2006.

Donato, Katharine M., Donna Gabaccia, Jennifer Holdaway, Martin Manalansan IV, and Patricia R. Pessar, eds. Special Issue, "Gender and Migration Revisited." *International Migration Review* 40, no. 1 (Spring 2006): 3–256.

Bibliography

Dror, Otniel E. "Creating the Emotional Body: Confusion, Possibilities, and Knowledge." In *An Emotional history of the United States*, edited by Peter N. Stearns and Jan Lewis, 173–94. New York: New York University Press, 1998.

Elliott, Bruce S., David A. Gerber, and Suzanne M. Sinke, eds. *Letters across Borders: The Epistolary Practices of International Migrants*. New York: Palgrave Macmillan, 2006.

"Emotionalism." *Merriam-Webster Dictionary*. https://www.merriam-webster.com/dictionary/emotionalism.

Epp, Marlene. "The Memory of Violence: Soviet and East European Mennonite Refugees and Rape in the Second World War." *Journal of Women's History* 9, no. 1 (Spring 1997): 58–87.

Erickson, Charlotte. *Invisible Immigrants: The Adaptation of English and Scottish Immigrants in 19th Century America*. Coral Gables: Miami University Press, 1972.

Fahrni, Magda. *Household Politics: Montreal Families and Postwar Reconstruction*. Toronto: University of Toronto Press, 2005.

Falicov, Celia J. *Latino Families in Therapy*. New York: Guilford, 1998.

Febvre, Lucien. "La sensibilité et l'histoire : Comment reconstituer la vie affective d'autrefois?" *Annales d'histoire sociale* 3 (January–June 1941): 5–20.

Feenberg, Andrew. "The Written World: On the Theory and Practice of Computer Conferencing." *Mindweave: Communication, Computers and Distance Education*, edited by Robin Mason and Anthony Kaye, 22–39. Oxford: Pergamon, 1989.

Fitzpatrick, David. *Oceans of Consolation: Personal Accounts of Irish Migration to Australia*. Ithaca: Cornell University Press, 1994.

Franzina, Emilio. *Merica! Merica! Emigrazione e colonizzazione nelle lettere dei contadini veneti e friulani in America Latina, 1876–1902*. Milano: Feltrinelli, 1979.

Frenette, Yves, Marcel Martel, and John Willis, eds. *Envoyer et recevoir. Lettres et correspondances dans les diasporas francophones*. Québec: Presses L'Université Laval, 2006.

Freud, Sigmund. "Mourning and Melancholia." In *The Standard Edition of the Complete Psychological Works of Sigmund Freud, Volume XIV (1914–1916): On the History of the Psycho-Analytic Movement, Papers on Metapsychology and Other Works*, edited by James Strachey in collaboration with Anna Freud. Translated by James Strachey, 243–58. London: Hogarth Press and the Institute of Psycho-Analysis, 1917.

Frevert, Ute. *Emotions in History – Lost and Found*. Budapest: Central European University Press, 2011.

Gabaccia, Donna R. "Is Everywhere Nowhere? Nomads, Nations, and the Immigrant Paradigm of United States History." *The Journal of American History* 86, no. 3. "The Nation and Beyond: Transnational Perspectives on United States History: A Special Issue" (December 1999): 1115–34.

– *Foreign Relations: American Immigration in Global Perspective*. Princeton: Princeton University Press, 2012.

– "Global Geography of 'Little Italy': Italian Neighbourhoods in Comparative Perspective." *Modern Italy* 11, no. 1 (February 2006): 9–24.

– *Italy's Many Diasporas*. Seattle: University of Washington Press, 2000.

Gabrielli, Patrizia. *Col Freddo nel Cuore: Uomini e donne nell'emigrazione antifascista*. Roma: Donzelli editore, 2004.

– *Il 1946, le donne, la Repubblica*. Roma: Donzelli editore, 2010.

Gerber, David A. *Authors of their Lives: The Personal Correspondence of British Immigrants to North America in the Nineteenth Century*. New York: New York University Press, 2006.

– "The Immigrant Letter between Positivism and Populism: The Uses of Immigrant Personal Correspondence in Twentieth-Century American Scholarship." *Journal of American Ethnic History* 16, no. 4 (Summer 1997): 3–34.

Giannotti, Marcello. *L'enciclopedia di Sanremo: 55 anni di storia del festival dalla A alla Z*. Roma: Gremese Editore, 2005.

Gibelli, Antonio. *L'officina della Guerra: La Grande Guerra e le trasformazioni del mondo mentale*. Torino: Bollati Boringhieri editore, 1998.

Gillis, John R. *For Better, For Worse: British Marriages, 1600 to the Present*. New York: Oxford University Press, 1985.

Ginsborg, Paul. *A History of Contemporary Italy: Society and Politics 1943–1988*. London: Penguin Books.

Glick Schiller, Nina, Linda Basch, and Cristina Szanton Blanc. "From Immigrant to Transmigrant: Theorizing Transnational Migration." *Anthropological Quarterly* 68, no. 1 (January 1995): 48–63.

Gobetti, Ada. *Diario partigiano*. Torino: Einaudi, 1972.

Goody, Jack. *Food and Love: A Cultural History of East and West*. London: Verso, 1998.

Gori, Claudia. "Cultural, Social, and Personal Ways of Experiencing Love – An Analysis of the Perception of Subjectivity." *Medical Science Monitor* 17, no. 11 (2011): SR29–SR33.

Granatstein, J.L. and David Stafford. *Spy Wars: Espionage and Canada from Gouzenko to Glasnost*. Toronto: McClelland & Stewart, 1990.

Grassi, Marie-Claire. "Des lettres qui parlent d'amour." *Romantisme* 68, no. 2 (1990): 23–32.

Bibliography

Grinberg, Léon and Rebeca Grinberg. *Psychoanalytic Perspectives on Migration and Exile*. London: Yale University Press, 1989.

Grondin, Mélanie. *The Art and Passion of Guido Nincheri*. Montreal: Véhicule Press, 2018.

Grossman, Edith. *Why Translation Matters*. New Haven: Yale University Press, 2010.

Hall, Kira and Mary Bucholtz. *Gender Articulated: Language and the Socially Constructed Self*. New York: Routledge, 1995.

Hamilton, Paula. "The Proust Effect: Oral History and the Senses." In *The Oxford Handbook of Oral History*, edited by Donald A. Ritchie. Oxford: Oxford University Press, 2011.

Hammerton, A. James. *Migrants of the British Diaspora since the 1960s: Stories from Modern Nomads*. Manchester: Manchester University Press, 2017.

Hanna, Martha. *Your Death Would be Mine: Paul and Marie Pireaud in the Great War*. Cambridge: Harvard University Press, 2006.

Hansen, Marcus Lee. *The Atlantic Migration, 1607–1860: A History of the Continuing Settlement of the United States*. Cambridge: Harvard University Press, 1940.

– "The History of American Immigration as a Field for Research." *American Historical Review* 32 (April 1927): 500–18.

Harney, Robert F. "Men Without Women: Italian Migrants in Canada, 1885–1930." *Canadian Ethnic Studies/Etudes Ethniques au Canada* 11, no. 1 (1979): 29–47.

Harzig, Christiane. "Immigration Policies: A Gendered Historical Comparison." In *Crossing Borders and Shifting Boundaries Vol. I: Gender on the Move*, edited by Mirjana Morokvasic-Muller, Umut Erel, and Kyoko Shinozaki, 35–58. Weisbaden: Springer Fachmedien Wiesbaden, 2003.

– "Women Migrants as Global and Local Agents: New Research Strategies on Gender and Migration." In *Women, Gender and Labour Migration Historical and Cultural Perspectives*, edited by Pamela Sharpe, 15–28. London: Routledge, 2001.

Hasse, John Edward. "Carmichael, Hoagy." In *The New Grove Dictionary of Music and Musicians*, vol. 5, edited by Stanley Sadie, 157. Oxford: Oxford University Press, 2001.

Hirsch, Jennifer S. and Holly Wardlow, eds. *Modern Loves: The Anthropology of Romantic Courtship and Companionate Marriage*. Ann Arbor: University of Michigan Press, 2006.

Hoerder, Dirk. *Creating Societies: Immigrant Lives in Canada*. Montreal and Kingston: McGill-Queen's University Press, 1999.

Hochschild, Arlie. *The Managed Heart: Commercialization of Human Feeling*. Berkeley: University of California Press, 1983.

Holloway, Sally. "'You know I am all on fire': Writing the Adulterous Affair in England, C.1740–1830." *Historical Research* 89, no. 244 (May 2016): 317–39.

Holmes, James, ed. *The Nature of Translation*. The Hague: Mouton, 1970.

Hondagneu-Sotelo, Pierrette. *Gendered Transitions: Mexican Experiences of Immigration*. Berkeley: University of California Press, 1994.

Hutchinson, Braden. "Objects of Affection: Producing and Consuming Toys and Childhood in Canada, 1840–1989." PhD diss., Department of History. Queen's University, 2013.

Iacovetta, Franca. "Ordering in Bulk: Canada's Postwar Immigration Policy and the Recruitment of Contract Workers from Italy." *Journal of American Ethnic History* 11, no. 1 (Fall 1991): 50–80.

– "Scrivere le donne nella storia dell'immigrazione: il caso italo-canadese"/ "Writing Women into Immigration History: The Italian Canadian Case." *Altreitalie* 9 (1993): 5–47.

– *Such Hardworking People: Postwar Toronto*. Montreal-Kingston: McGill-Queen's University Press, 1999.

Isnenghi, Mario. *Breve storia d'Italia ad uso dei perplessi (e non)*. Roma-Bari: Laterza & figli, 2012.

ISTAT. *Serie Storiche, Istruzione e Lavoro*, Tavola 7.1.

– *Serie Storiche. Popolazione. Emigrazione italiani e rimpatri. Espatriati per alcuni paesi di destinazione. Anni 1869–2014*.

Jacobs, Jane. *The Question of Separatism: Quebec and the Struggle over Sovereignty*. New York: Random House, 1980.

James, William. "What Is an Emotion?" *Mind* 9, no. 34 (April 1884): 188–205.

Jansen, Clifford J. *Italians in a Multicultural Canada*. Lewiston, MA: Edwin Mellen Press, 1988.

Jaroszynska-Kirchmann, Anna D. *The Polish Hearst: Ameryka-Echo and the Public Role of the Immigrant Press*. Urbana: University of Illinois Press, 2015.

Jolly, Margaretta. "Introduction: Epistolarity in the Twenty-First Century." *Autobiography Studies* 21, no. 1 (2006): 1–6.

Judt, Tony. *Postwar: A History of Europe since 1945*. London: Vintage, 2010.

Kamphoefner, Walter D., Wolfgang Helbich, and Ulrike Sommer, eds. *News from the Land of Freedom: German Immigrants Write Home*. Ithaca: Cornell University Press, 1991.

Kershaw, Ian. *Roller-Coaster: Europe, 1950–2017*. London: Penguin, 2019.

King, Mackenzie. "Canada's Postwar Immigration Policy," House of Commons Debates, 1 May 1947. In *Immigration and the Rise of Multiculturalism*, edited by Howard Palmer, 58–61. Toronto: Copp Clark, 1975.

Bibliography

Kirmayer, Laurence J., Lavanya Narasiah, Marie Munoz, Meb Rashid, Andrew G. Ryder, Jaswant Guzder, Ghayda Hassan, Cécile Rousseau, and Kevin Pottie. "Common Mental Health Problems in Immigrants and Refugees: General Approach in Primary Care." *Canadian Medical Association Journal* 183, no. 12 (6 September 2011): E959–E967.

Knight, Amy. *How the Cold War Began: The Gouzenko Affair and the Hunt for Soviet Spies*. Toronto: McClelland & Stewart, 2005.

Kristeva, Julia. "On the Melancholic Imaginary." *New Formations* no. 3 (Winter 1987): 5–17.

Kuplowsky, Adam. "A Captivating 'Open City': The Production of Montreal as a 'wide-open town' and 'ville ouverte' in the 1940s and '50s." Master of Arts thesis, Department of History and Classical Studies, McGill University, Montreal, July 2014.

Kushner, Tony. *Journeys from the Abyss: The Holocaust and Forced Migration from the 1880s to the Present*. Liverpool: Liverpool University Press, 2017.

Lakoff, Robin T. *Language and Woman's Place*. New York: Harper & Row, 1975.

Langhamer, Claire. *The English in Love: The Intimate Story of an Emotional Revolution*. Oxford: Oxford University Press, 2013.

Lawlor, Clark. "Fashionable Melancholy." In *Melancholy Experience in Literature of the Long Eighteenth Century: Before Depression, 1660–1800*, edited by Allan Ingram, Stuart Sim, Clark Lawlor, Richard Terry, John Baker, Leigh Wetherall-Dickson, 25–53. Basingstoke, UK: Palgrave Macmillan, 2011.

Leese, Peter and Jason Crouthamel, eds. *Traumatic Memories of the Second World War and After*. New York and London: Palgrave Macmillan, 2016.

Levine, Marc V. *The Reconquest of Montreal: Language Policy and Social Change in a Bilingual City*. Philadelphia: Temple University Press, 1990.

Levý, Jiří, *Umeni prekladu* [*The Art of Translation*]. Prague: n.p., 1963.

– *The Art of Translation*. Translated by Patrick Corness. Edited with a critical foreword by Zuzana Jettmarová. Amsterdam: John Benjamins Publishing, 2011.

Linteau, Paul-André. *Brève histoire de Montréal*. Montreal: Boréal, 2007.

– *Histoire de Montréal depuis la confédération*. Montreal: Boréal, 1992.

Liu, Haiming. *The Transnational History of a Chinese Family: Immigrant Letters, Family Business and Reverse Migration*. New Brunswick, NJ: Rutgers University Press, 2005.

Lorber, Judith. *Paradoxes of Gender*. New Haven: Yale University Press, 1994.

Lowenthal, Cynthia. *Lady Mary Wortley Montagu and the Eighteenth-Century Familiar Letter*. London: University of Georgia Press, 1994.

Lyons, Martyn. "Love Letters and Writing Practices: On Écritures Intimes in the Nineteenth Century." *Journal of Family History* 24, no. 2 (April 1999): 232–9.

Magni, Stefano. *"Carlo Sgorlon: Ideologia e Guerra."* *Images littéraires de la société contemporaine* 3 (2005): 235–51.

Mahler, Sarah J. "Transnational Relationships: The Struggle to Communicate across Borders." *Identities* 7, no. 4 (2001): 583–619.

Mai, Nicola and Russell King. "Love, Sexuality and Migration: Mapping the Issue(s)." *Mobilities* 4, no. 3 (2009): 295–307.

Marchetti-Mercer, Maria C. "Those Easily Forgotten: The Impact of Emigration on Those Left Behind." *Family Process* 51, no. 3 (September 2012): 376–90.

Martin, Simon. *Sport Italia: The Italian Love Affair with Sport.* London: I.B. Tauris, 2011.

Mascagni, Pietro. *L'Amico Fritz,* Act 2, Libretto by P. Suardon. In Nico Castel, *Italian Verismo Opera Libretti,* vol. 1, edited by Scott Jackson Wiley. Mount Morris, New York: Leyerle, 2000.

Matt, Susan J. *Homesickness: An American History.* Oxford: Oxford University Press, 2011.

Matt, Susan J. and Peter N. Stearns, eds. *Doing Emotions History.* Urbana: University of Illinois Press, 2014.

Mazzei, Filomena, interviewed by Antoinette Lo Busco. "Italians in Chicago." Typed transcript, 7, box 1. Oral History Project. Immigration History Research Center Archives. University of Minnesota.

"May 4, 1949: The Tragedy of Superga." Accessed 5 April 2019. http://torinofc. it/en/contenuto-storia/may-4-1949-tragedy-superga.

Maynes, Mary Jo, Jennifer L. Pierce, and Barbara Laslett. *Telling Stories: The Use of Personal Narratives in the Social Sciences and History.* Ithaca: Cornell University Press, 2008.

McClary, Susan. "Foreword: The Undoing of Opera: Toward a Feminist Criticism of Music." In *Opera, or the Undoing of Women,* edited by Catherine Clément, ix–xviii. Minneapolis: University of Minnesota Press, 1988.

Miller, Kerby A. *Emigrants and Exiles: Ireland and the Irish Exodus to North America.* Oxford: Oxford University Press, 1988.

Miller, Kerby A., Arnold Schrier, Bruce D. Boling, and David N. Doyle, eds. *Irish Immigrants in the Land of Canaan: Letters and Memoirs from Colonial and Revolutionary America, 1675–1815.* Oxford: Oxford University Press, 2003.

Milne, Esther. "Email and Epistolary Technologies: Presence, Intimacy, Disembodiment." *The Fibreculture Journal* no. 2 (2003): n.p. Accessed 30 May 2019. http://two.fibreculturejournal.org/fcj-010-email-and-epistolary-tech nologies-presence-intimacy-disembodiment/.

– *Letters, Postcards, Email: Technologies of Presence.* New York: Routledge, 2010.

Bibliography

Molinaro, Dennis. "How the Cold War Began ... with British Help: The Gouzenko Affair Revisited." *Labour/Le Travail* 79 (Spring 2017): 143–55.

Morris, Penelope. "The Harem Exposed: Gabriella Parca's *Le italiane si confessano*." In *Women in Italy, 1945–1960: An Interdisciplinary Study*, edited by Penelope Morris, 109–30. New York: Palgrave Macmillan, 2006.

Moscoso, Javier. *Pain: A Cultural History*. Translated by Sarah Thomas and Paul House. London: Palgrave Macmillan, 2012.

Nussbaum, Martha C. *For Love of Country?* Boston: Beacon Press, 2002.

Ong, Walter J. *Orality and Literacy: The Technologizing of the Word*. London: Routledge, 1982.

Parker, Roger. "La Traviata." In *The New Grove Dictionary of Opera*. Vol. 4, edited by Stanley Sadie, 802. Oxford: Oxford University Press, 1998.

Passerini, Luisa. *Autobiography of a Generation: Italy, 1968*, trans. L. Erdberg. Middletown, CT: Wesleyan University Press, 1996.

– *Europe in Love, Love in Europe: Imagination and Politics in Britain between the Wars*. London: I.B. Tauris, 1999.

Paul, Heike. "Expressive Individualism and the Myth of the Self-Made Man." In *The Myths that Made America*, edited by Heike Paul, 367–420. Bielefeld: transcript Verlag, 2014.

Pernau, Margrit, Helge Jordheim, Orit Bashkin, Christian Bailey, Oleg Benesch, Jan Ifversen, Mana Kia, Rochona Majumdar, Angelika C. Messner, Myoung-kyu Park, Emmanuelle Saada, Mohinder Singh, and Einar Wigen. *Civilizing Emotions: Concepts in Nineteenth-Century Asia and Europe*. Oxford: Oxford University Press, 2015.

Perry, Ruth. *Women, Letters, and the Novel*. New York: AMS, 1980.

Petris, Antonietta. Interviews with Sonia Cancian. September 20, 2011. http://purl.umn.edu/119661.

Plamper, Jan. "The History of Emotions: An Interview with William Reddy, Barbara Rosenwein, and Peter Stearns." *History and Theory* 49, no. 2 (May 2010): 237–65.

– *The History of Emotions: An Introduction*. Oxford: Oxford University Press, 2012.

Polizzotti, Mark. *Sympathy for the Traitor: A Translation Manifesto*. Cambridge: Yale University Press, 2018.

Portelli, Alessandro. *The Battle of Valle Giulia: Oral History and the Art of Dialogue*. Madison: University of Wisconsin Press, 1997.

– "What Makes Oral History Different." In *The Oral History Reader*, edited by Robert Perks and Alistair Thomson. London: Routledge, 2006. First published in 1979.

Pozzetta, George E. "Such Hardworking People: Italian Immigrants in Postwar Toronto by Franca Iacovetta" (review). *The Canadian Historical Review* 74, no. 4 (December 1993): 645–6.

Puccini, Giacomo. *Madama Butterfly*, Act 2, Libretto by L. Illica and G. Giacosa. In Nico Castel, *The Complete Puccini Libretti with International Phonetic Transcriptions Word for Word Translations*. Vol. 1, edited by Marcie Stapp. New York: Leyerle Publications, 1994.

Quirk, Randolph. *The Linguist and the English Language*. London: Edward Arnold, 1974.

Radice, Betty. "Introduction." In *The Letters of Abelard and Heloise*. Translated by Betty Radice. Revised by Michael Clanchy. London: Penguin, 2003.

Ramirez, Bruno. "In Canada." In *Storia dell'emigrazione italiana. II. Arrivi*, edited by Piero Bevilacqua, Andreina De Clementi, and Emilio Franzina. Roma: Donzelli editore, 2009.

– *The Italians in Canada*. Ottawa: Canadian Historical Association, 1989.

– "Montreal's Italians and the Socio-Economy of Settlement, 1900–1930: Some Historical Hypotheses." *Urban History Review* 10, no. 1 (June 1981): 39–48.

– "Sonia Cancian interviewing Antonietta Petris," University of Minnesota Libraries and the Immigration History Research Center Archives, University of Minnesota, 2011. http://purl.umn.edu/119661.

Reddy, William M. *The Navigation of Feeling: A Framework for the History of Emotions*. Cambridge, UK: Cambridge University Press, 2001.

Redford, Bruce. *The Converse of the Pen: Acts of Intimacy in the Eighteenth-Century Familiar Letter*. Chicago: Chicago University Press, 1986.

Reeder, Linda. *Italy in the Modern World: Society, Culture & Identity*. London: Bloomsbury Academic, 2020.

– *Widows in White: Migration and the Transformation of Rural Italian Women, Sicily, 1880–1920*. Toronto: University of Toronto Press, 2003.

Ricatti, Francesco. *Embodying Migrants: Italians in Postwar Australia*. Bern: Peter Lang, 2011.

– "First Love and Italian Postwar Migration Stories." In *Transnational Lives: Australian Lives in the World*, edited by Delsey Deacon, Penny Russell, and Angela Woollacott, 165–80. Canberra: Australian National University Press, 2008.

Rosenwein, Barbara H. *Generations of Feeling. A History of Emotions, 600–1700*. Cambridge, UK: Cambridge University Press, 2006.

– "Worrying about Emotions in History." *American Historical Review* 107, no. 3 (June 2002): 821–45.

Rosenwein, Barbara H. and Riccardo Cristiani. *What is the History of Emotions?* Cambridge, UK: Polity Press, 2017.

Bibliography

Ross, Peter. *"Amico Fritz, L."* In *The New Grove Dictionary of Opera, Vol. 4*, edited by Stanley Sadie, 109. Oxford: Oxford University Press, 1998.

Rudner, Martin and J. Laurence Black, eds. *The Gouzenko Affair: Canada and the Beginnings of the Cold War Counter-Espionage*. Manotick, ON: Penumbra, 2006.

Sbolci, Antonella. *Amore di terra lontana. Storie di emigranti attraverso le loro lettere (1946–1970)*. Firenze: Casa editrice Le Lettere, 2001

Scheer, Monique. "Are Emotions a Kind of Practice (and Is that What Makes Them Have a History)? A Bourdieuian Approach to Understanding Emotion." *History and Theory* 51, no. 2 (2012): 193–220.

Sciorra, Joseph. "'Don't Forget You Have Relatives Here': Transnational Intimacy and Acoustic Communities of WOV-AM's *La Grande Famiglia*." In *New Italian Migrations to the United States, Volume 2: Art and Culture since 1945*, edited by Laura E. Ruberto and Joseph Sciorra, 32–64. Urbana: University of Illinois Press, 2017.

Seymour, Mark. "Emotional Arenas: From Provincial Circus to National Courtroom in Late Nineteenth-Century Italy." *Rethinking History* 16, no. 2 (June 2012): 177–97.

– *Emotional Arenas: Life, Love, and Death in 1870s Italy*. Oxford: Oxford University Press, 2020.

Shawe-Taylor, Desmond and Alan Blyth. "Gigli, Beniamino." In *The New Grove Dictionary of Music and Musicians*. Second Edition. Vol. 9, edited by Stanley Sadie and John Tyrrell, 847–8. Oxford: Oxford University Press, 2001.

Shawe-Taylor, Desmond. "Tagliavini, Ferruccio." In *The New Grove Dictionary of Music and Musicians*. Second edition. Vol. 24, edited by Stanley Sadie and John Tyrrell, 925. Oxford: Oxford University Press, 2001.

Shefiel, Anna and Stacey Zembrzycki. "'We Started Over Again, We Were Young': Postwar Social Worlds of Child Holocaust Survivors in Montreal." *Urban History Review* 39, no. 1. Special Issue: Encounters, Contests, and Communities: New Histories of Race and Ethnicity in the Canadian City, Part 2 (Fall 2010): 20–30.

Simon, Sherry. *Cities in Translation: Intersections of Language and Memory*. New York: Routledge, 2013.

– "Introduction: Cultural Expressions." In *Engaging with Diversity: Multidisciplinary Reflections on Plurality from Quebec*, edited by Stéphan Gervais, Raffaele Iacovino, and Mary Anne Poutanen, 403–7. Bern: Peter Lang, 2018.

– *Translating Montreal: Episodes in the Life of a Divided City*. Montreal and Kingston: McGill-Queen's University Press, 2006.

Singer, Irving. *The Pursuit of Love*. Baltimore: Johns Hopkins University Press, 1994.

Sinke, Suzanne M. *Dutch Immigrant Women in the United States, 1880–1920.* Urbana: Illinois University Press, 2002.

Slaughter, Jane. *Women and the Italian Resistance 1943–1945.* Denver: Arden Press, 1997.

Stanley, Liz. "The Epistolarium: On Theorizing Letters and Correspondences." *Auto/Biography* 12 (2004): 201–35.

Stearns, Carol Z. and Peter N. Stearns, eds. *Emotion and Social Change: Toward a New Psychohistory.* New York: Holmes & Meier, 1988.

Stearns, Peter N. and Jan Lewis, eds. *An Emotional History of the United States.* New York: New York University Press, 1998.

Stephenson, George M. *Letters Relating to Gustaf Unonius and the Early Swedish Settlers in Wisconsin.* Rock Island, IL: Augustana Historical Society, 1937.

– "Typical 'America Letters.'" *Swedish Historical Society Year Book* 7 (1921): 52–93.

Stone, Lawrence. *The Family, Sex and Marriage in England 1500–1800.* New York: Harper & Row, 1977.

Sullivan, Erin. "The Art of Medicine: Melancholy, Medicine, and the Arts." *The Lancet* 372 (13 September 2008): 884–5.

Svašek, Maruška, ed. *Emotions and Human Mobility: Ethnographies of Movement.* New York: Routledge, 2012.

Templeton, Jacqueline. *From the Mountains to the Bush: Italian Migrants Write Home from Australia, 1860–1962,* edited by John Lack. Perth: University of Western Australia Press, 2003.

Tannen, Deborah. *You Just Don't Understand: Women and Men in Conversation.* New York: Morrow, 1990.

Thomson, Alistair. "Memory and Remembering in Oral History." In *The Oxford Handbook of Oral History,* edited by Donald A. Ritchie. Oxford: Oxford University Press, 2011.

Viganò, Renata. *L'Agnese va a Morire.* Torino: Einaudi, 2005. First published in 1949.

Viroli, Maurizio. *For Love of Country: An Essay on Patriotism and Nationalism.* Oxford: Clarendon, 1995.

Willson, Perry. *Women in Twentieth-Century Italy.* New York: Palgrave Macmillan, 2010.

Willcox, Walter F. and Imre Ferenczi. *International Migrations.* Vol. 1. New York: National Bureau of Economic Research, 1929.

Whittaker, Reginald. *Cold War Canada: The Making of a National Insecurity State, 1945–1957.* Toronto: University of Toronto Press, 1994.

Zanoni, Elizabeth. *Migrant Marketplaces: Foods and Italians in North and South America.* Urbana: University of Illinois Press, 2018.

Index

Page numbers in italics refer to figures.

Akhtar, Salman, 178
Ampezzo Carnico, *xxvi*, *xxxvi*,
8, 55n27, 131, *147*, 222, 231;
Antonietta's early years in, 11–12,
16, 43, 104, 124, 273, 276; Loris
and Antonietta meet and visit in,
xiii–xiv, xvi, 4, 7, 12, 18–19, 20, 21,
22, 26, 72, 128, 136, 138, 168, 252;
Loris visits while Antonietta is in
Canada, 27, 83, 142, 145, 171, 226,
228–9, 235, 236–9, 240, 242–3,
246–7, 248, 261, 262, 263, 264,
266–8
anxiety and fear, expressed in
letters, 68, 81–3, 121, 127, 132,
224, 258, 273–5; related to
immigration application, 188–9,
221, 247, 248; related to waiting
for letters, 25, 119, 174–6, 240–1,
246
April Fool's day, 229, 230, 230n18,
231
Archbald, Mary Ann,
correspondence of, 38
Australia: Italian migration to, 16,
28, 65

Baldassar, Loretta, 26, 32, 37, 214;
and co-presence, 26, 32–3

Ballarin, Aldo, 244
Ballarin, Dino, 244
Barthes, Roland, 26, 162
Beck, Ulrich, 9, 17; *Distant Love*, 9
Beck-Gernsheim, Elisabeth, 9, 17;
Distant Love, 9
Benjamin, Walter, 48
Biasetton, Francesca, 197
Blegen, Theodore, 40
Borges, Marcelo, 9; *Emotional
Landscapes*, 9
Braidotti, Rosi, 10; and
"retrospective" identity, 10–11
Brant, Clare, 197
Brescia, 112, 114
Brooks, Peter, 51; *The Melodramatic
Imagination*, 51

Canada: Christmas celebrations
in, 6, 123–5, 138–40, 145–6;
Italian communities ("Little
Italies") in, 29; Italian migration
to, 4, 5, 16, 21, 28–31, 65, 113,
182, 214–15; postwar period in,
4, 15, 30, 214; seasons in, 26, 97,
138, 145, 198, 223, 263–4, 266;
worldwide migration to, 214–15.
See also immigration to Canada,
policy and procedures for; Italy,

migration from: to Canada; Montreal

Cancian, Sonia, 9, *158*, 256, 271, 272, 275, 276, 280; *Emotional Landscapes*, 9

Caplow, Theodore, 123

Caramelli, Carlo, 13

Cartier, Jacques, 101

Cebotari, Maria, 106, 106n13

Champagne, John, 51

Chaplin, Charlie, 66

Chiswick, Barry R., 103

Christmas, xiv, 25, 83, 94, 114, 123–46, *139*, 170, 177, 273, 278; in Canada, 6, 25, 123–5, 127, 138–40, 145–6; and gift-giving tradition, 123–4, 145–6, 175, 176; in Italy, 123, 135–7, 141–3; and Santa Claus, 123, 124, 127

Cold War, 161, 207n21, 275; and fear of new war in Europe, 88, 94, 161

communication, means of: *fotoromanzi* magazines, 17; movies, 17, 78, 85, 106, 109, 207; radio, 12, 76, 78, 88, 89, 169; radiogram, 68, 72; telegram, 15, 259–60, 268; telephone, 15, 105, 125, 252, 260. *See also* letters, in context of migration; letter-writing, practice of; letter-writing, purpose of

co-presence, 6, 26, 32–3, 163, 195–6; creation of in letter-writing, 9, 10, 11, 26, 32–3, 143, 190, 192, 202, 218, 226, 243, 263

Cornille, Jean-Louis, 196; and *l'angoisse de la reception*, 196

correspondence. *See* letters, in context of migration; letter-writing, practice of; letter-writing, purpose of

Cuore di mamma (play), 190

Dante, 45

Dauphin, Cécile, 195

David, Jean-Louis, 10; *The Death of Marat*, 10

DeSalvo, Louise, 85, 86

despair, expressed in letters, 22–3, 33, 68, 78, 142, 168, 173, 206, 240–2, 276–7

determination and resilience, expressed in letters, 23, 46, 86, 96, 99, 117, 125–6, 136, 165–6, 168, 173, 194, 207, 229

de Tocqueville, Alexis, 65

digital correspondence, 41, 197–8, 280–1; and publication of migrant letters on digital platforms, 14, 41, 54n12, 271, 280–1. *See also* literacy: digital

Digitizing Immigrant Letters Project (DIL), 14, 54n12, 271, 280–1

Di Leonardo, Micaela, 125

distance: challenges of, 11, 15, 32, 41, 46, 52–3, 74, 80, 84, 116–17, 136, 137–8, 162, 176, 209, 237; sense of collapsed by correspondence, 10, 26, 105, 113–14, 196. *See also* love, expressed in letters: distant

Donizetti, Gaetano, 36, 58n80, 132n11; *L'elisir d'amore*, 36, 58n80, 132n11

Dureghello, Cornelia (mother of Loris), 12, 185, 191, 200–1, 213, 229, 231, 240, 245, 252, 254, 257, 260–1, 276

education: for employment, 12, 276; in Italy, 12, 16, 276; for language learning, 88, 95, 128, 174, 180, 200; and literacy, 16, 39

emotionality, in letter-writing, 52, 84–6, 280–1; in the letters of

Antonietta and Loris, 32–3, 39, 43, 50–1, 275, 279
emotions: connected to separation, 9–11, 14–15, 31–4, 38–41, 52–3, 67–8, 255–7; intersecting with gender, 34; and sense of "spiritual communion," 38–9. *See also specific entries for individual emotions*; emotionality, in letter-writing; emotions, history of
emotions, history of, 5, 31–4, 41; new research concerning, 31–2; and romantic love, 17
epistolary pact (*pacte épistolaire*), complicity, 33–4, 85

faith, expressed in letters, 91, 96, 99, 115, 120, 122, 133, 136, 173, 189, 212–13, 242; in love, 194, 220; in religious context, 68, 74, 121, 248
family, 79, 83; inclusion of in correspondence, 3, 7, 37, 72–4, 72n16, 77, 79, 100, 107, 140–1, 200–1, 213; letter-writing sustaining kinship support, 37, 66, 94, 100, 114, 169, 173–4, 177, 228, 231, 238–9, 246–7, 279; obligations to, 20, 129–30, 167, 169, 225, 254; reunion of, *xxxv*, 21–2, 30, 73, 143; silences concerning, 44
Febvre, Lucien, 31
Feenberg, Andrew, 197
Ferrara, 173, 219, 225, 258, 259, 261, 264
football. *See* soccer
France, 262, 264, 268; Antonietta's family in, 27, 250, 253
Freud, Sigmund, 33, 162
Fruchi, Dino, 13

Gabaccia, Donna R., 5, 6, 29, 37, 65, 66, 214; *Italy's Many Diasporas*, 5

Gabrielli, Patrizia, 163
gender, 4, 32, 34–7, 45, 275, 278; and kinwork, 124–5; and mothering, 166, 184, 277; norms and expectations of reinforced, 34–6, 82, 129–30, 167, 169, 176, 185, 202, 211, 225, 244, 275, 278; norms and expectations of resisted, 35, 79, 119; and women's agency in the migration process, 6, 16, 214–16, 266
Gerber, David, 7, 38
Gigli, Beniamino, 169, 169n18
Goody, Jack, 52, 84
grief, expressed in letters, 68, 171, 175–6, 243
Grossman, Edith, 48, 49

Hamilton, Paula, 46
Hammerton, James, 28, 56n37; and "discretionary migration," 28; and "migration of austerity," 28
Hansen, Marcus Lee, 40
Harzig, Christiane, 215
hope, expressed in letters, 5, 19, 77–8, 81, 91, 99, 115, 126, 129, 167, 190, 209, 224, 229, 247; coexisting with melancholy, 86, 97, 179; in religious context, 193, 248

identity, 47, 178, 190; and awareness of *italianità*, 272–4; fixed in time by photographs, 252; merging of with loved one, 177, 192; migration causing rupturing of, 178; retrospective, 11–12
Il Sipario di Ferro, 207. See also *Iron Curtain, The*
immigration. *See* migration, transnational; migration, transnational, impact of; migration, transnational, reasons for

Immigration History Research Center Archives (IHRCA), 281–2

immigration to Canada, policies and procedures for, xvii, 22–7, 30–1, 113, 181, 186, 191, 216–17, 245–7, 248–9, 252, 253–4, 274–5; and concern over Communist Party affiliation, 231, 274–5; and family unification program, 215; and fiancé(e) sponsorship, 25, 113, 115, 138, 214; medical examination and x-rays, xvii, 22, 245, 246, 248–9, 254; passport and visa, 245, 246, 248–9, 253, 260, 262; and requirement of boarding ticket, 245, 249, 250, 252, 262; role of travel agent in, 23, 76, 138, 145, 172–3, 186, 191, 208, 250; sponsorship application process, 23, 113, 130, 134, 181, 191, 208, 216–17

intimate letters. *See* love letters

Iron Curtain, The (film), 207n21

Italy, 15–17; Christmas in, 123, 135–7, 141–3; culture of, 273, 279, 281; during Second World War, 15–16, 44; education in, 16; gender roles in, 16, 34, 66, 275; and nostalgia for homeland (*la Patria*), 67, 98, 190, 212, 233, 247, 258, 273; popular association of with criminal violence, 271; popular association of with emotionalism, 6, 271–81; postwar period in, 4, 16–17, 18–19, 65–8, 161–2. *See also* Italy, migration from

Italy, migration from, 16, 21, 28–31, 65–8, 162, 271, 274–5; to Canada, 4, 5, 16, 21, 28–31, 65, 113, 214–15; emotional cost of, 67–8, 190, 233, 247, 256, 258, 266; by gender, 29, 215; and *i ritornati* (returnees),

66; and regret, 182, 191; and "white widows," 67

Italy, political parties in: Christian Democratic, 66, 274–5; Communist, 231, 274–5; Democratic Popular Front, 66; and general elections of 1948, 16, 66; Republicans, 66; Social Democrats, 66

jealousy and envy, expressed in letters, 168, 187, 231, 251–2

Jolly, Margaretta, 197

joy, expressed in letters, 68, 70, 73–4, 98, 112, 116–17, 122, 133–7, 146, 175, 194, 211–12, 224, 249, 268; anticipating, 70, 78–9, 81, 91, 97, 104, 107, 113, 166–7, 168, 184, 221, 248, 251, 259, 263; at receiving a letter, 77, 80, 99, 115, 125–7, 202, 227; remembering, 74, 131–2, 141–4, 203, 230, 234, 236–7, 243

Judt, Tony, 161

King, W.L. Mackenzie, 30

kinwork, practice of, 124–5, 215

Kirmayer, Laurence J., 178

Kristeva, Julia, 33, 162

L'America, myth of, 21, 65–6, 206

Langhamer, Claire, 17

language: and colonialism, 101; dynamics of in postwar Montreal, 6, 101–4; and finding employment, 186–7; learning as challenge to new migrant, 88, 101–4, 106, 128, 178, 179, 186–7, 190; learning as opportunity for civic engagement, 103. *See also* writing style, in letters

Laslett, Barbara, 42

La Traviata (film), 106, 209

Index

Leoncavallo, Ruggero: *I Pagliacci*, 169
Leopardi, Giacomo, 232–3
letter collection of Antonietta and
  Loris, 6–8, *156, 157*; preservation
  of, 7, 14
letters, in context of migration,
  38–41, 42, 84–6; artifacts
  included with, 32, 195, 240, 246,
  247, 250; and authenticity, 196–7;
  compared to oral histories, 41–7;
  legibility of, 14, 82, 83, 117, 167,
  183, 210, 217, 266, 277; materiality
  of, 6, 10, 195, 196, 197; reading and
  rereading of, 42–3, 87, 106, 125,
  127, 170, 208; and spontaneity,
  196; studies of, 5, 38, 40–1. *See
  also* letter-writing, practice of;
  letter-writing, purpose of; love
  letters; writing style, in letters
letter-writing, practice of, xvi, 5, 6,
  7, 15, 84–5, 125, 163, 195, 197–8;
  collapse of past, present, future
  in, xvi, 105–6, 113–14, 143, 145,
  164–5, 168, 172, 181, 195–6, 212,
  235; compared to face-to-face
  communication, 196–7; and
  creation of co-presence, 6, 9, 11,
  26, 32–3, 143, 190, 192, 195–6,
  218, 226, 243, 263; and creativity,
  85, 163, 197; emotional labour
  of, 32, 84–5, 195; and "emotive
  organization of memory," 85–6;
  and epistolary complicity (*pacte
  épistolaire*), 33–4, 85; frequency
  of, 53, 88, 112–13, 174–5, 189,
  201, 204, 206, 224, 227, 229,
  240, 265; and privacy, 7, 48,
  272; and reflexivity, 38, 52, 84;
  and self-censorship, 17, 44; and
  troubling delays, silences, 15, 25,
  68, 80–1, 82–3, 103, 108–13, 119,
  125, 129, 141, 171, 216, 235, 239–43,

246, 247–50. *See also* letters,
  in context of migration; letter-
  writing, purpose of; love letters;
  writing style, in letters
letter-writing, purpose of, 38–9;
  crucial to sustaining relationship
  over distance, xiv, xv, 17, 19,
  24, 28, 32, 52, 84; as emotional
  therapy, 85, 187–8; offering
  advice, 67, 96, 102–3, 104, 182;
  offering encouragement, 24–5, 52,
  70–1, 77, 80, 86, 91, 93, 96, 97, 99,
  107, 144, 169, 173; for preservation
  of memory, 113, 138, 140, 146,
  163, 164–5, 168, 183, 230, 237–8.
  See also letters, in context of
  migration; letter-writing, practice
  of; love letters; writing style, in
  letters
Levý, J., 47
literacy, 6, 38–9; creative, 197;
  digital, 41, 197–8, 280–1; in Italy,
  16; of migrants, 11, 38–9
Loik, Ezio, 244
love, expressed in letters: connected
  to suffering, 110, 176, 201, 209,
  212–13, 225, 241; destined, 90–2;
  distant, 9–10, 14, 17–18, 52–3,
  74–6, 99, 109, 176, 209, 212–13;
  and fading, 26, 162; familial, 35,
  37, 73, 98, 279, 280, 281; filial, 129,
  192, 225; physical, xiv, 72, 80, 90,
  96, 116, 120, 137, 145, 189, 223,
  239, 265; romantic ("modern"),
  14, 17, 28, 52, 104–5, 107, 119–20,
  162, 200, 203–4, 240, 252, 272,
  279, 280–1, 281n1–2; spiritual,
  mystical, 38, 80–1, 90, 98–9, 120–
  1, 122, 131, 184, 242–3, 244, 280;
  transnational, 9–10, 14–15, 52. *See
  also* emotions; emotions, history
  of; love letters

love letters, 4, 15, 28, 32–3, 38, 42, 85, 196, 271–2, 276–81, 281n1; influence of Italian literature on, 277–8; melodrama in, 15, 33, 51, 279; metaphor in, 276–7, 280; philosophy, metaphysics in, 276–7
Lyons, Martyn, 196

Mahler, Sarah, 34
Malipiero, Giovanni, 106, 106n13
marriage, 17, 130, 164, 241; involvement of kinship group in, 275; paperwork required for, 207, 217, 221–2, 228, 259–60, 262, 268; in the postwar period, 14, 17
Martinis, Lucia (mother of Antonietta), xv, *xxxv*, 11–12, 44–5, 73, 86–7, 94, 130–1, 141, *154*, 172, 189–90, 216, 223, 247, 252–3, 263; and decision to emigrate to Canada, xv, 20, 22; language challenges faced by, 104, 106, 179; and separation from husband, xv, 12, 16, 20, 22, 44, 278–9; suffers nervous breakdown, 44–5, 179–80, 182–5, 198–200, 202, 211, 213
Mascagni, Pietro, 12, 51, 164n15; *Cavalleria Rusticana*, 169
Matt, Susan, 179; *Homesickness*, 179
Maynes, Mary Jo, 42
Mazzei, Filomena, 179
Mazzola, Valentino, 244
McClary, Susan, 36
melancholy, expressed in letters, 6, 33, 41, 109, 123, 138, 161–3, 170, 277; coexisting with hope, 86; prolonging remembrance, 163, 237; related to imagination, 162–3
melodrama, 51; in the letters, 15, 279; inspired by opera, 28, 36, 279; writing as melodramatic experience, 33

memory: associated with pain, regret, 25–6, 71–2, 74, 143, 146, 165; evoked and expressed by nature, 234; intersectionality of oral and textual, 5, 41–7; involuntary, 46; letters as organizing principle for, 37, 85–6; letters as preservation of, 113, 138, 140, 146, 163, 164–5, 168, 183, 230, 237–8; and nostalgia, 31, 74, 83, 136, 164
migrant correspondence. *See* letters, in context of migration; letter-writing, practice of; letter-writing, purpose of
migration, transnational, 4–5, 14, 65–8, 178–80; between Canada and Italy, 4, 5, 16, 21, 28–31, 65–8, 162, 214–15, 271, 271, 274–5; collective emotional involvement in, 4–5, 37, 250, 269, 273; denial of for political reasons, 231, 274–5; and difficulty finding work, 186–7, 200; family-based, 22, 29, 30, 214–15; and language challenges, 88, 101–4, 106, 128, 178, 179, 186–7, 190; and men following women, 215–16; and migrants' regret, 182, 191; requiring reconstruction of social networks, 39, 76, 178, 190, 215; and "white widows," 12, 67. *See also* immigration to Canada, policies and procedures for; Italy, migration from; migration, transnational, impact of; migration, transnational, reasons for
migration, transnational, impact of: culture shock, 24, 124, 178; on gender relations, dynamics, 4, 5, 6, 16, 34–7; on kin, non-kin relations, 4, 5, 66, 67; on physical/mental health, 178–9, 182–5; on

Index

those left behind, 4–5, 27–8, 255–7, 260–1; on women's agency, 6, 16, 214–16, 266

migration, transnational, reasons for: discretionary, 28; motivated by love, 27–8, 31, 206, 207, 219, 255–8, 268; in pursuit of better life, 21, 28, 56n37, 65, 67, 162

Miller, Paul W., 103

Milne, Esther, 196

Montbriand, Louis-Roch, 29

Montreal, xvi–xvii, 6, 7, 11–12, 13, 20, 22–6, 29–30, 44, 101–3, 191, 215, 258, 276; Casa d'Italia (community centre), 30, 56n47, 198, 217; Christmas celebrations in, 123–5, 127, 138–40, 145; Italian community in, 7, 13, 23, 29–30, 56n47, 76, 102, 103, 113, 125, 137, 219, 273; language dynamics in, 6, 101–4, 200; Madonna della Difesa (Notre-Dame-de-la-Défense) church, 29–30, 56n46, 89, *152*, 209, 209n23, 228; St Joseph's Oratory, 77, 104

Moscoso, Javier, 33; "cartography of misery," 33

nature, 27, 39, 81, 232–5, 236, 252; correlation of to literary imagination, 6, 232–3; evoking and expressing memory, 234; inspiring nostalgia, longing, 232–3

Necas, Daniel, 281

Nincheri, Guido, 13, 29, 103

nostalgia, expressed in letters, 5, 19, 20, 24, 25–6, 31, 33, 43, 74, 83, 123, 141, 203, 235, 236, 242, 256; in connection with nature, 232–3; for Italy, 78–9, 89, 124, 174, 190, 228, 258

Ong, Walter, 84–5

opera, xiv–xv, 12–13, 39, 51, 85, 169; disseminating moral codes, values, normative behaviour, 36–7; letter-writers' identification with, 20, 33, 36, 85, 163–4, 279; popularity of in Italian culture, 36, 279, 281; as source of inspiration, 12, 28. *See also* operas

operas: *Cavalleria Rusticana*, 169; *I Pagliacci*, 169; *L'Amico Fritz*, 164n15; *La Traviata*, 209, 209n24; *L'elisir d'amore*, 36, 58n80; *Madama Butterfly*, xiv–xv, *xxxiii*, 20, 36, 58n80, 88, 132, 231, 231n19, 279

oral histories, 41–7

Palma, Loris, *xxv, xxvi, xxviii, xxix, xxxii, xxxiii, xxxiv, 151, 152, 153, 154, 155*; awareness of Italian identity (*italianità*), 273–4; Communist Party affiliation of, 231, 274–5; courtship and engagement to Antonietta, xiii–xiv, 5, 12, 19, 21, 31; cultural awareness of, 12–13, 276; death of, 6; and decision to emigrate to Canada, xv–xvi, 7, 20–2, 255, 257–8; delays to migration of, 81–2, 83, 87, 93–4, 117, 126, 264–6; education and studies, 12, 39, 90, 92, 111, 276, 277–8; employment, 12–13, 35, 73, 94, 112, 210–11, 226, 227, 262, 265, 266, 268; experience of Antonietta's departure, 33, 112, 237; experience of sacrifice in migration, 233, 235, 256, 258, 266; immigration process of, 27–8, 76, 113, 130, 134, 138, 143–4, 172, 176, 186, 191, 202, 206–8, 219, 238–9, 245, 248–9,

253–4; marriage to Antonietta, xvii, 30, 130, 134, *151*, *152*, 207–8, 268–9; military service of, 18, 24, 76, 81, 83, 87–8, 94, 115, 117, 122, 130, 131, 132–3; participation of in author's correspondence study, 6, 47; remembering Antonietta's reunion with her father (1947), 21–2, 130, 131–2, 134; responsibility of to support his family, 129–30, 169, 225, 254; return to Italy (1963), 13, 257; separation from Antonietta prior to emigration, xiv, 5, 7, 18, 19–20. *See also* Société de diffusion du patrimoine artistique et culturel des Italo-Canadiens

Palma, Luigi (Gigio) (father of Loris), 12, 257, 275–6; employment, 35, 129, 169, 275–6

Passerini, Luisa, 32, 232

Petris, Antonietta, *xxv–xxvii, xxxiii–xxxv, 148–55, 157–8*; agency and freedom in Canada, 24, 47, 145, 214–17, 266; arrival and adjustment to life in Montreal, xvi–xvii, 7, 22–7, 74–6, 78–9, 95–6, 128; awareness of Italian identity (*italianità*), 273–4; and challenge of language learning, xvi–xvii, 23, 26, 76, 88, 95, 97, 101–4, 106, 117, 128, 170, 190, 200; courtship and engagement to Loris, xiii–xiv, 5, 7, 12, 19, 21, 31; decision to emigrate to Canada, xv, 4, 20–2; departure from Italy, xvi, 22, 65, 109, 189–90, 191, 251; early life in Ampezzo Carnico, xiii, 11, 43; education and studies, 12, 16, 39, 88, 128, 174, 200, 276, 277; employment, 12, 24, 26, 79, 86–7, 94, 102, 105, 138, 170,

200, 208, 223, 263, 277; marriage to Loris, xvii, 30, 130, 134, *151*, *152*, 207–8, 268–9; and move to new home, 205, 209, 216, 218, 223; and reunion with father (1947), xv, *xxxv*, 21–2, 30, 43, 138; and return to Italy (1963), 13; separation of from Loris prior to emigration, xiv, 5, 7, 18–19, 96; and sharing of correspondence with author, 7–8, 41–2, 43–5, 46–7, 50

Petris, Vittorio (father of Antonietta), xvi, *xxxv*, 11–12, 20, 22, 30, 35, 44, 72, 73, 77, 78, 86–7, 94, 97, 104, 107, 108, 118, 134, 145–6, *154*, 185, 191, 194, 200, 211, 216, 217, 222–3, 229, 230, 277; employment, 11–12, 276; migration of in search of work (1920s), 11, 67, 276; migration to Canada (1928), xiii, xv, 11, 21, 43; return to Italy (1947), xv, *xxvii*, *xxxv*, 21–2, 30, 43, 130–1, 134, 138; support of for Loris's immigration process, xvii, 44, 76, 113, 173, 181, 182, 186, 245, 250

photographs, 15, 79, 87, 97, 131, 231, 244–5, 250; creating co-presence, 79, 87, 114, 203, 240, 244–5, 252; fixing identity, 252

Pierce, Jennifer, 42

Polizzotti, Mark, 48; *Sympathy for the Traitor*, 48

Proust, Marcel, 46; and "involuntary memory," 46

Puccini, Giacomo, xiv, *xxxiii*, 12, 36, 51, 58n80; *Madama Butterfly*, xiv–xv, *xxxiii*, 20, 36, 58n80, 132

Raoux, Jean, 10; *La Liseuse*, 10

Reddy, William, 31; emotives and emotional regimes, 31

Reeder, Linda, 9, 12, 67; *Emotional Landscapes*, 9; *Widows in White*, 12

religious faith, expressed in letters, 33, 68, 74, 89, 98, 115, 117, 130, 136, 164, 193, 203, 205, 248, 249, 260, 280

Rome, 24, 71, 87, 92, 248–9, 254, 258, 259, 261, 273; Canadian Consulate in, 22, 239, 245, 248–9, 254, 259; Ciampino International Airport, xvi, 22, 65, 109

Rosenwein, Barbara, 31, 37; emotional communities, 31, 37

Rossini, Gioachino, 51

Rousseau, Jean-Jacques, 51

Second World War, 4, 12, 15, 30, 44, 256–7; silence concerning in letters, 44; suffering related to, xiii, 14, 16, 17, 161

separation, emotional costs of, xvi, 4, 6, 9, 11–13, 19, 22–3, 40, 53, 68–70, 74–6, 178–80, 183, 189–90, 195, 205, 228, 233, 251–2, 256; migration of loved one experienced as social death, 6, 256; positive interpretation of, 87, 178. *See also* emotions

Simon, Sherry, 34, 49, 101

SISAL (Sport Italia Società e Responsibilità Limitata) lottery, 222, 222n12

soccer, *xxxii*, 26, 92, 111–12, 114, 176, 211–12, 222n12, 249, 274; and plane crash of Turin team, 27, 244, 274

Società Adriatica di Elettricità (SADE), xiii, 12, 19, 26, 134, 210–11, 250, 262, 268

Société de diffusion du patrimoine artistique et culturel des Italo-Canadiens, 13, 56n46

sorrow, expressed in letters, 23, 70–4, 78, 85, 93, 108, 110, 132, 138, 142, 175–7, 182, 192–4, 237, 240–4, 260–1

sponsorship program for immigration (Canada). *See* immigration to Canada, policies and procedures for

sports: identified as unifying migrants, 212, 219, 273–4. *See also* soccer

Stanley, Liz, 15; and the role of time in letters, 15

"Stardust" (song), 218, 218n9

Stearns, Carol, 31; and emotionology, 31

Stearns, Peter, 31; and emotionology, 31

Stephenson, George, 40

Tagliavini, Ferruccio, 169, 169n18

Thomas, William, 40; *The Polish Peasant in Europe and America*, 40

time, 46, 121; distorted sense of, 97, 98, 113, 129, 172, 188, 192, 220, 230, 263; and future projection, 3, 20, 31, 35, 80–1, 117, 136, 161–5, 166, 175, 188, 198, 211, 237, 248; preserved in letters, 15

transnationalism, 5, 14, 255, 255n1; among Italians, 5, 66–7; and creation of social spheres, 84, 102, 215; and emotional communities, 37; from below, 37; strategies for, 11, 24–5; transnational love, 9–10, 52, 162–3. *See also* migration, transnational; migration, transnational, impact of; migration, transnational, reasons for

transcription, challenges of, 45

translation, challenges of, 5, 45, 47–51, 280–1; and dialect, local/regional terms, 45, 50; and literary translation, 48; as transcreation, 47–51

Turin, 16, 27

United States, 123, 161; Italian migration to, 16, 65, 125, 179

Venice, xiii–xvi, *xxix, xxx, xxxi, xxxiii, xxxiv,* 8, 12–13, 18, 19, 21, 28, 44, 97, 202–3, 254, 256, 258, 259–60, 264–5, 273, 274; Teatro Goldoni, 13, 44, 190; Teatro La Fenice, xiv, xxxiii, 13, 44, 106n13

Verdi, Giuseppe, 12, 51, 98, 106n13, 107, 209n24; *La Traviata,* 209, 209n24

Vermeer, Johannes, 10; *Girl Reading a Letter at an Open Window,* 10

work, 17, 20, 21, 179; as expression of support, 79, 87, 138, 205; in factory, described, 87, 138; and language dynamics in Montreal, 102–3, 104, 186–7; migration motivated by, 11, 21, 65, 67, 73, 276; values, meaning, importance ascribed to, 4, 73, 112, 200, 210–11

writing style, in letters, xvi–xvii, 39, 45, 50–1, 85; Antonietta's, 45, 50, 144, 215, 276–7; and careful construction, xvi, 39, 84–5, 124; and employment of metaphors, 240–1, 276–7, 280; Loris's, 45, 50, 107, 110, 133, 210, 221, 240, 276–7; and melodramatic style, 15, 51, 279; and philosophical, metaphysical style, 277. *See also* translation

Znaniecki, Florian, 40; *The Polish Peasant in Europe and America,* 40